# SOCIETY:

## The Struggles of Hatred and Righteous Betrayal

*Written By: Misty L. Bishop*

*Cover Design By: Mack Bishop 3$^{rd}$*

*Publishing*

*"You never know what you're going to face;*
*You never know what you're going to take;*
*You never know what you're going to get.*
*All you can do is live and learn with strong faith day by day."*

*-Misty L Bishop*

## PREFACE:

*Society: The Struggles of Hatred and Righteous Betrayal* is a screenplay that revolves around a young African American woman by the name of Ashlyn Richardson who moves from a black community in Inglewood, California, in the summer of '97, the beginning of her senior year in high school, with her parents, Rev. Jeff Richardson and Debbie Richardson, and older brother, Carlton, to the suburban area, Sugarland, Texas. The Richardson family made this transition because Rev. Richardson had been promoted to be the director of Texas Health and Human Services in his childhood home state in the Southwest region. They reunite with Ashlyn's older sister, Vanessa, and her husband, Darnell, and also touch base with her oldest brother, Speedy.

In addition, the Richardson family reconnects with their old hometown church in the heart of Third Ward as their spiritual foundation. However, this physical transition brought about changes in young Ashlyn's life as she transforms from a teenager to a full-grown woman. In this transformation, society has exposed and placed obstacles, such as racism, loss of a loved one, early motherhood, betrayal, workplace animosity, and sibling rivalry in Ashlyn's life that will either hinder her from or strengthen her to become a successful television executive producer.

## ABOUT THE AUTHOR

Misty L. Bishop is a poet/screenwriter/author/publisher and an aspired attorney who resides in Houston, Texas. She is the wife of Mack Leon Bishop III and together they have three sons, Mansur Lemuel Bishop, Mack Leon Bishop IV (Onyi) and Malik Lali Bishop. She is also the daughter of Pastor Mary L. Shot low & Clarence Shotlow and Herbert Lee Edwards.

Misty is a native of Grimes County, Texas and an alumna of Anderson-Shiro Jr.-Sr. High School and Texas Southern University. She has a degree in Administration of Justice and Speech Communication, and a paralegal certificate from Southwestern Professional Institute. She also plans to pursue a degree in law.

## SPECIAL ACKNOWLEDGEMENTS

To the Creator of all living things in this world and far beyond of what we can not see. I give honor to this powerful Being, Spirit, and Source for allowing me to utilize my gift that will bring forth motivation and inspiration for others to not only dream but to live their dream.

I want to take time to acknowledge the presence and the pure spirit of my two blessings from God, Onyi and Malik, who motivate me day by day to be the wholesome person God wants me to be. I also want to thank my husband for being a man of his word by supporting, motivating, and loving me to the fullest.

I want to thank my mother for guiding, supporting, and inspiring me to be the best I can be, as well as my siblings: Michelle, Cameron, Clarence Shotlow, Jr. (CJ), Monica, LaTresia, Beatrice, Hershamber, and Kevin, for the unconditional love and support they have given me throughout the years. I also want to acknowledge my two fathers, Herbert Lee Edwards and Clarence Shotlow, Sr., for being there for me as their child. And for my aunts: Cheryl, Chandra, Bessie White, Zola Taylor, Jeralyn, Florence, Beverly Ann Lott, Gloria Bircher, Bobbie, Natalie Lyles, Lavadia Edwards, and Barbara Oliver; and my uncles: FD Calhoun, T. C., Clifford Edwards, Jezzell Lyles, Donny Jones, Alfred, Glenn, and Hulon Oliver; as well as my grandparents: Leroy and Gloria Edwards, and Dorothy Yancy, I thank you all for the love and support from the time I was born and forevermore.

I also want to share my gratitude toward my in-laws: Robbie Shaw, Cresta Robertson, Brenda Johnson, Mary Ann Childs, Ruby Faye, Gregory Gregg, Laura Phillips, Leola Comeaux, Vickie Robertson, Bubba Campbell, Darryl Bishop, Mack Bishop, Jr., James (Pete) and Charlotte Shaw and family, Catina Shaw and family, Shamecka (Shaw), April, Nikki Ray, Tiffany Ray, Candice (Childs), Eboni, Tyrone Johnson, and Lottie Lofton, who have given love and support toward me and my endeavors.

I also want to express my profound gratitude toward my godparents and family, Rose (Frank Smith) and family, and Floyd and Sheila Wolf and family, for their love and support throughout the years.

I also want to thank all of my family in Grimes, Brazos, and Harris County, Texas, as well as Central Florida and

Alexandria, Louisiana, for their love and support throughout my upbringing.

I want to thank my alma maters, Anderson-Shiro Jr.-Sr. High School and Texas Southern University for molding my mind to grasp for and achieve excellence.

I also want to express my spiritual gratitude to my hometown churches: McKenzie United Methodist Church and Yarbrough United Methodist Church, for giving me a strong spiritual foundation upon which to build as I travel this lifelong journey.

I also want to thank those who are not here physically, who have ventured out into another life, for their love, support, and aspiration that they have shown me from the time they were here: Earline Ruth Minor Calhoun, W.H. Buster Calhoun, Jr., Sonya Minor, Ervin Locke Minor, Sr., Ervin Minor, Jr., Mary Ellen Minor, Jake Minor, Willie and Lois Edwards, Frank Smith, Gloria Thomas, Alberta Minor, Anna Marie Minor, Erma Jean Campbell, Lovie Minor, Aunt Bessie –Tot Menefee, Kendrick –Kee Weell Smith; Kenneth Bay, George Calhoun, Sr., Dantwan and Chan Calhoun, Jimmy Calhoun, Tameka Jackson, and Gracie Mae Williams.

I also want to thank the following for your love and support for me and my endeavors in the literary field as a writer and publisher. May God bless you on your lifelong journey:

Texas Southern University-University Museum; St. Luke Episcopal Hospital- OR Scheduling Dept.; University of Houston-Bookstore; Texas Southern University-Bookstore; Hastings in Bryan and College Station; KCOH 1430 AM family; KTSU 90.9 FM family; KPFT 90.1 FM family; Ruby L. Thompson Elementary in Houston; St. Paul United Methodist Church in Anahuac, Texas; The Marker Group- Expediting Team in Houston, Texas; Devon Energy-Records Management and Imaging Department in Houston, Texas.

**Special Thanks To:**

Dr. Avia Wardlaw; Dr. Corliss A. Rabb; Eddie Marie Hearld and family; Cynthia Hunter; Kimberly Hughes; Melaine Robertson; Gloria Blankett; Marilyn Guidry; Diane Wilkerson; Vivian; Ida; Iris Lancaster; Bertha Eugene; Iris Cruz; Betty Benavides; Michelle Austin; Esperanza; Olivia Rule; Micale Clark; Clarissa Sharp; Carolyn Sanders; Antoinette Player; Brandi Taylor; Sofia Vaji; Tanika Lane; Diane Howard; Jessica Pete; Gayle Roberson; Rainey Mock; Linda Ingle: Angela Sinette; Kimberly Wulf; Sharon Womack; Lisa Mendez; LaToya Berry; Suzie Jones; Jeanne Langley; Tametria James; Melissha Hill; Autumn Hill; Tiyosha Turner; Dale Chambliss, Eric W. Elder; Tammer Cooper; Shikenah Jones; Aaron Ellison and family; Rev. Gerald & Paulette Bryant; Dr. Opolot; Dr. J. Domatob; Patrick Sawyer; Dr. Sarah A. Trotty; Orlando Ruiz; E. Lee Felder, Jr.; Karen Anderson; Rosemary; Brett Edwards; Linda Clark; Michael and Ruby Francis; Marla Blackmon; Ella Maxine Allen; Ruby W. Session; Gloria A. Clouser; Melaine J. Harvey; Marvin Mickey; Justine Baly; Meredith Collins Hamilton; Rachel Green; Heather Griffin; Janice Ward; Delores Cloud; Suesan Jordan; Terrie A. Valiare; Saundra Roberts-Brown; Earnestine Reeder; Tanita Rice; –Snookiel, and Mr. Dickerson.

# Part I

## The Transitional Stage of Teenage Years to Womanhood

*[During the transitional stage of Ashlyn Richardson's teenage to womanhood years, she begin to experience and struggle with the hatred that presides in her path as .well as losing a loved one and betrayed by another one until she feels God is betraying and punishing her. Therefore, she reacts in a rebellious manner that could cause her to deter from her ultimate goal in life which is becoming an executive producer at a television station.]*

# ACT 1

*Fade in*

## Scene 1

When: During school
Where: Class at Inglewood High School in Inglewood, California

*Ashlyn Richardson enters her government class with her friend Darnesia Woods at Inglewood High School for the last time in her junior year as classes will be closing for the summer of 1996. She will be moving to Houston, Texas, with her family because of the job offer her father, Rev. Jeff, has as a director of the Southwest region of the Health and Human Services Department in Houston, Tex.*

Ashlyn: (walks to her desk talking to Darnesia) Girl, I hope I did well on that final exam because I studied my behind off.
Darnesia: I know I studied for the first time of my life because I need to pass this class to raise my GPA to . . . (she pauses) uh . . . uh . . . um . . . go to college.
Ashlyn: Yeah, right. You go to college. (she laughs out loud) It's more like you chasing after my brother holding on to his you-know-what.
Darnesia: Oh, you funny. Oh, you got jokes. (she pauses) Uh-huh. Let's don't forget Mr. O.
Ashlyn: (she smiles) I admit I got nothing but love for my Oreo cookie, but you got it bad for brother man. It's a wonder you haven't sprouted one of his seeds.
Darnesia: (she laughs) And you *know* this woman!
[Mrs. Jones gets the class's attention when she walks into the room with the exams in her arms.]
Mrs. Jones: Well, class, how are you today? The class responds: Good!
Student 1: (shouts out) I'm glad this is the last day of the school year because next year, I am the man. (he jumps out of his seat and start stepping around the classroom) I am the man, I am the man!
Student 2: (jumps up and joins the male student 1) Yeah, we the men, class of '97, say what? Class of '97, we run this motherf—, hell, yeah.
[All the juniors join in, including Ashlyn and Darnesia. Then Mrs. Jones interrupts the celebration.]

Mrs. Jones: (she laughs) OK, class, I definitely get the picture. (she pauses)I have the exams graded and most of them were surprisingly good from some people I least expected it from. The lowest grades were in the 70s. The highest were in the high 90s, and only one person made a 100. That person is Darnesia Woods.

Darnesia: (looks at Ashlyn with a smirk on her face) I told you. I was not playing. Now, you believe me. *Who's* the woman that runs this house? (she walks up to the front of the class to get her exam with a diva strut and walks back to her seat flaunting her exam before Ashlyn)

Ashlyn: (looks at Darnesia in aah manner) Oh, I can't believe this. She got a perfect grade.

Mrs. Jones: (smiles) I tell you, Darnesia, you shocked me, but I knew you had potential as long as you focus on your books, not men. And I'm very proud of you. You just got to stay focused on the books to better yourself because education is very important, especially in this society. (she pauses and turns to Ashlyn) Miss Ashlyn Richardson, you were the next-highest grade behind Ms. Darnesia, surprisingly.

Ashlyn: (walks up to the front of the class smiling and pumping her hands up) Yeah, Mrs. Jones, it shocked me, but I still got a high A. (she sticks her tongue out at Darnesia as she walks back to her seat)

Darnesia: (she sticks her tongue back at Ashlyn) I'm still number one.

Ashlyn: Yeah, on *this* test, but overall, I am THE ONE. (she laughs out) Ha- ha-ha-ha!

[Mrs. Jones continues to pass out the exams, then she gets the class's attention one more time.]

Mrs. Jones: Since you guys did well on the exam and today is the last day of class, I bought some pizza and brought some CDs to listen to for our class. (she directs her attention to Ashlyn) Also, one of my brightest students in this class is leaving us to move to Tejas, Texas. That person is Miss Ashlyn Richardson. So, this is also going to be her farewell party. Miss Ashlyn, I wish you the best, and I pray you will continue to excel in life as you have done here at Inglewood High. I also want your address so we can keep in touch, OK?

[The pizza guy interrupts the class and gives the pizzas to Mrs. Jones while the students get into their cliques and put their CDs in the radio by Mrs. Jones's desk. The pizza man receives the money and exits the scene. The students get their pizza and dance to Ice Cube, –Today Was a Good Day.‖] Mrs. Jones: (approaches Ashlyn and Darnesia's clique and grabs her chair to eat her 2 slices of pizza with them) Well, ladies, what's up? What you talking about?

Ashlyn: (she speaks to Mrs. Jones) Oh, we just talking about me moving to Texas and getting acquainted with some Southern brothers. (the girls in the clique had laugh)

Mrs. Jones: Now, you see, Ashlyn, I think Miss Darnesia has rubbed off on you. (she laughs)

Darnesia: Oh, no, no. This chick here ain't got nothing or control on Ms. Thang. She's already hot to trot but on a down low. (the other three girls in the clique nod their heads to agree with what Darnesia stated)

Mrs. Jones: Really? (she turns to Ashlyn) Ashlyn, is that true, Ms. Thang? Ashlyn: Well, you know Ash needs love, too. Yet I know how to control myself ladylike. (smiles at Darnesia)

Darnesia: Oh, what you're trying to say? (stands up and holds her hands up in the air)

[Ashlyn gets up, too.]

Mrs. Jones: Okay, girls, let's chill. (turns to Ashlyn as she and Darnesia sit back down) Ashlyn, I'm going to give you my number and address to keep in touch with me. (she hands her a piece of paper; Ashlyn takes it and puts it in her purse) I also want you to know (then she turns to all of the girls), and you all to know, high school is just the prelude, and after graduation it's just the beginning on how life itself can make you or break you. Society gives you opportunities to take but also can hinder you from those goals that you have in sight. You never know what you're going to get. You never know what you're going to face. All I know is you all have to have faith in God and have the desire to overcome the obstacles that are placed before you with His help and your drive to claim what is rightfully yours.

Don't give in to the crime. Don't allow discrimination to give you fear and prevent success. Be who you want to be, not what someone else wants you to be. You are who you are. I want you to remember that just like I remember my mentor telling me this. Hopefully, you will pass down this advice to others that come along in your path.

[Darnesia, Ashlyn, and the other girls are in tears and hug Mrs. Jones for the advice.]

Ashlyn: Thank you, Mrs. Jones. (she wipes the tears from her face) I will remember that advice, and I will act upon it. Also, I will keep in touch. (she gets a piece of paper and a pen to write down her new address and number, then she hands it to Mrs. Jones) I'm going to miss you; you are like a big sista to me. You made sure I stayed in a straight line. I thank you for that, and I love you. (she hugs Mrs. Jones again)

Mrs. Jones: That's why I'm here.

Darnesia: I know I'm going to miss you too, Ashlyn. You are my ace, sista, and my best friend. (she hugs Ashlyn in tears)

Ashlyn: I love you too, Dee.

[Then all the girls in the clique join in with Mrs. Jones.]

*The scene fades away.*

## Scene 2

When: Friday at 3:30 P.M. Where: Omar's house

*Ashlyn and Darnesia go to Ashlyn's boyfriend's house, Omar, who is also her brother, Carlton's, best friend. Carlton and Omar are playing NFL Madden on PlayStation in the living room sitting on the couch in Omar's apartment.*

Carlton: (swinging back and forth) Yeah, boy-oy, what are you gonna do now? (leaning toward Omar) Oh, oh, I think I . . . ah, score another touchdown. Now what, nigga-nigga?

Omar: (pushes Carlton) Man, get out of my face. The game ain't over until I run this all (stands up) the way to the end zone! (jumps in Carlton's face) Now, punk-ass nigga, who's the loser, and who's the champ? Game over, B-I- T-C-H! (throws the controller down)

[Carlton tackles Omar. Then the doorbell rings.]

Carlton: (gasping for air as he's holding Omar around the neck) Don't make me whip your ass before I leave, punk. (Ashlyn and Darnesia continuously ring the doorbell and bang on door)

[Carlton lets Omar go and pushes him. Omar continues to laugh and runs to the door.]

Omar: (opens the door and grabs Ashlyn but pushes Darnesia and shuts door in her face) You don't belong here, Dee! (turns to Ashlyn) Why you bring her here 'cause every time she . . .? (pauses)

Darnesia: (bangs on the door hard) Oh, you betta let me in, or else I'll come around the back and whip your ass! I'm going to count to three. . . . 1 . . . 2 . . . Omar: (opens the door and she falls flat on her face) Uh . . . wee, somebody ate the floor! (starts laughing out loud) Darnesia: (gets up and jumps on Omar) You son of a bitch! You made me break a nail!

[Ashlyn laughs while trying to break them up. Then Carlton runs to them and grabs Darnesia. He takes her to the bedroom and shuts the door. Then opens the door and winks at Ashlyn and Omar and closes the door. Now Ashlyn and Omar go into Omar's bedroom.]

Ashlyn: Well, baby, you know this is my last day here, and I really want to make this special.

Omar: Um, girl, (he runs and jumps in the bed) let's get it on then. (he claps his hands and the song –Down Low‖ comes on)

[The lights dim as Omar gets on top of Ashlyn.]

*The scene fades away.*

**Scene 3**

When: Friday at 5 P.M.
Where: The Richardsons' family house

*Omar and Ashlyn are pulling up to Carlton and Ashlyn's house in Darnesia's car with Carlton.*

Darnesia: (speaks in sad tone) Well, you guys, this is it.
Ashlyn: (she grabs Omar's knee and rubs his leg while they are sitting in the car) Yep! This is it.
Omar: (opens the car door) Well, this is not the last time we will all be together. (he gets out) [Darnesia gets out and goes to Carlton and hugs him, then Carlton hugs her back. Ashlyn and Omar get out of the car kissing and telling each other they love each other. Then Jeff and Debbie come out of the house and walk toward them.]

Debbie: (smiling) Well, Jeff, look at the lovebirds.
Jeff: I see him. (looking at Omar all on Ashlyn) Son, (talking to Omar) you need to step back a little. (with a serious look)

Omar: Oh, my bad. I was just caught up in the moment. (he puts space between him and Ashlyn, holding her hand) I love you. (he whispers to Ashlyn)

Jeff: Yeah, you're bad. She doesn't need any babies right now. (then he turns to Carlton) That goes for you two over there also. (he points at both of the couples) I know what's up. I used to be your age. It's all right to be intimate but not sexually before you marry, especially when you haven't taken small responsibilities seriously.

I keep telling you four that society looks at us as a nobody already.

Don't make matters worse and let them be right.

You all are going to listen one day or else society is going to teach and show you the way. Darnesia and Omar, I love you two like you're mine. That's why I talk to you just like I talk to Ash and C. I want you two to know that. (he walks to Darnesia, then Omar, and hugs them)

I'm going to miss you two and hope you come and visit us sometime in H- Town so I can show you my stepping-stone. (he laughs) (Darnesia starts to cry and Debbie hugs her)

Debbie: Oh, sweetheart, I love you, too, and we're going to make sure you and Omar get the directions on how to get to H-Town since I know you already got the phone number and the address.

Darnesia: Yes ma'am. (wiping her face, then hugs Ashlyn) I'm going to miss you, girl. You are my sista I never had.

Ashlyn: (hugs Darnesia again) Oh, girl, you know it. I'm going to call you and check on ya as well as Omar, you know? (they do their handshake)

Darnesia: You know I'll keep my eye on him just like you keep an eye open on Carlton.

Ashlyn: Girl, you know you are my ace. (she hugs her again)

[Carlton, Omar, and Jeff shake hands.]

Jeff: Well, lovebirds, kiss each other good-bye.

[Jeff walks to the moving van with Debbie. Ashlyn kisses Omar with tears rolling down her face as she gets in the van. Darnesia cries as she holds onto Carlton until Omar has to grab her.]

Omar: (talks to Darnesia) Cuz, it's all right. We'll see them again, I promise. [The Richardson family pulls away from the driveway as Omar and Darnesia wave.]

*The scene fades away.*

**Scene 4**

When: Saturday at 12:30 P.M. Where: Houston, Texas

*The Richardson family arrives at their new home in the Sugarland area in Houston after 19 hours.*

Jeff: Well, family, we are finally at home.
Debbie: I hope Nessa got all of the furniture we shipped over here.
Jeff: I hope so, too. Let me call her. (he gets out of the van to call Vanessa; walks to the house and opens the door)
[Ashlyn and Carlton get out of the van next; then Debbie follows.]
Carlton: (turns around and looks at the houses, cars, and the people in the neighborhood) This is definitely not the hood-i-wood. It looks like a predominately white neighborhood. (talks to Debbie) I got an eerie feeling about this place even though the crib is tight. Moms, why we couldn't stay in the hood like we did back at home?
Debbie: Well, first of all, it was to introduce you to a new way of living in a new city, new state, but most of all, in a new society.
Ashlyn: I agree with Carlton, but I understand, Mom, your intuition that Carlton and I should be surrounded by people who are hardworking and well educated; yet, this is not a black neighborhood. It seems to be predominately white. All I see is white people outside; no blacks in sight. To me, this is not good.
[Jeff interrupts and comes out of the house talking to Vanessa, waving to Debbie, Carlton, and Ashlyn to come inside.]
Debbie: (talks to Carlton and Ashlyn as they walk into the house) You two have to realize we are trying to set an example that blacks can live just as well in a nice, quiet, clean, and tidy neighborhood with hardly any crime taking place.
Ashlyn: But still, Mom, this neighborhood is not predominately black. In case you didn't notice, we are *not* white.
Carlton: (smirks) She got you, Mom.
Debbie: Oh, hush. (she rolls her eyes at Ashlyn)
Jeff: (talks to Vanessa on the phone) Really? So, are you and Darnell coming over? (pauses waiting for a response) OK? (looking around the living room, then he walks into the kitchen and looks in the pantry) I'll see you later. I love you. Bye-bye.
Carlton: (looks in the pantry and cabinets, then shouts) Where's the food? Ah, man, I'm starving. I need some grub.
Ashlyn: Aw, you'll live.
Carlton: (shouts) Aw, shut up. You know you hungry, too. So, don't

(low tone)

Ashlyn: Seems like somebody been in the doghouse. (pauses and laughs) So, did she or didn't she?

Vanessa: Since he doesn't want to answer, the li'l skank did.

Carlton: No, no, brotha, that's a no-no. Creepin' is not allowed in the M- game. And plus, you're married to my sis. So when you mess over her, you gonna answer to me. (he pops his knuckles, then balls in hands in a fist and rubs his knuckles) So, did you jump on it or off it?

Darnell: First of all, Carlton, bro, dog, I'm a man with principles. That girl is nothing compare to my wife. She wanted me, but I rejected her. I turned away from it like a married man should do.

Ashlyn: Uh-huh. I pretty sure you did. Only God knows the truth. (pauses) Can I get an amen from somebody?

Jeff: Amen. Now, let's drop this subject into something more nondramatic and less personal, if you know what I mean. Can I get an amen . . .? (pauses) I *said*, can I get an amen?

Everybody: Amen!

Jeff: Do you think Bill is the best president we ever had for African Americans?

Vanessa: Well, I think so because he has kept Affirmative Action, even though some wanted to eliminate that policy, and he . . .

Carlton: He knows how to get the ladies with playa mentality. (pops his collar and grins)

Ashlyn: You *would* have to say something stupid. (rolling her eyes at Carlton) Anyway, Clinton has improved the standardized budget that was in a deficit. He also increased more job opportunities for all races, religions, colors, and creeds. Then he raised the minimum wage to $5.15.

Debbie: (looks at Ashlyn) Somebody has been studying governmental issues.

(she turns and look at everybody else) Well, in my opinion, in spite of the Watergate Scandal, students from any ethical and economical background can afford to further their education. Those that are poverty-stricken can receive grants that will cover all their expenses. Those that are not will be awarded at the time of income taxes. Of course, Clinton has raised taxes, but the payment of these taxes reduces the deficit to an even budget that will lead to a surplus. Also, the benefits for retirees and the disabled are receiving the maximum amount. Therefore, they will spend money just like everybody else, and the economy will continue to grow.

Vanessa: OK, I agree with you, Mom and Ash. No matter what has occurred in the first term, this term will matter for the premillennial era. The break of 2000.

Darnell: First of all, Bill Clinton is a black man (laughing) trapped in a white man's body. He's very decisive, strong-willed, assertive, but a free-spirited person. In spite of the Oklahoma and Nairobi Embassy bombing, he's still in touch with the people. He's making sure everyone has some sort of income, even if it is a welfare or disability check.

Jeff: Since I asked the question, I will answer it also. I agree with everyone at the table, including (looks over at Carlton, laughing at him) Carlton. Bill Clinton has faced the Watergate Scandal, World Trade Center bombing in 1995, and the Oklahoma bombing. Then he also suffered the repercussions from the bombing at the embassy in Nairobi that killed over 100 people.

Yet, he took charge and action to bomb the nuclear plants and the underground terrorist camps to prevent any other terrorist attacks. In spite of it all, he focused on how to have a surplus budget that will increase job opportunities and has extended health, retirement, education, and disability benefits. He boosted up the economy without hurting anyone.

Carlton: Yep. That's why I voted for him. 'Cause he gave me a chance to improve my life, even though I'm hardheaded and a juvy. I know there's a way out. Hopefully, one day, (grinning from ear to ear) I might enroll in college to get my MBA and have my own car dealership.

Ashlyn: Say what? (she looks at Carlton) Are you kidding me? You gots to be kidding me! (she rolls her eyes)

Jeff: Really, son. You (pauses) want to go to college? And own your own car dealership? (laughs out loud)

[Then everybody laughed except Carlton.]

Carlton: That's dirty, man. You don't believe me. You don't believe I can do it. I'm going to prove to each of you that I can. And let's see who's going to laugh then.

Debbie: Well, son, the matter is, do *you* believe in yourself enough to do it and achieve your career goals? Or you just saying it to feel good, or do it for others to see?

Carlton: For others to see that I've changed and I want to better myself.

Jeff: Okay, son. The first step is find a school that suits you. Then, get the application and complete it. And the rest will follow. (he gets

up from the table and pats Carlton on the head)
Debbie: That's what you have to do, Carlton. Find a school that will give you an opportunity to be a businessman.
Ashlyn: I'll help, Carlton, if you need me, bro.
Vanessa: Carlton, U of H has a decent business school. You can apply there. Darnell: Yeah, C., you can fill your application in my office. If I have time, I'll show you around.
[Vanessa's cell phone rings—it's Speedy, the older brother calling from Louisiana.
Speedy is sitting at his house in his office.] Vanessa: Hey, boy, what's up?
Speedy: Oh, a lot. So much to tell. (his fiancée walks by with her nightgown on) Um, have you heard from Mom and Dad?
Vanessa: Yeah, I'm sitting right here in the dining room at their new home in Houston.
Speedy: For real? Aw, man, they got there quick!
Vanessa: Yep . . . (pauses) Tell me what's up. (she crosses her legs)
[Darnell gets up with Ashlyn and Carlton while Debbie is still eating.]
Speedy: (fiancée starts kissing on him, and he's telling her to wait) I'm getting married.
Debbie: Married?
Ashlyn: (runs back in) Did you say Speedy? Speedy is getting married? To whom? And what she . . .?
Vanessa: (interrupts Ashlyn's questions, then talks to her and Debbie) Hold up, you two. (talks again to Speedy on the phone) So, who is she?
Speedy: She came down with me a lot of times in the past 4 years. (pauses) You remember her.
Vanessa: Speedy, you brought plenty of women to my house, and they were not the same girl.
Speedy: I know, but she was one of them. Only thing is, I brought her down more than four times to see you and Darnell . . .

She had long, coal-black hair, big slanted eyes with a bronze complexion. Vanessa: All the girls you brought fit that description. Speedy: OK, remember the woman who brought the Double Dutch Chocolate Cake for your B/D, and you told me to keep her? She's good with the family. Vanessa: Oh, her; oh, she's a good catch. She has moral values, and she's family-oriented. Yeah, I remember her. (pauses) Have Mom and Dad met her? Speedy: Yep. A couple of times when I came home to visit.

Vanessa: (look over at Debbie) What did Mom say about her? And how did the rest of the crew act?

Speedy: Mom told me she's the one after they had a long talk. Now, Ashlyn was like, she's fake and not all real. Carlton was just, it's whatever, man. Dad told me not to rush into anything and make sure she's what she claims to be.

Vanessa: That's good advice from him.

Speedy: Yep. (he looks at his fiancée while she sits on his lap)

Vanessa: Well, do you want to talk to Mom and Dad?

Speedy: Yeah, I would like to talk to both of them. (Vanessa hands the phone to Debbie, first)

Debbie: Hey, boy, how are you? I hear you gonna get married. Tell Momma who this lady is.

Speedy: The one you liked so much. I finally decided to settle down. (his fiancée drops her clothes in front of him) Oh, yeah. (smiling as he pulls her to him)

Debbie: Really? Tell Teresa I said hi and congrats, OK? (pauses) You want to talk to your father?

[Jeff walks into the dining room.]

Speedy: OK. (Debbie hands the phone to Jeff) Jeff: Say, man, you gonna get hitched?

Speedy: Yep. (his fiancée is kissing all over him) I'm ready, too. For that moment. (looks at her)

Jeff: Okay, let us know when the date is so we can help out. Hopefully, you'll come down soon, huh?

Speedy: Yeah. Probably next weekend. I'll call to get the directions from ya. Jeff: OK. (pauses) Do you want to talk to your young siblings?

Vanessa: Dad, my minutes! (whispers to Jeff)

Jeff: Oh, I'm sorry, Vanessa. (Vanessa smiles) I guess, Speedy, you have to talk to them later.

Speedy: Yeah, tell them I'll call later. I got the number from Vanessa. I love y'all.

Jeff: All right, see you later. Love ya. (he hangs up the phone)

[Vanessa retrieves the phone from Jeff.]

Vanessa: So, Dad, how you feel your eldest son is getting married?

Jeff: Well, the same I felt about you. Happy for ya and just hope ya have a prosperous marriage like me and your mother.

Debbie: (walks toward Jeff and hugs him around the neck) Yep, it's been 28 years since we've been married, and 33 since we've been together. Even though sometimes he makes my skin crawl and my hair rise off my arms, (she smiles and kisses Jeff on the forehead) I still love him. (she walks off)

Jeff: Vice versa. At times, it's a challenge, but you live, learn, and you love. As long as God is in the union, nothing can break it apart unless one is fierce and weak. (Jeff gets up from the table and hugs Vanessa)

[Vanessa and Jeff joined Carlton, Darnell, Ashlyn, and Debbie in the den watching *Menace II Society*.]

*The scene fades away.*

**Scene 6**

When: Sunday at 9:30 A.M.
Where: Bathroom at the Richardson household

*The Richardsons are getting ready for church. Carlton and Ashlyn are fighting over the bathroom.*

Carlton: Come on, girl, quit hogging the bathroom! Other people got to use it. (hitting the door)

Ashlyn: (just singing away) La . . . La . . . La . . . Oh, happy day, oh, happy day when Jesu—(Carlton bangs on the door) Stop it, Carlton! I'll be out in a minute!

Carlton: You said that an hour ago!

Ashlyn: (opens the door fully dressed) Shut up, dried bag of dog food that is purified with sh—it.

Carlton: (pushes Ashlyn out of the way and shuts the door) Got dang, girl. The mirror is all fogged up.

[Ashlyn runs downstairs to the kitchen where Debbie and Jeff are eating breakfast at the kitchen table.]

Debbie: (speaks to Ashlyn) You finally joined us. Jeff: (looks up at Ashlyn) Where's Carlton?

Ashlyn: He's getting ready. (she's pours orange juice and places pancakes on her plate; pours syrup on her pancakes)

Jeff: Ashlyn, you got to stop hogging the bathroom. You need to have consideration for other people.

Debbie: Your dad is right. You need to do unto others as you want them to do unto you.

Ashlyn: I know. I know.

[Carlton comes downstairs, grabs a glass of orange juice, and puts pancakes on his plate with syrup, sausage, and biscuits.]
Carlton: (sits down) Um, ummmm, ew-weee, good ol' breakfast.
[Debbie and Jeff get up from the table, rinse their plates, then put them in the dishwasher while Carlton and Ashlyn are eating.]
Carlton: Dad, are we going to meet Nessa and Dee at church, or are they coming over here? (he gets up and rinses his plate)
Jeff: Oh, we're going to meet them at church.
[Debbie goes out of the kitchen and Ashlyn puts her plate up and follows. Jeff and Carlton walk out last. The Richardsons get in their SUV and leave for church.]

*The scene fades away.*


## Scene 7

When: Sunday at 11 A.M.
Where: St. Mark United Methodist Church

*The Richardsons drive to the church parking lot. People are going inside the church. Darnell and Vanessa are waiting outside in front of the church on the bottom steps. Jeff, Debbie, Ashlyn, and Carlton get out of the SUV and walk to the church steps to greet Darnell and Vanessa.*

Jeff: (shakes Darnell's hand and hugs Vanessa) Good morning.
Debbie: (comes behind Jeff and hugs both Darnell and Vanessa) Good morning. How are you two doing?
Vanessa and Darnell: Fine.
[Carlton and Ashlyn hug both Vanessa and Darnell; they all walk in together. As they enter the church, it's packed and the choir is singing –Be Encouraged.‖ The congregation is waving their hands and shouting.]
Ashlyn: (touches Debbie's shoulder to whisper) Momma, are we late? Debbie: (looks at her watch then answers) About 15 minutes.
[The choir stops singing, then Rev. Lockett gets up to speak while the entire Richardson family sits.]
Rev. Lockett: May we please bow our heads and close our eyes. (he bows his head and closes his eyes, then prays) Father, we come here today to give all thanks and praise unto you for your magnificent

works and miraculous outcomes in our lives. We ask you to purify our hearts, minds, and our souls. Forgive us, Lord, for the sins we indulge in. Protect us from the wicked and dangers of this society. Heal the sick, and let those that are lost know they are loved, too. And keep us in the palm of your hand. In Jesus' name, we pray. Amen.

Let the church say amen. (the congregation repeats –amen‖) Say–amen again. (the entire church says –amen) That's a lil better. Today, we are going to first thank God for all that he has blessed us with! We should lift his name up and rejoice, for this is the day the Lord has made! So get up out of your seat and praise him & shout for glory!
Congregation: (shouts randomly) Hallelujah! Thank you, Lord! Thank you, God!
[The choir begins to sing –Praise Him‖ for about 6 minutes, then Rev. Lockett approaches the pulpit again while the congregation sings along with the choir. Rev. Lockett then signals the director to end the song. Everybody in church is praising God, including the Richardson family.]
Rev. Lockett: Oh, I feel good! Uhwee, wee, church, I feel fire burnin' so deep in me. (the music is playing as speaks) Oh, hallelujah! Oh, hallelujah! Oh, church, do you know him? Do you know him? Have you tried him?
Congregation: Yes!
Rev. Lockett: Have you tried God? (the music continues to play) (he pauses and looks at the choir, then the congregation; the congregation stands up and shouts) Oh, oh, (pauses, then shakes his head) we're going to move on along. We have an old friend that is here to join us, him and his family! Mr. Jeffery Richardson. Pastor Richardson! Come on up and let God use you! (laughs) I hope you have your sermon!
Ashlyn: (looks at Jeff) Sermon? We just got here. Debbie: Jeff, get up and let the Lord use you.
[The congregation claps their hands as Rev. Lockett flags him to come up to the pulpit. Jeff gets up and walks to the pulpit.]
Jeff: Well, well, well. (looks around the church and smiles) I said it is good to be in the house with folks that are not ashamed of praising him!

The one who had sent his only begotten son, Jesus Christ, who died for our souls to be saved and set free! We should jump up for joy physically, mentally, spiritually, whichever one, or all three! Praise be to God!

Congregation: (randomly) Hallelujah! Thank you, Lord!

Jeff: Today, church, I am so glad to stand here—right here where I had first begun my spiritual walk. This place is where I began to come out of the nutshell of iniquity and began to walk on the narrow path that leads to salvation and glory! I want to thank God for my beautiful family, my wife, Debbie, my two daughters, Ashlyn and Vanessa, my son, Carlton, and my son-in-law, Darnell; also my son, Jeffery Jr., who is in New Orleans preparing for the football season and marriage. Amen.

Congregation: Amen.

Jeff: I'm so blessed to have my family. My youngest son, Carlton, said, –Dad, I want to go to college to become an owner of car dealerships. I'm tired of being noticed as a troublemaker.

Instead, I want to be an entrepreneur in a positive way.‖ (he pauses and looks at Carlton) I'm proud of you, son, even though we are skeptical of him keeping this goal in mind. God has allowed me today to realize he is sincere this time. All he needs is our support as a family. (Debbie grabs Carlton's hand, then Ashlyn hugs him) Amen.

My youngest daughter, Ashlyn, is a straight-A student with such talent on the basketball court and the track and field. She plans to be an executive producer at a television broadcasting network. When she was in Inglewood, she was the producer of the school's network. She was also the editor for the yearbook and newspaper. Amen.

My oldest daughter, Vanessa is the English and drama professor at U of H, while her husband, Darnell, is a computer engineer and an engineer professor at U of H, too.

Last, but not least, my wife, the love of life and my backbone with her beautiful self. Oh, oh well, she is . . . a self-reliant RN to the T! That's why I love her. She knows her stuff. (Debbie laughs)

Well, like I said before, I thank God for my family. No matter what society has placed in front of me or tried to take away, I've learned to live and have faith in God and to love those that love me. (pauses) I tell my children all the time in society you never know what you're going to face; you never know what you're going to take; you never know what you're going to get. All you can do is live and learn and have strong faith day by day. And have hope and dreams and love within your soul and spirit. Be fruitful and truthful of thyself! Let no man take away your faith, destiny, and life! It is *you* that will allow harm as well as help that comes your way. It is *you* that can be your best friend but also your worst enemy!

It is *you* that makes you or breaks you. It is *you*, my sistas and brothas! Stop all the backbiting. Let us help each other! Let us build up our community! I am talking about the black race! Society is teaching the children of this generation to be ignorant, to be Uncle Toms, to be who they want us to be—

to be scavengers, brutes, the slaves that have never been freed! It is time to wake up, black people! Our children need us!

We are losing our children day by day due to violence, drugs, prostitution, STDs! Wake up! Where did we go wrong? Do you think Martin Luther King Jr. or Malcolm X would be happy to see a higher percentage of our black males in prison? Or our black females selling their bodies not only for money but for drugs, too? And the only way to survive is to commit crime? Or live on welfare? Babies having babies not knowing who the father is?

Black people in the church, *what* is going on? (pauses and shakes his head) You don't hear me!

Debbie: (hollers) Preach, baby! Elder: Tell it like it is, son!

Deacon: Go 'head! Congregation: Amen!

Rev. Jeff: That's not all, church! You see, the church needs be cleansed, too. There's too much homosexuality, adultery, fornication, and lies. I mean the hidden truth.

Debbie: Come on, preach!

Rev. Lockett: Go ahead, boy! (hits him with his towel)

Jeff: Y'all don't hear me! There is also idolatry, envy, jealousy, and greed! And GREED!

That's why we fight among ourselves! That's not godly; that's not even Christlike!

Debbie: Preach, preach!

Jeff: You see, I was a pastor at a 1,500-member church known as Trinity UMC in the heart of Inglewood, California. I-wood is nothing nice, especially in the black community. There's always somebody getting jumped, stabbed, shot, robbed, and killed. Getting run down by the police. There was never a dull moment where my family and I used to live.

We had a nice house and cars. Of course, that environment had caused my children to fall time after time again, but we managed to keep harm away. I even contributed my finances that I received from the church to help build a community center.

A center that has social workers to help people with their finances, counselors for domestic issues, a clinic for STD and pregnancy testing, tutorial programs, youth camps in basketball, baseball, tennis, golf, swimming, flag football, track, and field. This is one step I took, but I was not by myself. There were other pastors and ministers who had contributed just as much as I did for the past 5 years. It helped quite a few children to get out of the streets and get in their books so they could receive a full scholarship to go to college and achieve their career goals.

But it's sad to say the community had such a slave mentality. They had a fear of success. They always looked for an easy way out. That's not supposed to happen because easy money is an easy way out; it's also a destructive way that will destroy one's soul in no time. Drugs are the main element that has harmed and destroyed our community. Society has placed that in our community to eliminate our brothas and sistas and to keep us in a slavery bondage. They make it seem like selling or taking these drugs will help us get over, yet this stuff controls our minds, to destroy our own, who then commit more violent crimes against one another.

Church, we need to wake up today and stand up for what is ours! Our children need us! So God help us! We need to come together as one like during the Harriet Tubman Era, George Washington Carver Era, Martin Luther King Jr. and Malcolm X Era! Black men, women, and children, we need to march on like we did during the Civil Rights movement and the Million Man March! (the congregation shouts) This time, we march every day with the same aspirations—the same attitude that we are black people who want to be known and looked at as human beings that are devoted fathers and mothers; supportive siblings; trustworthy friends; well organized, intelligent, open-minded employees. A person who has high moral standards; who knows not to do wrong but to make it right!

Oh, y'all don't hear me! Can you hear me clearly, church?

Congregation: Yes! Oh, yes!

Jeff: People, we (he points to himself and everyone that's around him) need to stop tearing each other down; instead, let us lift each other up! I know some of you are mad at me for what I've said thus far. (pauses and shakes his head) You know what? I don't care! 'Cause God is laying this on my heart and spirit! For those of you that speak and do wrong against your brotha and sista, shut up and move along! If you can't talk to them about your dislikes and disagreements of their lifestyles, shut up and move along! You and you, (points out to the congregation) we all need to look in the mirror very closely before chastising someone because there are more fingers pointing back at you then the one you use to point at them. Then you are heavenly judge by the Father!

So, wake up, wake up, wake up, my brothas and sistas! Let us join together and build this great foundation for our community so our ancestors' work and faith will not go in vain! Let us prosper! (pauses and wipes his face with a towel) Oh, oh, let us read a scripture or two, maybe three. The first one is Matthew 7:1–6. So, please open your Bible and read with me silently. (he reads the scripture while everyone else reads to themselves quietly)

Verse 1, *Judge not, that you be not judged.*
Verse 2, *For with what judgment you judge, you will be judged; and with the measure you use, it will be measured back to you.*
3  *And why do you look at the speck in your brother's eye, but do not consider the plank in your own eye?*
4  *Or how can you say to your brother, Let me remove the speck from your eye: and look, a plank is in your own eye?*
5  *Hypocrite! First, remove the plank from your own eye, and then you will see clearly to remove the speck from your brother's eye.*
6  *Do not give what is holy to the dogs; nor cast your pearls before swine, lest they trample them under their feet, and turn and tear you in pieces.*

Now, turn to Matthew 7:18–20 and follow with me as I read to you. (reads the scripture)

18  *A good tree cannot bear bad fruit, nor can a bad tree bear good fruit.*
19  *Every tree that does not bear good fruit is cut down and thrown into the fire.*
20     *Therefore by their fruits you will know them.*

Reading those versus in the seventh Act of Matthew lets you and you know who's the true judge and how he advises us to bear a foundation with seeds of wisdom that is not of wickedness. That will grow and prosper.


So, read and meditate these versus, my brothas and sistas, every day if you have to in order to live by it. Listen to what God is trying to tell you and you, my brothas and sistas today.

The message today is to stop judging one another and correct our demeaning ways so we can build a stable foundation with a profound and pure spirit in truth!

(shakes his head and closes his Bible, then walks away from behind the pulpit to the center of the platform) My God, my God, I don't think they hear me!

Congregation: (shouting) Yes! Amen! Hallelujah! Preach! Debbie: (stands up) Come on, break it down for them. [The musicians began to play a slow melody.]

Jeff: (shakes his head) God, himself, wants us to come together; not be apart. That's why he sent Jesus, the Messiah, thousands of years ago to built the foundation of love and unity among us. We should follow and dwell on that foundation because our Father of all beings, want us to stop that sista sowing so-and-so did this, brotha John did that; how come he doing that? Why I can't? I saw him last night. He was with you know who. If that was me in sista's shoes, I . . . um . . . um, child. (pauses and looks into the congregation as he steps down from the platform) Y'all don't know me. Only God knows me. I don't know you. Only God knows you. So who are you to judge? And who am I? Nobody compared to God, yet I am somebody trying to tell somebody to sweep around your own front door before you try to sweep around mine.

I'm trying to tell you God wants you, and you, and me to put away that jealousy, envy, those betraying ways, brothas and sistas. That wickedness will produce bad fruit that deteriorates the foundation that should hold up for generations to generations; let us plant the fruitful seed of wisdom and love.

Let us work together as one so this foundation that God has prepared us to have is prosperous. (pauses and sighs)

Do you want to stand on a foundation of wickedness that will lead to destruction and death? Or do you want to stand on a foundation that bears good fruit that will lead to salvation, glory, and prosperity? Congregation: (shouts) Good fruit! Hallelujah! Praise God!

Jeff: Oh, I feel good right now! I feel like preaching another sermon! (he jumps up and down to the music) Praise God! Oh, praise God!

[The music gets louder; congregation shouts and dances along with the choir.] Carlton: Ashlyn, I feel funny. Do you feel funny?

Ashlyn: (clapping her hands to the music) No. It's just the Spirit moving in you.

Carlton: (stands up) The Spirit?

[Debbie, Vanessa, and Darnell look at Carlton while he's standing up.]

Jeff: Oh my God, if there is anybody here today who wants to join this spiritual unity movement, come on.

[The choir sings, ‒We've Come Too Far,‖ while people are coming around the altar.]

Darnell: (talks to Vanessa) Seems like the whole church is coming around.

[Vanessa is slain in the spirit, waving her hands with her eyes closed. Carlton moves to the altar with tears in his eyes.]

Carlton: (walks in front shouting and jumping up and down) Oh, God, forgive me, Lord! Help me, Lord! I want to do right by you! Please, help me!

[Ashlyn and Debbie go to him and hug Carlton. Vanessa has passed out. Darnell is fanning her. Jeff comes down from the platform and hugs his son. Then 3 minutes later, Vanessa and Darnell join the family and embrace each other while the choir continues to sing ‒We've Come Too Far.‖]

*The scene fades away.*

# ACT 2

## Scene 8

When: The end of summer
Where: Kemptner High School

*Ashlyn begins her senior year at Kemptner High School. Carlton drives her to school before he goes to U of H downtown to attend his fall semester.*

Carlton: Well, sis, this is it. You need me to carry you in or escort you? Ashlyn: (rolls her eyes at Carlton) Carlton, don't start what you can't finish. I'm a grown woman, now.
Carlton: Really? Uh-huh. You sure about that? (he laughs)
Ashlyn: (opens and closes the car door) Ha-ha, that's funny. Just pick me up at 3:30, punk.
Carlton: (he laughs) A'ight, sis. I can't do that 'cause I sho' can't carry ya! (he pulls off)
[Ashlyn walks into the building, then goes to her classroom getting ready for Literature AP.]
Student 1: [white female] (talking to her li'l clique) Check it out, a black girl in AP Literature. Yeah, right. (laughs)
[Ashlyn sits in the front desk on the far left, close to the window.]
Student 2: [Asian male] (pointing out Ashlyn to his clique) Wow, who's that? She's too fine to be in this class.
[The teacher comes into the classroom. She notices Ashlyn and smiles at her.] Ms. Patrick: Good morning, my upperclassmen. If you don't know my name, my name is Ms. Patrick. (she turns to the chalkboard and writes)
I am your English Literature AP teacher. This is my second year at Kemptner, so, I'm still considered a new person at this campus. I would love everyone to introduce themselves by addressing their name, hobby, and goals. If you don't want to, just tell me your name so I can mark you down on the roll call. OK! Any volunteers? [No one stands up] All right, let's start at the last row, last desk by the window. Go ahead.
Student 3: [Anglo-American female] I'm Leslie Wright.
Student 4: [Hispanic male] I'm Ricardo Mendez.
Student 5: [Asian female] I'm Amy Veal.
Student 6: [Anglo American male] I'm Trent Coburn. Student 7: [Anglo-American male] I'm Joshua Simmons.
Ashlyn: Hi, my name is Ashlyn Richardson. I'm from Inglewood,

California. My hobbies are dancing, playing basketball, running track, and writing news columns; also reporting and producing news. My career goal is to become a television producer at CBS, FOX, UPN, or a cable network. I also love to go to church and sing.

Ms. Patrick: Wow, Ashlyn, I'm glad to hear your introduction. What school do you plan to go to?

Christopher Wilet: (interrupts) A nigga school. (he says it loud among his peers)

Ms. Patrick: (loud tone) Excuse me! Who said that? (looking around the class with disappointment) Tell me now! I need to know 'cause that in intolerable! Ashlyn: (turns around with rage and shouts out) Who called me a nigga? (she walks to the back where there were white boys huddling and snickering among themselves)

Ms. Patrick: Ashlyn, calm down. I know you're upset.

Christopher: (jumps up at Ashlyn) What are you going to do about it?

Ashlyn: (grits her teeth with anger and balls her fists at her side) You betta be glad this is my first day at this school 'cause I will knock your natural sour beaver teeth gonzo-looking ho-ass white boy down. You don't know me! You just don't know who you're messing with. [Ms. Patrick calls the principal to come to the room using the intercom.] Ms. Patrick: Dr. Berg, I need you to come to the classroom right now!

Christopher: (laughs and spits on Ashlyn's shoes; the saliva reflects back to lynching and slavery of what blacks went through) Obviously, you're in the wrong class, bitch. Go back to Africa.

Ashlyn: (turns her back to him then swings around and hits him two times with her fist) You're going to respect me, you white motherfucker! (before she could hit him again, the principal, Dr. Berg, pulls her back while Ms. Patrick pulls Christopher back)

Christopher: (wipes his hand across his nose and mouth; he's bleeding) That bitch hit me! I *know* she didn't hit me!

[Ms. Patrick and Dr. Berg escort Christopher and Ashlyn out of the classroom. A few minutes later, Ms. Patrick and Dr. Berg sit Ashlyn and Christopher in Dr. Berg's office while the students are out of their seats discussing the incident in Ms. Patrick's classroom. Ms. Patrick leaves the office and goes back to her classroom.]

[In Dr. Berg's office]

Dr. Berg: (speaks loudly behind his desk and points his finger at Christopher) Mr. Christopher, racial slurs and disrespect toward another student are intolerable. I don't care if you are a scholar and an outstanding athlete; this behavior is not acceptable in the classroom, on the field, or the court!

(he leans over his desk) Do you hear me? It is prohibited on school property! Do you hear me? Answer me NOW!

Christopher: (smirks at Dr. Berg) I hear you.

Dr. Berg: I surely hope so, because you are suspended for 4 days.

Christopher: (stands up) You can't do that! I'm the star quarterback! That's not fair! (he looks at Ashlyn with a mean frown on his face)

Dr. Berg: Mr. Christopher! Sit down right now!

[Christopher sits down slowly staring at Ashlyn.] (Berg speaks to Ashlyn) I apologize for this behavior for your first day at Kemptner High School. However, hitting a student does not solve the problem. Next time, keep your hands to yourself so you will not be punished. I'm going to give you after- school detention for 2 days.

Ashlyn: (looks at Christopher, then turns to Dr. Berg) That's fine. (pauses) I apologize for lashing out so soon.

Dr. Berg: What do you mean so soon?

Ashlyn: I shouldn't have made any physical contact until he did because it would have been self-defense in your sight, (starts talking sassy) even though I defended myself against this white boy that overstepped his damn boundaries and who could've received more bruises! (she looks at Christopher) Ignorant-ass white boy!

Dr. Berg: Ms. Ashlyn, I know you are upset, but fighting is not tolerated at this school. Do I make myself clear, Ms. Richardson? Ms. Richardson?

Ashlyn: (sassy tone picking at her fingernails) Yep. Just make sure he doesn't cross my path.

Dr. Berg: OK. I'm going to call your parents to let them know what happened. (he looks in his contact information folder to locate the parents) Mr. Chris, I want you to stay right here with me, and Ms. Ashlyn, you go back to the classroom.

Christopher: What? That black bi—um, uh. I hate this!

[Ashlyn gets up, walks out of the office, and walks into the classroom. She goes to her seat. Ms. Patrick stops and looks at her as Ashlyn sits down.]

Ms. Patrick: Ashlyn, these are the assignments on your desk. (Ashlyn looks at the papers on her desk while everybody was staring at her) OK, back to what I was discussing. I want you to write a five-page critical analysis on Othello in

2 weeks. Use the simple format I placed on your desk as a guideline. Remember, there are going to be pop quizzes between now and then over Othello, so make sure you read this literature every night.

[The bell rings for the next class to start and the previous class to end. Christopher walks up to Ashlyn as she leaves the classroom.]

Christopher: You betta watch your back, black bitch.

Ashlyn: (ignores him and keeps walking to her next class) Whatever! (she walks into her calculus class; there were some blacks in this class. She smiles with relief as she takes her seat)

*The scene fades away.*

## Scene 9

When: Noon
Where: School cafeteria

*The lunch bell rings at noon, and Ashlyn leaves her class and goes to the school cafeteria. She gets in the Pizza Hut food line and is approached by four black girls.*

Tamara: Hi, you must be Ashlyn, the new girl that beat down Christopher, the quarterback.

Ashlyn: Well, actually, I only hit him once or twice. And yes, my name is Ashlyn Richardson.

Deniece: And my name is Deniece Broudeaux. I'm a senior and the captain of the basketball team and track.

[The girls get their pizza and walk outside to the picnic area where the blacks and Latinos hang out. They sit down at a bench across from a group of athletes and so-called troublemakers.]

Tamara: Ashlyn, I'm sorry for not introducing myself. I'm Tamara Jones. I'm in your calculus class. I apologize for not talking to you in class, but I was trying to fill out some college applications when you came in. I'm also on the b-squad as the point guard, while she's the p-forward. Nevertheless, I'm a chess master and a tennis pro. (she eats her pizza)

Courtney: Oh, (puts down her breadsticks) I'm Courtney Swift. I also run track and play volleyball. I'm the school asst. editor for the yearbook and newspaper. So, (she takes a sip of her soda) where are you from? And what are your talents, or should I say skillz? (she laughs)

Ashlyn: (wipes her mouth) Well, I used to live in Inglewood, California. I went to Inglewood High School that was predominately black. I participated in basketball, track, and I was the school's broadcasting network producer and editor. I also acted in school plays and danced on the marching squad.

Tamara: So, what do your fam do?

Ashlyn: First of all, they are strict. My mother is a registered nurse, and my father is a director of HHSC of this region and an associate pastor at St. Mark United Methodist Church at Sunnyside.

[The black students across from them are getting louder while listening to their DJ Screw and dancing.]

Tamara: Ashlyn, (points over to students across from them) you don't belong over there. They are troublemakers; all they do is smoke dope and party all the time. Then they love to start fights.

Courtney: Yeah, the majority of them live on welfare or their parents are either divorced or on drugs; they're just a disgrace to our race, you know?

Tamara and Deniece: (laughs sarcastically) Yep.

Ashlyn: (sarcastically speaking) What's so funny? I guess you think you are better than them because of their lifestyle. I don't think so 'cause you all are black. And I don't appreciate that at all. You see, white people want us to be divided so they can manipulate any situation that will give them authority over us. I guess y'all not black; y'all are the Uncle Toms. The ones that use their brothers and sisters in order to get where they want to be, then backbite them in their ass! I see you three have to wake up and see what's really going in society. Apparently, you all need to sit in the cafeteria with the whites and Asians 'cause you all got something in common: you disrespect the entire black race. (she stops talking and stuffs her mouth with pizza)

Tamara: You know, you are a smart-ass! You got some nerve to call me *Uncle Tom* when you don't even know what my family has gone through. I've been on welfare before, but my parents did not give up on their dreams to become entrepreneurs as a hairstylist and a barber. So, I think those students over there are a disgrace to the race because they lay on their asses expecting everything to be handed to them instead of working for what they want to achieve.

Ashlyn: My point exactly. You see, you shouldn't laugh 'cause you'll be laughing at yourself. (she bites into her other slice of pizza)

Courtney: You right, Ashlyn. We should all stick together. For instance, Christopher, the so-called star quarterback, made racial slurs about you. We all should kick his ass because that was a NO . . . NO . . . NO!

Deniece: Yeah! I oughta (points at the guy across from them) tell

Dannybo over there, who plays football with him.
Ashlyn: That's all right. I can defend my own problems. Deniece:
OK, suit yourself.

[Deniece, Courtney, Ashlyn, and Tamara are walking down the
hallway to go to their next class laughing and joking around until
Christopher knocks Ashlyn's notebook out of her hand from behind
while he's walking with his clique.]
Christopher: Oops, (impersonating Steve Urkel in *Family Matters*)
did I do that? (he walks away laughing with his clique)
[One of the football player saw that while he's walking with his
girlfriend to her classroom, then he turns around to help Ashlyn pick
up her papers along with Deniece, Tamara, and Courtney.]
Corey: What's up? I'm Corey. I'm sorry he did this to you. (hands
Ashlyn her notebook and her papers) My boys and I are going to
jump him after school, away from school property 'cause I'm aware
that he called you a ‒niggaǁ in class.
Tamara: Yep. Get his ass.
Ashlyn: He did, but I can handle it. Trust me; I grew up in the
hood, I-wood, CA.
Corey: Fa' real! No shit! (laughs out) Ooooh! You got an older
brotha? Ashlyn: (nods) Yep! I surely do.
Corey: Ah, somebody gonna get their ass kick tonite! (he walks to
the classroom laughing with a group of the football players)
[Tamara, Deniece, and Courtney look at each other.] Tamara: I guess
so.
Courtney: Does your brotha have a girl? Deniece: Yeah, does he?
Ashlyn: Yep. My best friend, Darnesia. Tamara: In Cali, right?
Ashlyn: Yep.
Courtney: Oh, girlfriends, (looks at her watch) we're going to be late.
We only got a minute to get to our classes.
Tamara: Oh, shoot. (she runs upstairs)


Ashlyn: My class is r . . . ight here.
Courtney: Mine is, too. (turns to speak to Deniece) Dee, where you.?
[Deniece had left already. Ashlyn and Courtney just walk into their
journalism class together.]

*The scene fades away.*

*Scene 10*

When: The end of the school day Where: The front of the school building

*Hours pass and the school bell rings while the students are going to their cars or getting on the bus. Carlton parks the car in front of the building where he had dropped Ashlyn off earlier. He notices Ashlyn isn't around. He waits 15 minutes. Then he begins to get fidgety. He waits an additional 15 minutes. Ashlyn still hasn't shown up so he gets out of the car and goes into the building.*
*He looks around to see if he can spot her; he walks around looking inside classrooms. Finally, he reaches the 4th classroom, where he sees his sister. She is doing her homework, then he reads the bulletin stating, "After-school detention" in a whisper.*

Carlton: (speaks in disappointment to himself) Aw, Ashly! What did you do? Damn, girl, you just got here. (his beeper goes off; it's Debbie) Oh, shit, somebody's in trouble. (he goes down the hall to the pay phone and calls his mother) Hello.
Debbie: (she's on her car phone pulling in the driveway) Carlton, are you picking up Ashly right now?
Carlton: Yes.
Debbie: OK. I came home early because Ashly got into a fight and the principal wants me to meet him at the school. So, C., it's up to you to come on home 'cause I have to meet with the principal because of Ms. Thang.
Carlton: Do you know why she got in a fight?
Debbie: He told me he wanted me to meet him in person to disclose that information.
Carlton: Really? It must be something dealing with race because Ash don't fight unless she's defending herself.
Debbie: Well, I don't know, but I'll be there in a minute, soon as I change clothes.
Carlton: OK. I'm going to stay here. Debbie: All right, I'll be there in a minute.
[Carlton hangs the phone up and goes down the hall to see where the administration is; he goes into the office and sits down.
No one was in there until Ash walks in.]
Ashlyn: Why are you here? Did you get the message from Mom? (she sits down by Carlton)
Carlton: I just talked to Mom. I didn't go straight home. I came

here. (he pauses; Dr. Berg and Ms. Patrick enter the office)

Ashlyn: OK, I guess you want to know what hap—!

Dr. Berg: (interrupts Ashlyn and Carlton's conversation while he's opening his office door) Ashlyn, come on in my office while we wait on your mother. [Ms. Patrick sits down by Carlton.]

Ashlyn: (gets up) OK. (walks into the office and Dr. Berg shuts the door behind her)

Ms. Patrick: Hi, my name is Ms. Patrick, and your name is?

Carlton: I'm Ashlyn's brother, Carlton Richardson. So, who are you supposed to be?

Ms. Patrick: I'm Ashlyn's literature teacher. She was in my class when she got in a fight.

Carlton: Oh, so you witnessed the fight. (pauses) Who started it? And what was said or done in order for my . . .? (his voice tone gets louder; Debbie walks in)

Debbie: (interrupts) Carlton, keep it down. (she looks at Ms. Patrick) Hi, I'm Debbie Richardson, (she shakes Ms. Patrick's hand) Ashlyn's mother. (she looks at Dr. Berg's office) Are they already inside the office?

Ms. Patrick: (stands up) Yes, Ms. Richardson. (she directs Debbie to the office) Let's go inside 'cause he's waiting for you.

[Debbie and Ms. Patrick open the door and walk in. Ashlyn and Dr. Berg are talking, then stop when the door opens.]

Ms. Patrick: Dr. Berg, this is (points to Debbie) Ashlyn's mother, Debbie Richardson. (she sits down beside Dr. Berg)

Dr. Berg: (reaches over his desk to shake Debbie's hand) Nice to meet you, Mrs. Richardson. Have a seat by your daughter. (Debbie sits down by Ashlyn and Dr. Berg sits in his chair) Well, Ms. Richardson, sorry for the incident involving your daughter's first day at Kemptner.

Debbie: I appreciate the sympathy, but what is the incident you told me on the phone you could only explain in person?

Ashlyn: Hmm, I wonder why.

Debbie: Ashlyn! (she looks at her with a scowl on her face)

Dr. Berg: Well, Ms. Richardson, a student in the AP Literature class used racial slurs and profanity directed to Ms. Ashlyn.

Debbie: (puzzled with anger) Racial slurs?

Ashlyn: (shouts with aggression) Yeah, he called me a ‖nigga.‖ A ‖nigga bitch.‖

He even told me to go back to Africa where I belong. Dr. Berg: Look, Ashlyn. I know you're upset—

Debbie: (spoke with authority) Upset? You think she's upset? I am very disappointed and angry at you people who should have control of your students by making sure they are at least respecting one another. This is a disgrace! I can't believe you have the audacity to be calm about this incident that has occurred at your school on the first day! Explain to me why my daughter is in after-school detention when she was only defending her identity! How would you feel if it were vice versa? In other words, my daughter calling him a –honky‖ or a cracker? (she rocks in her seat) Tell me that!

[Dr. Berg and Ms. Patrick blush when Debbie made that statement.]

Ashlyn: Oh, by the way, Mr. Quarterback (she emphasizes) knocked down my books while I was going to class after lunch. He even threatened me. (pauses) Oh, don't forget he spit on my shoes in Ms. Patrick's classroom. *That's* why I retaliated.

Debbie: (turns to Ashlyn and touches her hand while Dr. Berg and Ms. Patrick look nervous) He *spit* on you? He spit on you in the *classroom*? Then he knocks down your books in the hallway. (she turns to Dr. Berg, taking a deep breath) I want to know, did all this happen to my daughter on the first day at this school? And be truthful.

Ms. Patrick: (looks at Dr. Berg) Yes, the part where Christopher spit on her shoes, but I wasn't aware of him knocking her books out of her hands.

Dr. Berg: I'm aware of Christopher spitting on Ashlyn's shoes, but she didn't notify us that Chris had knocked her books down (Ashlyn rolls her eyes at Dr. Berg) and threatened her.

Debbie: Um, so what type of punishment are you giving him? (she folds her arm and leans into the chair)

Dr. Berg: I'm giving him a 4-day suspension from school and from all extracurricular activities.

Debbie: *That's it?* You just giving him 4 days to forget what he has done wrong to a fellow classmate? That's more like a slap on the hand instead of the behind. What kind of school is this?

Ashlyn: A school that makes minorities feel meaningless.

Ms. Patrick: That's not true, Ashlyn. That's why I immediately acted on his abominable behavior.

Ashlyn: (rolls her eyes at Dr. Berg) Well, Dr. Berg needs to control the so- called superstar QB, or else . . .

Debbie: Or else you're not going to do anything, Ashlyn. Let me and your dad handle this. (she looks at Dr. Berg) Dr. Berg, if you don't handle this young man and his disrespectful attitude, I will file charges against this school. 'Cause a school is for education; it's a definite tool for our children's success. Therefore, the child needs to have a comfortable, civilized, well-structured environment that has zero tolerance for disrespect, discrimination, or any other negative behaviors. Do I make myself clear on this matter? (pauses for seconds to hear a response) I don't hear—

Dr. Berg: Yes, I hear you, and I understand. I will make sure Mr. Christopher does not bother Ms. Ashlyn. If so, we will expel him for disorderly conduct. (he smirks)

Ms. Patrick: I definitely agree. I think he should be suspended from the property for 2 weeks, including football games and practices, along with other school functions.

Debbie: I agree.

Dr. Berg: Well, ladies, I will grant the extended suspension.

Debbie: (she smiles) Thank you.

Dr. Berg: Oh, Miss Ashlyn, today is your last day in after-school detention, OK? (pauses) Well, I guess you can sign the papers, and we can leave. (he smiles)

[Debbie signs the papers, shakes Dr. Berg's hand and Ms. Patrick's, too. Ashlyn and Debbie leave the office and get Carlton. Carlton walks with Ashlyn and Debbie to Debbie's car.]

Carlton: Everything is cool, right? Debbie: Yep.

Ashlyn: Where did you park, C.?

Carlton: Oh, I parked in the front parking lot not back here. (pauses) Ashlyn, what happened? [Debbie gets in the car.]

Ashlyn: (opens the door and sits in the car with Debbie in the driver's seat) It's a long story. I'll tell you when we get home. (she shuts the door and they pull off)

[Carlton looks puzzled and weary, then he goes to his car; he gets in and leaves the premises.]

*The scene fades away.*

## Scene 11

When: Minutes later
Where: The Richardson home

*Carlton, Ashlyn, and Debbie arrive home. They walk in the den; Carlton turns on the television while Ashlyn sits in the recliner and Debbie sits in the love seat.*

Carlton: (turns around and sits down at the end of the couch close to Ashlyn) Ashlyn, you were going to tell me what happened.

Ashlyn: (reclines the chair and kicks her shoes off) Carlton, what happened was I got in a fight because a white boy, who happens to be the star quarterback, called me a ‒nigga bitch‖ and spit at me when I was trying to introduce myself to the class.

Carlton: He called you a ‒nigga bitch‖ (pauses and stands up with rage) and spit at you?

Ashlyn: Yes.

[Carlton pacing back and forth with anger, clinching his fists.]

Debbie: Carlton, you need to sit down.

[A door slams.]

Ashlyn: (talks to Debbie) Did you hear that?


Debbie: Yeah. (she pauses) I think that's your father. (speaks loudly to Jeff) Honey, is that you?

Jeff: (responds) Yeah! (he walks into the den with his tie loose and his jacket hanging on his arm)

Carlton: (still pacing back and forth) I can't believe this! I should have known! Especially in this area!

Jeff: (jumps in front of Carlton) Hey, man! What's wrong? What's up? You got into it with somebody? (Carlton still manages to move back and forth) Slow down, Carlton! Stop, son! You're making me nervous! (he turns to Debbie, and then looks at Ashlyn with her lips sticking out) OK, somebody tell me what happened today!

Debbie: Ashlyn got into a fight at school.

Jeff: Say what? (shakes his head and put his hands on his hips) How in a world could (looks at Ashlyn with a stern look) you get into a fight on your first day at a new school? Tell me *now*!

Debbie: (gets out of her seat and walks toward Jeff) It's not her fault, Jeff, so calm down.

Jeff: What do you mean (turns to Debbie) it's not her fault? Huh? You know how arrogant and sassy she can be, just like Vanessa was at her age. (he turns back to Ashlyn) What did you do?

Ashlyn: (rolls her eyes at Jeff) I defended myself. *That's* what I did.

Debbie: Ashlyn, watch your tone.

Jeff: What did you do?

Carlton: Say, man! Get off of her! (he jumps in between Jeff and Ashlyn) OK! (pauses and shakes his head) Ash was called a ‒nigga bitch‖ and spit at in her English AP class, a'ight? (he walks out of the den) Oooh, I can't wait to get my hands on that white boy. (pauses) That ol' cracker!

Jeff: All right, Carlton, that's enough! And do not use that language in this house! (then he looks at Ashlyn) Ash, (he walks to her and bends down beside her) baby girl, I'm sorry, I'm so sorry. (he leans over and kisses her on the forehead) You know this is just a test for all of our faith to live in this neighborhood. It's going to take some time. I just, (clears his throat) we just pray to God that this doesn't happen to you again. If it does, may God help (stands up with so much fire and anger gritting his teeth) whoever does it to you..

Debbie: (swallows hard on her Coke) Jeff, baby, it's been taken care of. (she walks to him and grabs him) The lil white boy is going to be suspended for 2 weeks. (pauses and sighs) And if it happens again, he'll be expelled.

Jeff: Good! 'Cause nobody—I mean *nobody*—messes with my family! And if they do, they will pay! So help me God! (he walks out of the room, goes upstairs, and slams the bedroom door)

[Ashlyn and Debbie look at each other in a state of shock at how Jeff reacted toward her situation.]

*The scene fades away.*

# ACT 3

## Scene 12

When: Two weeks after the incident  Where: In the school

*Ashlyn has joined the journalism club and is working on the yearbook and the school broadcasting station. In her spare time, she hangs out with Courtney, Tamara, Deniece, and Corey, along with the black athletes. Everything seems to be OK until Friday, Sept. 8th, the beginning of the weekend after Labor Day weekend. The school bell has rung. Everyone is going to their cars, dancing, and talking out loud with one another. Ashlyn walks with Courtney, Tamara, Deneice, and Corey, along with the other black athletes. She walks to her brother Carlton's car (she borrows it from him sometimes) and notices someone had written, "Go Home, Nigga Bitch!" on her brother's windshield, and the car window was busted in with a noose hanging on the rearview mirror.*

Ashlyn: (throws her books down and yells) I don't believe this shit! Who did this?
[Corey, Tamara, Deniece, and Courtney run over to her while everyone else cuts off their music to see what happened.]
Corey: (running over to Ashlyn) What's wrong, Ash? Ash?
[Ashlyn paces back and forth, then points to the car as they approach her. Corey, Courtney, Tamara, and Deniece look at the writing on the car with anger.]
Tamara: What the f—uck! This can't be!
Deniece: I told you, Ashlyn. You should have let the guys beat that ol' white- ass punk.
Corey: That's it, Ashlyn! This is W..A..R, baby! I'm going to kick some white ass! (he looks over at the black athletes) Say, fellows! Check this shit out! Check it out!
[The athletes come over to the car and read it.]

Athlete 1: Ooooooh no, no, this is not the Kunta Kinte or Harriet Tubman era! (pauses) This white boy got some nuts!
Athlete 2: In practice today, let's eat this white cracker's ass up in the locker room and on the field, you know what I'm saying? (giving everybody dap) Shit! Let's do this, Corey!

Corey: Oh, I'm ready!

You ready, fu?

Athletes: Hell, yeah!

Corey: Hey, Ash, we going to handle this; just watch us at practice. (he huddles with the other athletes at his car across the way)

Ashlyn: OK! But I'm going to let Dr. Berg see this shit before he leaves! Tamara: (grabs Ashlyn's arm) Girl, don't do it until they finish doing what (points at Corey) they're gonna do.

Deneice: No, no, tell Dr. Berg first while the guys handle whenever they want to handle it.

Courtney: I agree with Dee and Ash.

Ashlyn: Cool, I'm going to tell Dr. Berg right now.

Corey: (walks back over to Ashlyn) Do that while we handle this so you won't get in trouble. A'ight? (he looks up and sees Christopher and his clique walking together laughing and pointing at Ashlyn's car) Yeah. He laughing now. (he looks at his teammates) Let's go, hommies. It's time to regulate! (they walk to the stadium)

Deneice: Somebody getting their ass kicked!

Tamara: OOOOOH! I feel sorry for the white boy, but he had it coming. Courtney: Yep.

[Ashlyn picks up her books and puts them in the car.]

Ashlyn: (shuts the car door) Hey, y'all want to go with me to get Dr. Berg? Tamara, Deneice, and Courtney: Hell, yeah! Let's go!

[They all walk with Ashlyn side by side to Dr. Berg's office. They walk into the office. The secretary is typing.]

Ashlyn: (speaks with sass and arrogance) I need to speak with Dr. Berg. It's an emergency.

[Tamara, Deneice, and Courtney frown at the secretary; the secretary looks at them nervously.]

Secretary: OK. (she picks up the phone and calls Dr. Berg) Mr. Berg, you need to come to the front. It's an emergency.

[Dr. Berg runs out of his office half-dressed, and Christopher's mother comes out right behind him. Tamara, Courtney, Ashlyn, and Deneice look at each other in disbelief.]

Ashlyn: Dr. Berg! Someone has put a racial slur on my car . . . busted my windows and hung a noose inside of it! (Christopher's mother rolls her eyes at Ashlyn.) I need you to come see this right now!

Dr. Berg: OK. Let's go.

[They all walk out of the office to the parking lot. When they got to the parking lot, there were police cars, ambulances, and fire trucks at the football stadium.]

Ashlyn: (speaks under her breathe) Oh, shit. (she looks at Deneice, Courtney, and Tamara)

Dr. Berg: I wonder what's going on there. (they approach Ashlyn's car) Oh, Ashlyn! I'm (pauses) shocked! I thought everything was all right! I can't believe it!

[Then one of the white teammates runs to Chris's mother; he stops and tries to catch his breath.]

Teammate: Ma'am, they're trying to kill us out there. The whole defensive squad and some of the offense. Chris is banged up pretty bad.

Chris's mother: (shaking and trembling) Oh my gosh! (grabs the player's hand) Take me to him! (she runs with the teammate)

Dr. Berg: This has gotten out of hand! (he stares at Ashlyn's car)

Ashlyn: So, what are you going to do about this, Dr. Berg?

Tamara: Yep, Mr. Berg, what's up?

Dr. Berg: We're going to investigate this. But now, I got to go see what's going on at the stadium. (he runs over there)

[Ashlyn, Courtney, Tamara, and Deneice just stand there without emotion; just shocked.]

Ashlyn: Damn, they really did handle it. They even got the emergency response over here. (pauses and sighs) I didn't want them to kill him. Courtney: Sista girl, welcome to the South.

[They walk over to the stadium. When they approach the stadium there is a puddle of blood going toward the field house; the police officers have players in handcuffs; Christopher's mom is crying as she gets in the ambulance with Christopher, who is fighting for his life; he wasn't the only one; Corey was too. Someone had shot him with a double-barreled shotgun. The girls couldn't believe their eyes; it was the Civil Rights movement all over again.]

*The scene fades away.*

## Scene 13

When: Later that day
Where: The Richardson home

*Ashlyn walks slowly toward the house. Her mom and dad run out to her. She breaks down and starts crying.*

Ashlyn: (crying) It's all my fault Corey is in the hospital. I should have told him, –No, don't do it.‖ None of the guys would be hurting or in jail if I would have stopped them.

Carlton: (comes out of the house to greet Ashlyn) Ashlyn, you all right? (he grabs and holds her in his brotherly arms) Oh my God, sis, why didn't you call me? I wanted to handle it. (pauses and sighs) But that's OK; Chris got what he deserved.

[They all look at the busted window, the noose, and the writing on the car, then walk in the house together, comforting Ashlyn. The television is on in the den informing the public about the brawl at Kemptner High School. They also announce Chris's condition as critical, and Corey's also.]

*The scene fades away.*

## Scene 14

When: A week later
Where: Memorial Herman Southwest Hospital

*Corey is in stable condition, and Ashlyn pays him a hospital visit. His mother, two sisters, a brother, and his girlfriend are at his bedside at Memorial Herman Southwest Hospital.*

[Ashlyn walks in with balloons and a teddy bear; his mother and girlfriend greet Ashlyn.]

Corey's mother: Hi, Ashlyn, come on in, sweetie. Corey's girlfriend: Hey, girl, it's about time you came by.

Ashlyn: Yeah, I apologize. I just did not want to see my boy suffering like that. (she hits Corey on the arm that is not wounded)

Sister 1: Oh, that's sweet.

Sister 2: I guess we adopt another li'l sista. (she hugs Ashlyn)

[Everybody smiles; Ashlyn gives the teddy bear to Corey.] Corey: Thanks.

Ashlyn: No. Thank you.

Corey: Ash, don't beat yourself up about me being here. What matters is that we black people should always have each other's back, especially in the South. No matter what it is, unity and love are the only ways God wants us to build the black community. So, keep ya head up, sis. 'Cause in society, you never know what you are going to face; you never know what you are going to take or to give; you just got to do whatever it takes and have faith as you live, learn, and love. (he smiles and touches her on the cheek)

Ashlyn: (weeps softly) Thanx. (pauses and sighs) You kinda sound like my dad. (pauses and cocks her eyebrow) Did he come by?

Corey: Yep. He surely did. He thanked me for protecting you like a brotha supposed to.

[Corey's mother and sisters were wiping tears from their eyes.]

Ashlyn: Well, I guess I have to go so I can practice on my jump shots and free throws to get in shape for tryouts 2 weeks from now. (pauses and hugs Corey) You take care, my black bro. (she gives him dap and hugs the sisters, the mother, and the girlfriend as she departs from the hospital room)

*The scene fades away.*


## Scene 15

When: Oct. 1, 1996 (Friday) Where: The school gym

*Ashlyn has been practicing and conditioning for tryouts for weeks. Now it's time for her to show what skills she has in the game of basketball on Friday, Oct. 1. Ashlyn walks into the gym filled mostly white people, then she sees Deniece, Tamara, and Courtney. They run to her; Deneice and Tamara are in their practice uniforms.*

Tamara: (dribbling the basketball) Are you ready to play some B-ball? Ashlyn: And you know this wo-MAN!

[They laugh.]

Deniece: Well, come on with yo' bad self! [Coach Matthews blows her whistle.]

Coach Matthews: All right, ladies! Let's get in four lines behind the baseline to run some suicides!

Ashlyn: Coach! Are we supposed to stretch first? Coach Matthews: Yes, if you were on time.

Ashlyn: What?

Deneice: (walks with Ashlyn to the baseline along with Tamara) Oh, Ash, you were 15 minutes late when we were stretching.

Ashlyn: Oh, now you tell me. (sighs) Uh, y'all can be (smirks) so trifling. [Deneice and Tamara laugh while they get in line to do suicides.]

[Coach Matthews continues to blow her whistle to have the players run the four suicides. Ashlyn is worn out already on the last one. She is the last one out of her bunch to finish the suicide.]

Coach Matthews: (yells at Ashlyn) What's wrong, Richardson? You tired? Ashlyn: (yells back catching her breath) No!

Coach Matthews: I can't hear you! Speak louder!

Ashlyn: (yells louder) I said –No‖! (she stops at the baseline to take her break bending over, then stands up with her hands on her head.)

Coach Matthews: All right, ladies!! Let's get in line to do the three-man weave! (she looks at Tamara and Deniece) Tamara and Deniece, you two are up first, along with Ms. Richardson!

Ashlyn: Say, what? Aw, man.

Coach Matthews: What was that, Richardson? (everybody looks and laughs softly) I can't hear you! (the predominately white team continues to laugh) Ashlyn: I need to watch first before doing it. Don't you think (sassy tone), Coach?

Coach Matthews: (walks up to Ashlyn and speaks in a soft, sarcastic tone) Are you teaching me how to coach, Richardson? I sure hope not (raises her tone at Ashlyn) 'cause the attitude will not be tolerated. (pauses and turns her back to Ashlyn) Better yet, give me a sprint right now under 10 seconds. (she walks to the corner of the baseline) Better yet, give me four! Get on the line, Richardson. Now! Or you will not be on the team! (Deniece and Tamara shake their head at the baseline with the rest of the team)

Deniece: (speaks softly to Tamara) This is some shit. Tamara: I know it. It's all 'cause of her rep.

Coach Matthews: (she turns to Tamara and Deniece) What is that, Deniece and Tamara? I can't hear you. (she walks up to them) If you want to play basketball, you keep your mouths shut.

[Ashlyn finishes the four sprints under 10 seconds each.]

Coach Matthew: OK, Richardson, get in line to do the three-man weave. Ashlyn: I don't know how to do it, Coach. (she's breathing hard)

Coach Matthews: Really? So what did you do in Inglewood High basketball, superstar? (pauses) You didn't think I knew what type of player you are. (she walks up to her) Ms. All-American, 1st team in the State of California 2 years in a row! You just an arrogant, sassy black athlete, which I somewhat have a problem with. (she smirks at her) So, show me what the three-man (she grabs the ball from one of the players and throws it at Ashlyn) is.

Ashlyn: (catches the ball and grits her teeth while she gets in line) OK, I'll show you.

[Ashlyn, Deniece, and Tamara run the course under 15 seconds; Ashlyn takes a 3-pt shot at the end of the course and makes it.]

Coach Matthews: (yells) Do it again! I want a layup!

[Ashlyn stares at Coach Matthews and does it with Tamara and Deniece again, but this time shoots a layup.]

[Coach Matthews stays on Ashlyn throughout the whole tryout when the players do the defense one-on-one drill, passing drills, free throws, and dribbling drills. After the free throw drill, Coach Matthews gathers the girls in a huddle to call the names of who made the team.]

Coach Matthews: Tamara, Deniece, Ashlyn, Amanda, Yvonne, Crystal, Tricia, Susan, Jennifer, Alexandria, and Maria, congratulations! You made the team. Practice starts next week after school.

[The girls go to locker to get their practice squad and game jerseys.]

Amanda: (greets Ashlyn) Welcome aboard (shakes her hand), Ashlyn! Ashlyn: Thanks. (smiles) I appreciate it.

Tamara: Ash!

Deniece: Ashlyn is in the house!

Tamara and Deniece: (start chanting four times) –Ashlyn is in the house! Say, what? Ashlyn in the house!‖

[They all leave the gym, get into their cars, and drive off.]

*The scene fades away.*

### Scene 16

When: Shortly after leaving the gym Where: The driveway of Ashlyn's house

*Ashlyn pulls up in the driveway to her house; she notice Darnesia's car is there. She jumps out of the car and opens the door and sees Carlton and Omar talking in the hallway.*

Ashlyn: (she runs to Omar) Omar! Omar! Omar: (hugs and kisses her) Hey, baby! Ashlyn: When did you get here?

Omar: Oh, we got here about 30 minutes ago.

Ashlyn: We?

Omar: Yeah. Darnesia is in the living room stuffing her face.

(Ashlyn continues to hug him)

We're . . . we're (she keeps kissing him) going to be here until Monday. Darnesia: (hears the conversation in the hallway and yells out) Naw, Wednesday. I have College Day at U of H!

Ashlyn: For real? (she pulls Omar into the living room)

Darnesia: (jumps out of her seat and runs to Ashlyn) What's up, sis? What you been doing?

Ashlyn: Uh, it's been so much trouble here.

Darnesia: Yeah, your moms told me about the white boy calling you a n—b— and writing on Carlton's car stating that. (pauses and shakes her head) Girl, if I was there, I would have whipped his A-S-S (spells it out, not say it) my damn self.

[Omar rubs Ashlyn's back as they sit down on the couch together, and Darnesia sits by Carlton in the love seat.]

Omar: So, baby, is this guy back in school? Ashlyn: Yeah, but he's scared to come near me.

Omar: Man, when Carlton told me that when we got here, I was like, why she didn't tell me over the phone or in the letters? (looks at Ashlyn) I'm your man. I need to know these things 'cause I would have flown down here and whopped his white ass! You know!

Carlton: I hear ya, man. I wanted to, but before you knew it, there was a brawl at the school. So, everything is a'ight, now. They know not to mess with her. Jeff: (leaning back in his recliner) Yep, I thought I was going to lose my religion and take to the ol' school like how we used to do it to defend ourselves down here in H-Town. Shoot, we were bad back then. Boxing was the sport.

[Carlton and Omar laugh.]

Omar: Boxing was the sport, huh? Jeff: Shoot, ask Debbie. Ask her.

[Omar laughs.]

Debbie: Yeah. He's right. We were feisty back then. Not everyone turned the cheek. (she chuckles)

[Ashlyn and Darnesia look at each other and laugh.] Ashlyn: So, that's why I'm so sassy, huh?

Jeff: Yep. Just like your ol' mama. (Debbie gets up and hits him in the back of his head.) And me, too.

[They all laugh.]

Carlton: Say, y'all want go to cuz Trent's club tonite since y'all down here?

Omar: Yeah, we can do that. Jeff: Y'all be careful out there. Carlton: Oh, we will, trust me.

Debbie: Uh-huh, trust you. (she smiles) Whatever you say. Ashlyn: I guess we could do that.

Darnesia: I don't. I want to go to the movies. Let's go to the club on our last night here.

Carlton: A'ight, we'll do that.

Ashlyn: Oh, Darnesia, girl, let's go tonite, then go later on to the movies. Carlton: Naw, let's show them around first, then go before they leave. (looks at Ashlyn) Is that cool, Ashlyn? So, you and my boy can spend one-on-one. You know what I mean.

Ashlyn: (she cuddles up with Omar) OK. That'll do. First, let me go take a shower and get myself together. (she gets up and goes upstairs; Darnesia follows)

Omar: Maybe I need to freshen up, too. (he gets up to follow Ashlyn) Jeff: (walks back into the den) Say what, Omar? Omar, what (he sits in his recliner eating ice cream) you say?

Omar: Oh, I'll freshen up later when Ashlyn is through. Jeff: (gets up and pats Omar on the shoulder) That's better.

Omar: So, Jeff, where are we staying tonite, me and Darnesia? (pauses and flashes a crooked smile) Here?

Jeff: (sitting down in his recliner) No. You two are going to Vanessa and Darnell's.

Omar: Oh, Ash and Carlton's sister's house? (nods his head) That's cool.

[An hour later, Carlton, Omar, and Darnesia are ready and waiting on Ashlyn. She finally runs into the den 30 minutes later.]

Ashlyn: A'ight, everybody! (rubbing her hands with strawberry and champagne lotion, hypnotizing Omar)

Omar: Dang, girl! I'm going to have to watch you. Um-umm, (turns her around) girl, you just don't know.

Jeff: Omar, I'm still here. (smacking on his toothpick; Omar blushes) [Carlton and Darnesia get up.]

Carlton: A'ight, let's go, my peeps.

[Carlton, Ashlyn, Darnesia, and Omar leave the house and jump into Carlton's car. They drive off.]

*The scene fades away.*

# ACT 4

## Scene 17

When: Late in the evening. Where: At the movies.

*Carlton, Ashlyn, Darnesia, and Omar leave the Richardson's' house to go to the movies at Tinseltown to see* B.A.P.S. *Carlton and Darnesia are hugged up at the ticket booth while Omar and Ashlyn are shoulder to shoulder receiving their movie tickets for* B.A.P.S. *They move out of the line, then Darnesia and Carlton get theirs while Omar and Ashlyn stand on the side of the ticket booth waiting on them.*

Carlton: (looks at Darnesia and grabs the tickets) Well, baby, you know how we do it when we come to the movies. (he holds her hand and leads the way to Omar and Ashlyn)
Darnesia: Yep. I know how we do it, but I want to go check in a room 'cause I'm a little more classy now, boo. (she grabs his behind)
Carlton: (he smiles) Hold that thought.
[Carlton and Darnesia meet up with Omar and Ashlyn, and they all go through the gate to get to the movie scene.]
Ashlyn: Darnesia and Carlton, behave yourselves in the movie. (they enter into the movie room)
[The audience is laughing at the movie previews. Carlton and Darnesia sit toward the top, while Omar and Ashlyn move closer to the screen. The movie presentation finally starts. Both couples are lip-locked.]
Omar: (talks to Ashlyn) Do you want to spend one-on-one at the hotel room tonight that's nearby or do you want it right now?
Ashlyn: Right after the movie we can check in a hotel that's close by.
Omar: Um, I can't wait. (he licks his lips) Um, um, girl, I've been, eh, wee, ready to rock your world.
Ashlyn: Really? (she grins as he nibbles her neck)
[Carlton and Darnesia are still kissing and groping each other.]
Carlton: Ooh, baby, I can't wait. (whines) I can't wait . . . got to have you now. (kisses her all over her neck)
Darnesia: You got (pauses) 1 hour 10 minutes.
[The audience is laughing at the table scene; 1 hour and 10 minutes pass and both couples are racing out of the theatre to the car.]
Darnesia: Ooh, baby, crank up the car.
Carlton: (laughs) Oh, my, my, you just can't wait to get some—
Ashlyn: (interrupts) All right, you two, we're in the car. (Omar just smiles)

[They drive to a Holiday Inn. Omar and Carlton get out of the car to get the rooms while Darnesia and Ashlyn wait in the car.]

Ashlyn: Girl, Omar just don't know how much I have saved for him. I feel like I'm in a drought season that needs some rain, you know what I mean?

Darnesia: I feel ya, girl, 'cause I'm 'bout to explode!

[Carlton and Omar jump into the car; Carlton drives to the rooms around the corner.]

Darnesia: You got the key, baby? Carlton: (driving) Yep.

[They pull up to the rooms; both couples get out of the car and run to the rooms. Darnesia and Carlton fall into the door on top of each other; then Carlton gets up and shuts the door; Ashlyn and Omar walk into the bedroom kissing.]

Ashlyn: I'm going to the restroom. Just wait right here. (she goes into the bathroom and shuts the door)

Omar: (pulls out the condom, then strips down and hops into the bed) Goddamn, Carlton. (he hears Darnesia screaming Carlton's name and the bed banging against the wall) Man, that brotha was faithful for a change.

[Ashlyn walks out with a towel around her and stands over Omar in the bed, then drops the towel.]

Omar: (amazed) Damn, where have you been? Ashlyn: Waiting on you.

Omar: Ah, shit, I'm think I'm already having an orgasm. (he swallows hard) [Then he pulls her down and covers her up with the bed comforter; he lies on top of her grinding and kissing her neck.]

Omar: Ah, baby, you feel so good to me. Can I take the condom off to get the real deal again? (kisses her neck)

Ashlyn: (moans) Yes. I'm on the pill.

Omar: Was you on it the last time, boo?

Ashlyn: No. I want to make it special.

Omar: (he kisses and continues grinding without the condom) Oh, oh, oh, baby, it feels so . . .

[Darnesia and Carlton steadily moan and bang on the wall.]

Ashlyn: Damn, C., you really was faithful. (listening to the noise; Omar laughs, then grinds Ashlyn pretty hard) Oh, baby! Omar, do it again.

[He continues.]

*The scene fades away.*

***Scene 18***

When: 1:00 A.M.
Where: The Richardson house

*Darnesia and Carlton, and Ashlyn and Omar leave the hotel around 12:30 A.M.; they arrive at the Richardson's' at 1:00 A.M. The lights are off when they drive up, but the porch light cuts on when Carlton turns off the ignition. Everybody sits in the car waiting to see if anyone will come out of the house. No one comes out so they quietly get out of the car. Each couple walks side by side to the front door of the house.*

Carlton: (putting his house key in the door) Man, I thought we were in trouble until I realized Darnell and Vanessa are still here. (he opens the door)
Ashlyn, Omar and Darnesia: (respond) Yep.
[They walk in the house, going straight through the kitchen to the den.] Vanessa: (stands up to greet them with a stern look on her face) Well, it's about time you all got home 'cause me and Darnell was fixin' to leave.
Darnell: Yep. (he stands up) We surely was. Your mom and dad are already asleep, but they were very disappointed in you guys.


Vanessa: (walks in front of Ashlyn) 'Cause you didn't call to let anyone know where you were . . . Anything could have happened to you guys!
Darnell: Calm down, Vanessa. They're here, and that's all that matters. OK? (looks at Vanessa, then kisses her on the forehead)
Vanessa: OK. But (sighs) I'm not pleased, especially about you (she points at Ashlyn), Ashlyn.
Ashlyn: What the hell is that supposed to mean? (she rolls her eyes at Vanessa) You can kiss my ass 'cause you did the same exact things I did, and even worse. So if I was you, I would shut the hell up to let bygones be bygones.
Omar: (smirks) Damn, baby, that's ya sista. She was just worried.
Ashlyn: So? I don't care. She just don't have a right coming up to me like that. (pauses) (looks at Vanessa) Bitch.
[Omar grabs Ashlyn and takes her into the kitchen while Darnell pulls Vanessa away from the kitchen.

Darnesia and Carlton just look at them and shake their heads.]

Vanessa: (trying to get in the kitchen) Oh, I got ya, bitch. You like a li'l skank ho!

Darnell: (holding onto Vanessa trying to calm her down) Baby, baby, that's ya li'l sista.

Vanessa: And? The truth is the truth. Somebody needs to ruffle her feathers, or else society will teach her the hard way.

Darnell: (shakes his head) Vanessa, Vanessa, let's go. Enough is said. (he walks through the kitchen pulling Vanessa, but she goes through the hallway while he goes through the kitchen and speaks to Omar)

Hey, hey, (Ashlyn and Omar were kissing) a'ight, lover boy, let's go.

[Omar kisses Ashlyn on the forehead, then walks out of the kitchen. Darnesia and Omar get into their car and follow Vanessa and Darnell to their home.]

*The scene fades away.*

## Scene 19

When: 9:00 P.M. Wednesday
Where: Upstairs at the Richardson's' house

*The weekend has ended quickly; Wednesday has arrived. Ashlyn practices basketball the whole week; Omar watches her practice every day as well as joining her in the ladies' locker room after everybody has left. Carlton and Darnesia walk around the campus together at U of H. During their free time, they're either eating or making out somewhere. Late Wednesday night at 9 P.M., Ashlyn and Darnesia are upstairs at the Richardson's' house getting dressed to go to Carlton and Ashlyn's cousin, Trent's, club. Carlton and Omar are downstairs in the den watching television with Debbie and Jeff while waiting on Ashlyn and Darnesia.*

Omar: Dang, how long is it going to take them?

Carlton: Shoot, you know how these women are. It takes 2 hours and 30 minutes for them to get fully dressed. (pauses) Shoot, I'd rather for them to take a long time 'cause I don't want to walk around with a dried-up, ashy, stanky female. I want her to be, you know, a Coca-Cola-shaped black Barbie with strawberry aroma.

I swear, man, tainted women that smell like catfish and ashy, like they jumped into the freezer being frostbitten. Me, I can't have it.

[Omar, Debbie, and Jeff laugh. Darnesia and Ashlyn come downstairs, finally.]
Debbie: (looks at Ashlyn) Oh, no, no, sista, you are *not* wearing that.
Jeff: Aw, Debbie, you bought it for her, remember?
Debbie: No, I didn't.
Jeff: Yes, you did, honey. I can recall me and you had a disagreement about it. I told you it was going to bite you in your behind. (he laughs)
Debbie: That's not funny. I didn't know it was—
Ashlyn: Mom, chill a little. I'll adjust it. (she ties the shirt close to her belly button instead of her chest where you can see her stomach) Is that better?
Debbie: I guess. (she rolls her eyes at Jeff)
Omar: (jumps up) I guess we ready. (he smiles at Ashlyn) Carlton: (grabs Darnesia's hand) Yeah, let's go.
Jeff: (walks out with the couples) Remember, call us to let us know y'all are all right, OK?
Omar, Ashlyn, Carlton, and Darnesia: (respond) OK! [They all get in Carlton's car and drive off.]
*The scene fades away.*

## Scene 20

When:
10:30 that night Where: Trent's club

*Carlton, Darnesia, Omar, and Ashlyn pull up to Trent's club, "Mr. T" on MLK around 10:30 P.M. after eating and making out at the park for the last time. Carlton gets out of the car first, then Ashlyn, to see if they can speak to Trent. Trent comes out of the club and greets Ashlyn and Carlton.*

Trent: Hey, li'l cuz, what's up, man? Long time no see. (he looks at Ashlyn) Girl, you sexy as hell and finer than a motherf—
Ashlyn: Say, T., it's me, Ashlyn.
Trent: Naw, fa' real? Li'l Ash? (he looks at her) Give cuz some love then. (he hugs Ashlyn) Shoot, I was waiting for y'all to come through.
Carlton: Shoot, you know how our T. Jones is.

Trent: I know it. Shoot, man, this club has kept me out of trouble. I don't smoke weed or sell crack anymore. (he looks up at the sky) I thank God for allowing me to have my own business, you know what I'm saying?

Carlton: Yeah. That's why I'm going to get my degree.

Trent: Fa' show, welcome to the (he gives Carlton dap) party.

Carlton: Say, Trent, we got our peeps in the car from I-wood; is it OK . . .? Trent: Yeah. It's on me, cuz. If you hungry I'll hook y'all up, too.

[Ashlyn and Carlton signal Omar and Darnesia to get out of the car. They walk up to their partners and go into the club together. The music is loud; people are shoulder to shoulder. They walk with Trent through the club.] Carlton: Damn, Trent, it sho' is crowded.

Trent: Yeah. I know it. Follow me to the VIP.

Carlton: A'ight. (holding Darnesia's hand tightly and follows Trent)

Omar: (holding Ashlyn's hand and follows Carlton and Trent) Damn, it's crowded tonight, you know?

Trent: Yep. (they reach the VIP where Bulldog, Dr. D, and Master C. are sitting at the bar) This is it.

Darnesia: Oh, shit, that's Dr. and Bulldog and Master C. Bulldog: Hey, ladies, what's crackin'? What's up, fellas? Dr.: What's up? Master C.: What's up? You're hanging with the big dogs today, you heard? Carlton: (gave them dap) Yeah, we just checking our cuz's franchise, you know?

Master C.: Fa' real. That's good, man. Family support is needed.

Carlton: Yeah.

Trent: Say, if yo' wanna dance, you got to go through this door (pointing to the door on his left) to get to the dance floor quicker.

Darnesia: You know I'm ready to shake this big a-s-s.

Ashlyn: Come on, sista. (she walks toward the door pulling Darnesia's arm) Bulldog: Aw, y'all don't wanna dance in here. That's cool.

[Ashlyn and Darnesia laugh and walk out of the VIP to the dance floor; Omar and Carlton look at each other, then follow them. Ashlyn and Darnesia reach the dance floor where 2Pac is playing; the music is very loud.]

Darnesia: Hey, that's my song! (she starts dancing)

Ashlyn: Girl, you betta stop before some guy come behind ya! (dancing from side to side)

Omar: Look at Dee. She would be the wild one.

Carlton: I know it. (he dances behind Darnesia) Hey, baby, I like the way you work it. (Darnesia smiles and dances harder)

Ashlyn: Oh, oh. (the song, ─I Like The Way You Work‖ by Blackstreet comes on) (pauses and listens to the beat of the song) That's Blackstreet. Oh, yeah, I'm ready to roll now!

Omar: (jumps behind Ashlyn) Let's show Carlton and Darnesia how we work it!

[Omar and Ashlyn take dancing to another level.]

Carlton: Aw, hell, naw, that's rated triple X! (looking at Ashlyn and Omar) Trent: (walks behind Carlton) Cuz (looking at Ashlyn dancing) ain't li'l no mo.

[Everybody starts watching Ashlyn and Omar dance; the song ends then a slow jam by R. Kelly, ─You Remind Me of Something,‖ comes on; Carlton caresses Darnesia while Omar and Ashlyn are slow dancing and kissing.] Omar: Ashlyn, I want a baby with you so bad. I prayed all last night that you'll carry my child, my firstborn.

Ashlyn: Omar, I would love to, but baby, I'm not ready yet.

Omar: You don't love me enough to bear my child? (pauses) Ash, I love you, girl. That's all I'm asking for. [Carlton and Darnesia stop dancing and look at Omar and Ashlyn beginning to argue.] Can you at least do that for me before I leave tomorrow? (he grabs her face with both hands and looks into her eyes) Please, baby, I want you to be the mother of my child and be my wife!

Ashlyn: Oh, Omar, you're talking crazy. You're moving too fast. I cannot do that right now. Plus, I want to have my degree to get a stable job in order to start a family, you know? Baby, I love you, but right now, we have to find our identity before bringing a child in this world.

Omar: Ash, (he backs away) you still can go to school and get your degree. I'll be there for you. I just want a child to keep my name going, you know? That's all I ask, baby. (he walks away)

[Carlton runs after Omar; Darnesia walks up to Ashlyn.]

Ashlyn: Girl, he's talking crazy! I wonder why he's acting that way!

Darnesia: Sista, girl, Omar loves you! He wants to settle down with you. He told me that he wants to move up here and marry you when you graduate from high school.

Ashlyn: Darnesia, are you serious? He plans to do that? (she looks confused) [Carlton finally catches up with Omar outside of the club.]

Carlton: Say, man, what's up? Why you run out on my sista like that?

Omar: I think Ash loves someone else. She's just not telling me, and the only way I know is because she doesn't want to settle down with me.

Carlton: Damn, bro, you serious. (pauses) Man! Damn, you really do love Ash.

Omar: (he wipes a tear off his face) Yep. She makes me feel like a man, you know, but if she don't wanna be down, it's cool.

Carlton: Oh, I'll talk to her to see what's up, a'ight? (he gives Omar dap) [Carlton walks back into the club; Darnesia and Ashlyn are sitting at the table talking; guys are flirting and smiling at them as they pass by.]

Darnesia: (looks at the guys and smiles) Damn, I see why you don't wanna settle down. All these sexy brothas up in here.

Ashlyn: Naw! I just want to have a decent life like my mother and father. I don't wanna be stuck in poverty and be a statistic, you know?

Darnesia: Girl, Omar is a hardworking man. He's a licensed carpenter with his GED, and he's good enough for you to be able to live your dreams as well.

Ashlyn: I know. I'm being a li'l shallow. I guess I can reconsider next year or the following year. Just don't tell Nessa or my parents.

Darnesia: (smiles) OK! Let's go find him. (she pulls Ashlyn out of her seat) [Outside of the club, there is a confrontation between Omar and some other black guy who is a Blood; Carlton is trying to get through the crowd.]

Omar: Look, man! I don't know you, a'ight? I apologize for running into your girl. I didn't see her there! I apologize! I don't want to cause any trouble, man!

Guy: She said you touched her ass, you ol' ho-ass nigga!

Omar: What? She told you that? I did not grab her ass; only my girl's ass tonight! The bitch is lying. (he's getting hostile) Now, if I was you I would leave me the hell alone 'cause where I come from, it ain't no pretty sight!

Guy: Really? Well, maybe you betta change your tone, nigga, cause the South don't play that West Coast shit!

Omar: How you know I'm from the West Coast?

Guy: I have my sources. I did a li'l investigate on ya 'cause what you did to my girl who is *not* a bitch like you!

[Carlton finally gets through the crowd.] Carlton: Aw, shit!

[Ashlyn and Darnesia come outside of the club; Trent runs past them; Omar and the guy are fighting, then a gun goes off twice. Ashlyn and Darnesia run to the crowd; Omar is on the ground; the security gets

the guy in handcuffs. Carlton is crying on his knees beside Omar.]
Carlton: Omar, (holding Omar's head up from the ground; crying) man, don't die, man! Don't die, man! Don't die, I love ya, bro!
Omar: I'm trying (spitting up blood and looks at his hand covered with blood) not to. Where's Ashly?
Ashlyn: (runs to him screaming) Omar, baby! I love you! (she cries out to him and falls beside him, hugging him) I want your baby! Baby, don't leave me!
Darnesia: (walks slowly; crying) Omar, Omar, O . . . (Carlton grabs Darnesia)
Carlton: Man, where is the ambulance? (he looks at Trent) Trent, are they coming, man? My dawg is dying, man!
[Darnesia holds onto Carlton, crying and screaming.]
Omar: (fighting for his life) Ashlyn, I love you, baby. I will always be here. (he touches her chest then closes his eyes)
Ashlyn: (crying and rocking Omar) Why, (she kisses him on the lips) baby, why you leave me here by myself? I love you.
[She continues to hold him while Darnesia is hollering and screaming and Carlton is crying out. The ambulance arrives.]
Trent: (looks at Carlton with tears in his eyes) I'm sorry, cuz. I'm so sorry, cuz. (he walks to the EMS)
[EMS pulls Ashlyn away from Omar, and Trent grabs her; Ashlyn is in a state of shock and passes out as the ambulance takes away Omar's body. Carlton and Darnesia run to Ashlyn to comfort her, but she's not responding so Trent has another unit rush Ashlyn to the hospital. Darnesia rides with her while Trent and Carlton follow them in Carlton's car and call home to tell the bad news.]

*The scene fades away.*

### Scene 21

When: Later that night
Where: The hospital emergency sitting room

*Twenty-five minutes after the ambulance brings Ashlyn in and pronounces Omar's death, Jeff, Debbie, Darnell, Vanessa, Darnesia, and Carlton sit in the waiting room for the status on Ashlyn since she had passed out and her heart was beating erratically. Everyone is shocked, gloomy, and badly shaken up.*

Jeff: (looks at his watch) It's already 12:30 P.M. We still haven't heard from Dr. Garza yet, Debbie. I'm nervous. My faith has been trampled. I can't believe this happened so suddenly; just three hours ago, Omar was here in a joyous mood and full of life. He even planned to go to college down here. (tears roll down his eyes as looks at Debbie) I just can't imagine how I can be strong for my daughter when I feel so weak. Now, I am worried about her. I just can't . . .

Debbie: (hugging and wiping the tears from Jeff's face) Baby, we can do this together. Surely (tears coming down her face) we are going to miss Omar; he was another son (she sniffs and wipes her face) that we took in since he was barely walking. We just got to pray about it and support each other through this loss.

[Darnesia is still crying and looking at Omar's clothes while Vanessa is comforting her; Darnell is comforting Carlton as he cries on Darnell's shoulder. Dr. Garza walks into the waiting room to give the family an update. Everyone focuses on him.]

Dr. Garza: (speaks in soft voice) Well, family, Miss Ashlyn is physically fine, but mentally she's not. So, (he sighs) you guys are going to have to support her through this crisis. Her heart was erratic because of shock. It could have led to a minor heart attack, but it didn't. She stopped breathing on her own, which initially slowed down her heartbeat. Therefore, I, (he sighs) I highly recommend you get her some counseling and watch her closely to make sure she doesn't try to commit suicide, OK?

The family: (responds) OK. Darnesia: So, can we go see her?

Dr. Garza: Yes. I'm going to discharge her in another hour. So feel free to see her. (he walks up to Jeff and pats him on the shoulder, then turns around and walks out of the room)

Carlton: Well, family, let's go in.

[Everyone follows Carlton through the swinging doors to Ashlyn's room; they walk in together. Ashlyn is in a fetal position in her hospital bed with tears rolling down her face. Darnesia and Debbie walk to the bed; Darnesia walks to the right side of her while Debbie walks to the left side where Ashlyn is turned to.]

Debbie: (pulls a chair up to the bed, sits down, and pushes Ashlyn's hair back) Hey, Ash, we're here for you. We want to see life back (her lips tremble as she speaks) into your eyes; we know it's going to take some time to heal, and that's why we are here to love you and support you through this. (pauses) OK? (she kisses Ashlyn's forehead)

[Darnesia sits down in a chair on her side waiting for Ashlyn to respond, but she doesn't.]

Debbie: (looks at Darnesia) You wanna come over here?

Darnesia: (gets up and walks over to Debbie to speak to Ashlyn) Hey, Ash, I want you to know that I'm here for you, too. (she starts crying again and runs out of the room)

Debbie: (looks at Jeff) Jeff, you and Carlton come over here so she can see you while I go talk to Darnesia. (Debbie leaves the room while Carlton and Jeff talk to Ashlyn)

Jeff: (tears falling from his eyes; holding her hand as she stares at the wall) Hey, baby girl, Daddy is here for you. I promise, you will not go through this alone, OK? (he wipes the tears from his eyes) We will get through this together. I can't afford losing you. You have a promised and bright future; I'm going to fast, pray, and fight for us to get you back to normal. (pauses) Oh, baby girl, I am so sorry. Daddy loves you. (he kisses her hand, then her forehead, and moves out of the way so Carlton can talk to her)

Carlton: (grabs her hand and rubs it) Hey, sis, I love you. I want you to know I am here no matter what. Just come back to us. I know it's hard, but you got to let it go and move on. I understand 'cause he was a brother to me since day one. So, I (he starts crying) know what you feel inside, but just come back and be your old self again. 'Cause I can't stand seeing you like this, Ash. I love you, baby sis. (he leans over and hugs her, crying on her)


[Vanessa and Darnell walk over to him; Darnell grabs his shoulder while Vanessa rubs his back crying. Within 2 minutes, Carlton lets go of Ashlyn and walks toward Jeff while Vanessa and Darnell speak to Ashlyn.]

Vanessa: (wiping tears from face) Oh, God, sis, I am very speechless right now. All I know is I love you so much I can't bear to see you like this. I want to help you and support you through this so I can see the ol' Ash again. The sassy one. (she laughs, then cries again) I love you and Darnell does, too.

Darnell: (he touches her forehead) Yeah, li'l sis, we are here for you, and we love you.

[Darnell and Vanessa walk away, then Darnesia and Debbie come back in the room.]

Jeff: Well, family, let's circle around Ashlyn's bed and pray over her.

Debbie: OK.

[The family circles around Ashlyn's bed; Ashlyn just bats her eyes with no body movement.]

Jeff: (shuts his eyes and prays) Father, we come here today to lift up our loved one . . .

*The scene fades away.*

# ACT 5

## Scene 22

When: A month has passed. Where: The gym locker room

*Everything is somewhat normal, but Ashlyn is still resentful and rebellious; yet, she still plays basketball. At this time, she's in the locker room with her teammates getting ready for their big game.*

Tamara: Say, Ash, you ready to whoop some ass? Ashlyn: Hell, yeah, let's do this!
[Tamara and Ashlyn get in line with the rest of the team waiting for their theme song, ‒Space Jam,‖ to run out; 5 minutes later, the song came on, and they run out. The crowd is yelling and shouting at the team as they make their entrance. The girls do their warm-ups, then 10 minutes later the horn blows; the announcer gets on the mike to announce the visiting team first.]
The announcer: Ladies and Gentlemen, it is time! Basketball time! Starting out the visiting team: Cy-fair Bulldogs; the coach, Patrice Walton. (she waves to the crowd, and they clap on the visiting side, but on the home side they boo) Now, for the starting lineup, at Guard #23, Lindsay Hunt (she runs out and hi-fives her teammates as she runs out to the center of the court); #15 at Guard, Mandy Morris (she runs out to greet her teammates); #5 at Forward, Danyell Miles (she runs out); the other Forward, #16 Trina Kyle; and #00 at Center, Melissa Johnson. (the lights began to dim and the spotlight came on focusing on the Kemptner Bulldogs team) Everyone get out of your seat for your Lady Bulldogs.
Now, for your home team coach, give it up for Coach Melinda Matthews. (the crowd went crazy as she waves at them) Now, for your starting lineup, (‒Whoomp, There It Is‖ came on) starting at Guard #15, Tamara Jones (she gives her teammates hi fives and runs to the center of the court); for the other Guard, #20 Ashlyn Richardson (the crowd went crazy; she ran to greet her teammates all crunk, pumping, and bouncing her shoulders); #21 at Forward, Amanda Caldwell (she runs out); at Power Forward, #19, Deniece Broudeaux (she runs out doing the ‒raising the roof motion); and at Center, #50, Alexandria Colburn! Ladies and Gentlemen, your Lady Bulldogs of '96‒'97, 8‒0, so stand up and make some noise!
[The crowd went crazy; the lights are cut back on, and the players greet each other, then get ready for the tip-off in the center of the court. The

horn blows; the referee tosses the ball up; Ashlyn gets the ball after the tip-off; she takes it to the basket and scores the first points. Throughout the first half, Kemptner dominates the game leading 38–15; at halftime,

Coach Matthews acknowledges the good efforts and wants more out of her players in the locker room.]

Coach Matthews: (holding her clipboard with the game stats) Keep up the good work, ladies! I want to see more defense, OK? I'm going to let y'all rest and look at the stats to see what you need to improve. All right! Keep up the good work, ladies. (she leaves the locker room)

[Ashlyn is bending over and holding her stomach when Coach Matthews leaves the locker room; Tamara walks over concerned.]

Tamara: (bends down) Hey, Ash, you all right, dog?

Ashlyn: (grunts) Yeah, I'll be all right. (Ashlyn sits down holding her stomach and looks at the stats) Man, I shot a lot. I got to pass the ball more.

Deniece: You keep shooting; that's why you're a shooting guard and Tamara is the point. You know, just keep doing what you doing. (gives Ashlyn dap) Give those girls a can of whoop A-S-S!

[Tamara laughs. The horn blows, and the girls leave the locker room; the 2nd half begins; 30 minutes pass by. Ashlyn is shooting free throws to give Kemptner 82 pts to Cy-fair's 57; she made both. Vanessa, Darnell, and Carlton cheer her on;

Jeff left the game to pick up Debbie from the hospital. Five seconds are left in the game; Kemptner wins their 9th game of the season.

Ashlyn is the high scorer at 35 pts., 7 asst., 5 rebs., 1 blk., and 4 steals. She goes into the locker room with the team to celebrate the victory.]

Coach Matthews: (shouts) Good job, ladies! I am *very* impressed! Ashlyn, outstanding game MVP with 35 pts, 7 assts, 5 rebs., 1 blk., and 4 steals! Keep it up!

Tamara: That's how you do it, Ash. I told you it's all good! (she chants) Hey, oh, a'ight! (pauses) Hey, oh, a'ight! (pauses) Hey, oh, a'ight!

[The team joins her and starts dancing; Ashlyn dances, too, then she runs to the bathroom stall leaning over the toilet; Deniece follows her while the other players leave the locker room chanting.]

Deniece: Say, Ash, you a'ight, shorty?

Ashlyn: Yeah. I think. I must have eaten something that upset my stomach. I'll be fine. (she flushes the toilet)

Deniece: A'ight. Just making sure.

Ashlyn: (walks out of the stall and grabs her items) I hope I'm not . . . Deniece: Pregnant?

Ashlyn: No! The flu, girl!

Deniece: Oh, tell me something!

[Deniece and Ashlyn walk out of the locker room. Ashlyn's family greets them; Carlton walks up to Ashlyn.]

Carlton: What's up, champ? You were doing it like MJ. Vanessa: Not Michael Jordan but Magic Johnson.

Darnell: All but razzle and dazzle! Ashlyn: (smiles) Where's Dad?

Vanessa: Oh, he went to pick up Mom. Ashlyn: Oh, okay.

[They all walk out of the gym together.]

*The scene fades away.*

**Scene 23**

When: Tuesday morning two days later Where: The Richardson home

*Ashlyn is sick in bed thinking she has the flu; she takes Theraflu, and it doesn't help. So, Debbie tells Vanessa to take Ashlyn to the doctor even though she doesn't want to go. Ashlyn is at home on a Tuesday morning waiting for Vanessa; she looks out the window. Vanessa drives up and gets out to ring the doorbell; Ashlyn opens the door.*

Vanessa: Hey, girl, (walks into the house) you ready? (walks through the hallway following Ashlyn)

Ashlyn: Nope. I don't want to go. I want to go to the game. (she coughs) Vanessa: You are not going to the game! Ashlyn, you are going to the doctor to see what's wrong with you!

Ashlyn: Oh, like you really care? The reason why you doing it is because Momma told you to. You didn't volunteer.

Vanessa: Ash, don't start. You need to put your shoes on so we can make it to the doctor's appointment, OK? Do it for your well-being, sis. (her hands are on her hips)

Ashlyn: I don't want to go! (she stands up from the love seat and walks toward Vanessa) I want to go to school and to the game and play! It only takes a week for the flu to completely leave my body,

Nessa! Nessa, this is the only way I will get better and that is moving around and getting involved in some sort of activity! You know. Come on, sis. With all the things I've been through, (she starts crying) I surely don't want go to any hospital or doctor's office.

Vanessa: (hugs her) OK. OK. It's just between us. I will take you to school and the game. OK?

Ashlyn: (wipes the tears off her face) OK. (she smiles) Let me go get my bag and put on my shoes. Then we can go.

[Ashlyn grabs her shoes and puts them on, then she runs upstairs to get her bag; she runs back downstairs.]

All right, I'm ready, Nessa.

Vanessa: OK, let's go. (she hugs Ashlyn again) You know I'm doing this 'cause I love you?

Ashlyn: I know.

[They walk out of the house; Ashlyn locks the door while Vanessa goes to the car and starts it; then Ashlyn jumps in; they drive off.]

*The scene fades away.*

### Scene 24

When: 10 A.M.
Where: Calculus class at school

*Ashlyn returns to school as an excused tardy for visiting the doctor's office which she didn't. She goes to her calculus class. Everybody is in a state of shock to see her. The hours pass; it's game time for the girls' varsity basketball team at 7:30 P.M.*

*Ashlyn walks in the locker room; everybody is already dressed at 6:45 P.M.*

Deniece: Say, Ash, (tying her shoes on the bench between the lockers) welcome back! (pauses) Coach going to give you PT even if you missed practice?

Ashlyn: I hope so . . .

Coach Matthews: (interrupts) Ash, suit up. (she smiles at her) You are not going to start, but you will receive PT if necessary.

Ashlyn: Okay. (she smiles) I can handle it. (she goes to her locker and gets her jersey from the manager, then puts on her uniform)

[The team cheers and runs out to their theme music –Space Jam,‖ including Ashlyn. The team is playing against Willowridge;

Ashlyn participates in the warm-up with no problem; the horn blows to begin the game. Within 45 minutes of the game in the 2nd quarter, 30 seconds are on the shot clock. Ashlyn still hasn't touched the court. Willowridge is beating Kemptner 38 to 22. Coach is not pleased, especially when Amanda turns the ball over by throwing it to Deniece when she is double-team.]

Coach Matthews: Goddamn, girls, come on! Work together! Communicate! (the horn blows; coach grabs her clipboard in anger and walks toward the locker room.) Shit!

[The girls follow with their heads down; they enter into the locker room.] Coach Matthews: I don't want to hear any excuses! We are getting our asses kicked out there! I know you play better than this! Come on, y'all! (she looks at Ashlyn) Ashlyn, get ready for the second half. You're playing your position! Amanda, (she looks at Amanda and Crystal) you're out. Crystal, you're in at the forward position! I want to see crisp, sharp passes, a high percentage of shots made, and crash the boards! Communicate! Communicate! Defense! Defense! Execute the plays! OK? (she looks at all her players) OK! Let's go and show these girls whose house this is! (all the players got in a circle around Coach Matthews and put their hands on top of each other) 1 . . . 2 . . . 3 . . .

Team: Victory!

[They run out of the locker room and shoot around for the last 2 minutes. Then the horn buzzes for the second half to start. Ashlyn is ready; she checks in and looks up to see her sister, Vanessa, and her brother, Carlton; she walks on the court.]

Carlton: (shouts) Let's go, Ashlyn!

Vanessa: Go, Ashlyn!

[The crowd cheers for Ashlyn, including Corey.] Corey: Go, Ashlyn!

[Ashlyn had the ball dribbling in between her legs and takes it all the way in. The crowd cheers! Ashlyn defends the shooting guard #6 on Willowridge when she gets the ball; Ashlyn watches her hips closely, then reaches in to steal the ball at the 3-pt line on Willowridge side; she steals the ball and takes it all the way in; the crowd gets louder! The score is now 26 to 38. Toward the end of the 3rd quarter with 15 seconds left, Ashlyn scores 11 pts, 3 steals, 3 assists, and 2 rebs, giving her team a lead 45 to 43. The opponents call a timeout.]

Coach Matthews: (talks to the team in a huddle) All right, ladies! I love it! I love it! Keep it up! (she puts her hand in the middle, and they put their hands on top) 1 . . . 2 . . . 3 . . .
Team: Hustle!

[They walk back on the court; Ashlyn feels dizzy and rubs her eyes a little bit to adjust them. The ref blows the whistle; Ashlyn gets on defense by making sure her man didn't get the ball. The team throws the ball to the post player
#35. She shoots the ball and makes it at the buzzer. The score is tied at 45. Coach Matthews claps and calls the girls over to the bench.]
Coach Matthews: All right, girls, let's play ball! Go into the 3–2 zone and run the motion 1 on offense. I want you to execute the play! Let's go! Let's win this game! This is our house! (girls huddle around with the hands on top of hers) 1! 2! 3!
Ashlyn: (yells) Whose house is this? Team: (yells) Our house!
Ashlyn: Whose house is this? Team: Our house!!!
Coach Matthews: 1, 2, 3! Team: Win!


[Team gets on the court; Deniece throws the ball to Tamara, then Tamara throws the ball at half-court to Ashlyn, and she takes it all the way to the basket and shoots it but gets fouled hard; the ball rolls into the goal; nothing but net. The crowd cheers. Ashlyn shoots her free throw and makes it. Then Willowridge brings the ball down the court while Kemptner is in a 3–2 zone defense. Willowridge passes the ball fast to one another around the perimeter; Ashlyn, Tamara, and Amanda run all over the court until Ashlyn leaps in front of the pass and steals it; she takes it all way in to the basket; Kemptner is leading Willowridge about 5 points within 4 minutes in the 4th quarter; the lead continues to grow.
At 45 seconds, Kemptner has the ball. The score is 63 to 52. Amanda throws the ball to Tamara; Tamara throws it back to Amanda; Amanda holds the ball and dribbles toward Deniece; she passes back out to Ashlyn; Ashlyn has the ball at 20 seconds; she dribbles to the basketball full force with her eyes closed, spinning around, then does a jump shot with elevation. As she's up in the air she is hammered real hard; she falls to the ground on her back, then she grabs her back. The crowd boos the Willowridge players. Carlton and Vanessa run out to the court but are stopped by the police officer. The trainer and Coach Matthews run to Ashlyn's side. Ashlyn holds her midback crying. Deniece and Tamara bend down to her.]
Tamara: Yo', Ashlyn, stop moving . . . be still . . . you can make it

worse.

Deniece: Uh, Ash, you fell hard . . . can you get up or move . . .?

Coach Matthews: (pushes Tamara and Deniece out of the way and bends down to Ashlyn) Ash, is that the only place it hurts? Ash? Can you respond?

Ashlyn: (cries out loud) Yes! It hurts bad! Oh, God!

The trainer: (bends down) Ash, I'm here to help you. I'm going turn your body where you will lay on your back, OK? I'm going to take it slow. (she turns her body)

Ashlyn: (screams in agony and pain) Ouch, ow, ow! That hurts!

Trainer: (rubs her arm) I know . . . I know . . .

[The ambulance comes with a stretcher.]

Vanessa: (runs out on the court) Excuse me! This is my sister! *I* will take her to the hospital!

EMT 1: Ma'am, she's in bad shape. We have to take her because she has a back injury that could be serious enough to mess up her spinal cord.

Carlton: I'm her brother! What's wrong?

Vanessa: (crying) Ash has a severe back injury, and you know how she is about hospitals, but she has to go.

EMT 2: Calm down. We don't know if it's major or not, OK? Just calm down. [The crowd is angry and cursing the Willowridge players. The EMTs takes Ashlyn out of the gym and put her in ambulance; Vanessa rides in the ambulance with Ashlyn while Carlton drives Vanessa's car. The game resumes, but before they start, the players, coaches, and fans pray for Ashlyn in a silent prayer. Kemptner wins the game 65 to 52; Tamara and Deniece run out of the gym and get in their cars to go to the hospital.]

*The scene fades away.*

### Scene 25

When: Minutes later
Where: Emergency room at the hospital

*Ashlyn arrives at the hospital in the ambulance in pain and agony with Vanessa and Carlton right beside her; they send Ashlyn straight to the ER since they noticed she's hemorrhaging and bleeding.*

Nurse: OK, this child is bleeding from her vaginal area! This is not good! I need some assistance here!

Doctor 1: What?

Nurse 1: She's bleeding!

Vanessa: What did she say? (runs to Ashlyn's side)

Nurse2: She's hemor—(she grabs Ashlyn's legs because Ashlyn is having a seizure.)

[Doctor 1 and Nurses run over to Carlton and Vanessa to get to Ashlyn because she's having a seizure.]

Doctor 2: OK! Let's turn her to her side! (they turn Ashlyn to her side)

Nurse 3: She's bleeding, and it seems like her water (looks puzzled) has broken!

Vanessa: (paces back and forth) Say what?

[Debbie, Jeff, and Darnell run into the ER to meet Carlton and Vanessa.] Debbie: (talks to Vanessa) What's going on, Nessa? Nessa?

Vanessa: I don't know! I don't know, all right?

[The doctors finally stabilize Ashlyn; they wipe their faces as a sign of relief and talk among themselves about Ashlyn's condition for 10 minutes before talking to Jeff and Debbie. Deniece and Tamara arrive at the hospital in the ER waiting room 5 minutes later after the doctors stabilized Ashlyn; Carlton sees Deniece and Tamara and walks over to let them know what is going on.] Carlton: (worried) Hey, you two. I'm glad you're here. I'm surprised they let you come back here.

Deniece: Oh, we, just ran in here when we saw the door open.

Tamara: (asks with concern) Is Ash a'ight?

Carlton: I hope so. (sighs) They stabilized her. (he wipes his head and face) I tell ya, my li'l sis has been through a lot in the past 4 months since we've been here, you know?

Deniece: I know.

Tamara: She surely has. (then she looks back and sees the security officer walking toward them, then looks at Carlton and Deniece) Well, C., I think we have to go now. (looking at the security officer) And please make sure you tell Ashlyn we were here.

Security Officer: (walks up to Tamara) Ladies, if you are not family you have to leave. OK?

Deniece: Oh, we're leaving. We just want to make sure our friend is all right. Tamara: (turns to Carlton) Carlton, make sure you tell her to call us.

[Deniece and Tamara wave at Carlton as they exit the ER. Carlton walks back to Vanessa and Darnell. Dr. Kabolo leaves the area with a clipboard in his hand where the doctors are standing to talk to Debbie and Jeff.]

Dr. Kabolo: (walks to Debbie and Jeff) Are you the parents? (they nod yes)

 I'm Dr. Kabolo, your daughter . . ., (pauses and clears his throat) your daughter has a badly bruised back but not severe. However, Miss Richardson has experienced a miscarriage due to the back injury. We are trying right now to make sure she's not bleeding internally, so we will keep her overnight and maybe 48 hours after, just to make sure she's fine, OK?

Debbie and Jeff: (respond) OK.

Dr. Kabolo: So, you guys will have to sit in the waiting room while we can get that excessive embryonic fluid and blood out of her system. Stay tight and near, OK?

Debbie: (in a state of shock, crying) My poor baby. Oh my God! (Jeff hugs her for comfort; she lets go and turns to Vanessa) Why didn't you take her to the doctor like I told you to? You just don't listen! You never listen to anybody! I told you to take her since I'm working a 12-hour shift back-to- back! Now, look; she ends up in the hospital! Nessa, you—!

Jeff: (interrupts) Debbie, calm down. Ashlyn is going to be fine. Don't blame it all on Vanessa. You know how Ashlyn can get since the loss of her boyfriend.

Debbie: But (points at Vanessa) she—!

Jeff: Deb, cool it; chill out! It is *not* her fault! We need to be here in unity (grabbing Debbie's arm and looking into her eyes) for Ash! My God in heaven, woman!

Debbie: (stares at Vanessa) OK, Jeff. (he lets go) I'll calm down.

Carlton: (asks his father) So, how long is it going to take?

Jeff: I don't know. We just have to wait.

Darnell: Yep. (he hugs Vanessa and rubs her back) Everything is going to be all right. We just got to stick together like Jeff said, (he kisses Vanessa on her forehead) you know?

[The Richardson family stands together in a huddle praying silently to themselves; an hour later, Dr. Kabolo comes in smiling and greeting the family with good news.]

Dr. Kabolo: (smiles) Well, family, Miss Ashlyn is doing fine. The procedure went successfully. We are going to keep her for 2 days to make sure she's fine.

Vanessa: What about her back injury?

Dr. Kabolo: She has a bruised spinal cord in the midsection of her back. She will have to wear a brace for 4 weeks. Then she can take it off. However, she will have back spasms due to the injury. The good thing is she's here with mobility. So, (sighs) you guys can follow me to her room. (he walks in front of them to Ashlyn's room)

[The family walks with Dr. Kabolo into Ashlyn's room; Ashlyn is asleep. Debbie walks to Ashlyn and sits down in the chair next to her; she leans over and kisses her forehead. Darnell, Vanessa, and Carlton sit on the sofa. Jeff sits in the love seat.]

Carlton: Dang, she is out. Po' sis, she just don't get a break, you know? Vanessa: Yep. But that's life.

Darnell: I agree. You love, lose, learn, and you live. Carlton: Damn, brother-in-law, that's poetic justice.

[Darnell smiles and holds onto Vanessa. Ashlyn wakes up and sees her mother, Debbie, beside her.]

Ashlyn: Mom, why (looks around the room with a puzzled expression her face) am I here? I don't remember how I (she scratches her head and sits up carefully) got here.

Vanessa: (looks at Carlton and speaks softly) She don't remember. [Darnell nods yes.]

Carlton: (shrugs his shoulders) I guess so. [They look at Ashlyn.]

Jeff: (walks over to Ashlyn's bedside) Don't worry about it. (leans over and kisses her on the forehead) All we know is, you won the game. (he smiles) [Ashlyn smiles, then Debbie smiles along with Jeff and Ashlyn. Vanessa, Carlton, and Darnell walk to Ashlyn and hug her.]

*The scene fades away.*

## Scene 26

When: Four weeks later Where: Gym at school

*Ashlyn is in school and back on the court. It is 5:30 P.M.; basketball practice has just ended. Ashlyn, Deniece, and Tamara are walking out of the gym. Corey and some of the guy athletes are just sitting around talking. Ashlyn walks up to her car while Deniece and Tamara get into their own cars. Corey runs behind Ashlyn as she opens her car door.*

Ashlyn: (swings back) Boy! Don't play! You was just about to get slapped! Corey: (laughs) What's up, sis?

Ashlyn: Nothing, just getting ready for the big Friday. Hopefully, the doctor will allow me to play since he ordered the coach to allow me to practice, but I still have to do back exercises and shoot the ball while everyone else is doing the offense and defense drills. (sighs) I kinda felt left out and out of place. Hopefully, I'll be back soon 'cause it's getting old. I can't wait no longer.

Corey: I sure hope so 'cause the girls need you; they lost five in a row. (holds up his hand while Ashlyn is sitting in her car and starting it) Me and the boys were like, Ashlyn needs to come back; these girls are hurtin'.

Ashlyn: Well, keep ya fingers crossed. (she's backing up the car while Corey backs away from the car)

Corey: (stands with his fingers crossed) I will. [Ashlyn drives off, and Corey runs back to the guys.]

*The scene fades away.*

## Scene 27

When: Two days later Where: The doctor's office

*Ashlyn is at the doctor's office with her sister, Vanessa, around 3:55 P.M.*

Ashlyn: (sitting on the hospital bench with a gown on waiting for the results on her back) Damn! Sis, they are taking a long time!

Vanessa: (sitting in a chair beside Ashlyn) Ash, I know it. They need to hurry up (looks at her watch, then the clock on the wall) before you miss practice. [Dr. Kabolo walks into the room with his clipboard in his hand.]

Dr. Kabolo: (speaks softly) Ashlyn, (sits beside her on a stool) I have good and bad news. (sighs) The good news is your back has healed, but the bad news is it is not 100 percent; you cannot play ball until next month, probably. The reason why is because your spinal cord is still tender, and if anyone hits you, that's it; no more basketball because the injury was in the middle of your back. (sighs) I'm sorry. I advise you to—

Ashlyn: Go to hell! (she puts on her clothes underneath the gown) I don't need this! I don't need to hear this negative shit! I'm gone! (she walks out of the room)

Vanessa: (touches the doctor on the shoulder) I'm sorry you had to—

Dr. Kabolo: I know. (he hands her the papers) Make sure you keep an eye on her.

Vanessa: (walks out) I will!

[Vanessa goes to her car. Ashlyn is sitting there pouting; Vanessa gets in the car and starts it, then pulls off from the parking lot at the doctor's office. She is driving to Ashlyn's house.]

Vanessa: (driving) Ashlyn. Ashlyn, (pauses and stops at a red light) I know you didn't want to hear the bad news, but you still will be able to play next month, which is January, the beginning of the district games. That's all that matters.

Ashlyn: (shrugs her shoulders and smacks her lips) Really?

Vanessa: (drives through the green light) Look, Ashlyn, (pauses) Ash, I advise you to listen to the doctor and focus more on your academics—

Ashlyn: (turns to Vanessa and yells) Just shut up, Nessa! I don't need to hear any lectures from you, all right? Just shut up! Shut the hell up!

Vanessa: (stops the car two blocks from the house) Ash, you will not disrespect me! I'm trying to help ya li'l trifling ass!

Ashlyn: (smirks at Vanessa) Trifling? Trifling? Oh, I got ya trifling, bitch! Bitch! Bitch! Bi-it-ch!

Vanessa: (pulls off fast) I don't need this! Next time, Mom will take you wherever you need to go!

[Vanessa pulls into the driveway almost hitting Carlton's car. Debbie, Jeff, Carlton, Corey, Trent, and Darnell are in the garage playing dominoes.] Darnell: (looks up toward the car) Oh, oh, oh, something is going (he gets up and runs to the car) on!

Ashlyn: (gets out of the car and slams the door shut) I hate that bitch! She's always trying to boss someone!

Vanessa: (gets out of the car and gently closes her door) You are out of line, Ms. Thang! You keep calling me names and I will whoop your ass just like I did when you were small! Just because you're my size, li'l sis; oh, you will *know* who's the big sista at the end!

[Jeff, Debbie, Carlton, and Darnell jump up and get between Vanessa and Ashlyn. Corey and Trent just watch the altercation.]

Ashlyn: (jumps around Carlton and Debbie) C'mon, bitch! Show me! Show me! Betcha ya can't whoop my ass, bitch!

Vanessa: Betcha I would! (Darnell and Jeff stand in front of Vanessa) Betcha I (she charges at Ashlyn) would! (Darnell grabs her and pulls her to the opposite side of Ashlyn on the lawn) Let me go; let me get her. I'm tired! I'm tired of trying to cater to her fucking alter ego!

Ashlyn: (Carlton pushes Ashlyn toward the house) Naw, let her c'mon. I will show her up! I know that much!

[Carlton and Debbie push Ashlyn into the house.]

Debbie: (yells at Ashlyn) What the hell is going on, Ash? (she grabs her arm to get Ashlyn's attention) Ashlyn! Ashlyn, speak to me right now!

Ashlyn: (yanks away) Don't you yell at me. (grits her teeth) I heard you. Debbie: (points her finger at Ashlyn but speaks in a softer but aggressive tone) What is the problem? Tell me now or I will raise my voice again 'cause I AM YOUR MOTHER AND YOU WILL ANSWER ME!

Ashlyn: What if I don't? (pauses and begins to walk out of the front area) I don't have to if I don't want to. (she walks upstairs)

Debbie: (turns to Carlton, then Jeff walks in) That girl! Uh-uh, I can't believe she . . .! Um, humph, I . . . I can't think straight! Lord, help us! Oh, I can kick her black ass all over these damn stairs. (she walks upstairs fussing and cussing)

Jeff: (talks to Carlton) Carlton, what happened in here? Where's Ashlyn? Carlton: All I know, Ash is on her trip mode. She didn't want to give Mom an explanation so she went to her room.

Jeff: (shakes his head) Ash, oh, Ash. (pauses) Ummm, (pauses) Nessa told me Ash was upset 'cause the doctor told her she couldn't play ball until next month. So Ash cursed the doctor out and stormed out of the office. Then on the way home, Nessa tried to talk to her to let her know she gets to play, but she just has to wait a little longer. Ash snapped at her and cursed her out. (sighs) So, that's what happened between them two. Now, I got to calm Debbie down and talk to Ashlyn later. (he walks toward the stairs) I'm going to let her calm down, but I (walking up the stairs) definitely got to calm Debbie down before Ashlyn catches a case.

Carlton: Yep! That's the best thing to do, you know? (pauses and shouts out to Jeff) Say, Pops! Darnell and Vanessa (peeks out the window) are gone?

Jeff: (yells from upstairs) Yep! Carlton: What about Trent and Corey?

Jeff: They're in the garage! (a door slams)

[Carlton walks out into the garage. Corey and Trent are sitting down discussing the sister quarrel between Vanessa and Ashlyn.]

Carlton: (sits down beside Trent) Man, oh, man, it's just drama after drama with Ash, man. She's just like a bomb ready to explode. (leans back into the chair) Goddamn, (he leans up) she acts just like Vanessa when Vanessa was her age.

Trent: Yep. That's why they can't get along 'cause they are too much alike on a fa' real trip.

Corey: So, where's Ashlyn?

Carlton: In her room. (pauses) My advice to you is to not go in there. Man, trust (laughs) me.

Corey: Oh, I was just wondering where she was. That's all. Trent: Yep. Li'l cuz need her space. She's been through a lot. Corey: Yeah, ain't that the truth.

Carlton: Hopefully, she won't veer into my bad habits. That's my only concern.

*The scene fades away.*

## Scene 28

When: Two days later on a Sunday morning Where: Ashlyn's bedroom

*Ashlyn is getting ready for church in her room. As she finishes dressing, she looks at the pictures of her, Omar, Carlton, and Darnesia. She pulls down the picture of her and Omar taken when they were at the movies in Houston; tears fall down her eyes as she holds the picture on her chest.*

Ashlyn: (cries and looks up at the ceiling) Oh, baby, I miss you so much. My life has not been the same. I'm so sorry I lost our child. I wish I could have that chance again.

Debbie: (walks in) Ashlyn, Ash, (she grabs her and holds her in her arm) baby, you just got to be strong. I know it hurts like hell, but you are not going through this alone. (she rubs her head)

Ashlyn: (looks into her mother's eyes) Mom, why am I going through so much turmoil? Why is God punishing me? (she lets go of her mother) I just don't understand what I've done to deserve this pain that will not leave. Ever since I got here in this racist city and school, my life has been tarnished. Why is that? I'm just being who I've always been but not receiving no respect and good vibes here.

Debbie: Ashlyn, I know it seems that God is punishing you, but he is testing your strength, perseverance, and trust in him. (pauses and looks at the picture of Ashlyn, Omar, Carlton, and Darnesia) You see, God is not punishing you, Ashlyn. He wants you to know that he is there at all times of sorrow and pain, just like when there's happiness and well-being.

He allows us to have free of choice in our lives, even though in society you never know what you are going to face or going to take. It all depends on what avenue you want to steer on. Whatever avenue you steer on, there are always going to be obstacles that can hinder you if you allow it to or help you gain more strength and faith to overcome it to reach whatever you want to reach. All of us have to learn this concept about life in our society. Ash, you just never know what will be given to you or taken from you. All you can do is pray to God for guidance and strength to endure and overcome whatever comes your way. (she hugs her) Baby, we are here for you. Don't ever think we don't love or care for you because we do, OK?

Ashlyn: (wipes her tears from her face) I know. I just don't know what to do at times. That's why I rebel so much, 'cause I feel God is upset with me.

Debbie: Well, Ashlyn, all I can tell you is that God does get angry at us when we go against his will, but he loves us enough to forgive us and pick us right up, baby. (she smiles) Just keep Omar and the baby in your heart and live like (points at Omar's picture) he wants you to. 'Cause, Ash, Omar doesn't want you to stop living because he's not physically here. He wants you to be you. The strong, aggressive, ambitious, intelligent, and independent woman he fell in love with. Can you do that for him?

Ashlyn: (smiles and tears fall from her eyes again) Yes.

Debbie: Come here, baby girl. (she holds Ashlyn's hands and faces her) I know it's hard, but you got to live. Don't let the devil turn you away from your dreams and goals in your life. Be strong in God 'cause he's here. (she points at her chest) You just got to hold on and believe in him.

It's hard, but that's life. (sighs) OK, enough of the short talk. We need to go downstairs so we can get our praise on!

[Jeff and Carlton are in the SUV blowing the horn; Debbie looks out the window.]

Debbie: Yep. It's time to go.

[Ashlyn walks out before Debbie. Debbie turns the light off and slowly looks at Omar and Ashlyn's prom picture as she closes the door.]

*The scene fades away.*

**Scene 29**

When: An hour and a half pass Where: Church

*Jeff is closing his sermon and opening the doors of the church. (invitation of Christ)*

Jeff: Church, this is the hour (wiping his face with his handkerchief) for an individual to make a choice that will help him or her on the road to salvation and glory.

Congregation: Amen!

Jeff: I know there is someone here today who wants to start on the right foot or wants to get back on track in their life.

I know there is someone who is looking for guidance, perseverance, and hope in their life.

Who has lost touch with their spiritual connection (he looks at Ashlyn in the choir stand) and faith in God. (he turns back to the congregation) Or someone is just looking for a church home where they can grow spiritually in their calling. If you are that person today, come on.

Don't be scared or embarrassed 'cause God loves you enough to give you an opportunity to join with his Son, Jesus Christ, to teach you while the Holy Spirit guides you! So, come on, children of God! Come on, come on down! I want you all to know that society cannot take what God has given you or cannot give you what God has already promised to you. (pauses) The sermon I have delivered to you is that in this society, (musicians play and people are coming to the altar; Ashlyn grabs the microphone to sing –So Good) you never know what you are going to face; you never know what you are going to get; you never know what you are going to take. All you can do is to live, learn, and have faith. (stretches his arm out as he walks down the altar) God loves you, (he speaks to people at the altar) and he forgives you enough to give you another chance; you (points at the people), another chance.

[Ashlyn sings the first verse of –So Good, then the choir follows.]

Ashlyn: When I lift my hands, I'm telling you thank you!

Choir: I'm telling you thank you!

Ashlyn: When I shed tears of joy, I'm saying I love you! Choir: I'm saying I love!

Ashlyn: Because I realize you didn't have do what you did, (choir joins in) but you did it anyhow. Oh, I'm not ashamed to tell the world that you have been  .

. .

Choir: So Good!

[Ashlyn repeats the verse and walks down to the altar with tears flowing down on her face; Debbie, Vanessa, Carlton, Jeff, and Darnell hug her when she stops, but the choir continues to sing the chorus of −So Good.‖]

Choir: (sings it four times) God has been . . . He's Been So Good.

*The scene fades away.*

# ACT 6

## Scene 30

When: 10 A.M. Monday morning Where: Classroom

*Ashlyn is sitting down trying to look over her book report that is due. One of Christopher's friends backs into Ashlyn's desk.*

Brandon: (turns around and looks at Ashlyn) Oh, my bad, Miss Richardson. I'm sorry to interrupt your reading. (he smirks at her)
Ashlyn: It's OK. Just watch where you're going next time. (she smiles at him) Brandon: All right. I will. (he walks to his desk)
[A group of white football players come in the classroom sit and talk to Brandon. As they walk in, they look at Ashlyn and smile at her.]
Player 1: (turns back and looks at Ashlyn) Hey, Brandon, could you hit that, (looks at Ashlyn) (softly speaks to him) that nigga bitch, if you wanted to?
Brandon: (smiles) Yeah. I'll make her call me Master.
[The football players laugh. Ashlyn gets up and turns in her paper on the teacher's desk; Brandon runs and gets behind her. Ashlyn backs into him on accident; Brandon touches her behind with his privates.]
Ashlyn: (yells at him) Uh, Brandon, excuse me! Didn't I tell you to watch where you were going?
Brandon: (smiles at her) Ashlyn, baby, I did. You backed up on me. (turns to his friends and smiles)
Ashlyn: (pushes him to the side so she can get to her desk) Uh-huh. I bet. I guess you got a handful of my ass, too. (she sits down and rolls her eyes at him)
[Ms. Washington, the economics teacher, walks in and picks up the book reports.]

Ms. Washington: Well, class, I see (she flips through the reports) everyone has turned in their book report. I guess you guys can get started on your final exam project.
Brandon: OK, Ms. Washington. (he smiles at Ashlyn when she looks back at him)
Ashlyn: Ms. Washington, this project is due next Friday, right?
Ms. Washington: Yes. And you have to have all your account ledgers, expense accounts, capital accounts, and annual reports of your stock dividends of your stocks in your business. OK, class?

Class: (respond) OK!

[Everybody gets in their groups if they choose to. Ashlyn is doing hers by herself. Brandon keeps smiling at Ashlyn. Ashlyn just shakes her head at him.]

Ashlyn: (talks in her mind) This white boy is driving me up a wall.

[Forty-five minutes later, the class ends. Ashlyn is still calculating her expenses. Brandon passes by and drops a note on her paper.]

Ashlyn: (silently reads it to herself) I would love to get to know you because you are so fine to me! Call me if you want to get to know me (281) 328-6248. [Ashlyn closes her book and gathers her items, then exits out of the classroom; she goes to her locker; Corey walks up to her.]

Corey: What's up? Ashlyn Richardson?

Ashlyn: Hey (smiles), bro! What's up with you and ol' girl? Huh?

Corey: (smirks) Oh, I caught her in the backseat of your brother's car.

Ashlyn: (shock) Say what? Oh, no . . . no . . . no, you got the wrong Carlton. I
*know* you do.

Corey: Yep. It happened last week.

Ashlyn: Wait a minute. (she walks to her calculus class with Corey) You was at my house (she sits down at her desk, and he sits beside her) Friday after school.

Corey: I know it, but Carlton had left while me and Trent was sitting down talking about you. Then we left 30 minutes after. I drove down the street that night around 7:30. (Tamara walks into the classroom and sits on the other side of Ashlyn)

Tamara: What's up, y'all?

Corey: Oh, we just talking about how her brother took my girl.

Tamara: Say what? (she looks at Ashlyn) Ashlyn, I thought Carlton was in love with Darnesia.

Corey: NOT!

Ashlyn: I am shocked, Corey.

Corey: (pulls his desk a little bit closer to Ashlyn's) Back to what happened. (sighs) I passed the park; I spotted Carlton's car and my girl's; I stopped the car and noticed that Carlton's car was rocking. I covered my eyes for a second and wiped my face 'cause I couldn't believe this shit. All I know, Ash, is that your brother told me he was seeing her sister so I assumed he was telling the truth—until I got out of the car and walked to Carlton's car. I looked down and saw three condom wrappers.

[Tamara and Ashlyn's mouth are wide open and amazed at what Carlton had done.]

Ashlyn: So, did they see you? What was their reaction? Tamara: Yeah.

Corey: Ol' girl jumped up and pushed Carlton off her, pointing at me. Boy, I was hot! Man, I wanted to kick your brotha's ass 'cause he lied to me. (shakes his head in disappointment) Then Carlton jumps out of the car, buckling his pants, trying to explain that it just happened. (he pauses)

[The teacher walks in, then walks out.]

Carlton told me that Lyn had followed him from her house 'cause he got mad at Leslie. He got mad at Leslie because he found numbers and men's shirts under her bed so he left. Then he went to the park to chill for a while. It so happens Lyn followed him and got out to talk to him about Leslie, that she's no good and he needs someone better. Then she seduces him, and all he can see is revenge.

Tamara: Damn!

Ashlyn: Just like that? Did Lyn deny it?

Corey: Nope. She told me that she thought I wanted to be with you instead of her, and she liked Carlton since day one when he started seeing her sister. Man, I wanted to slap that ho.

[Ashlyn and Tamara laugh.]

Ashlyn: I can't believe Carlton, on a serious note. I'm going to kick his ass. My friend Darnesia loves that jackass. Wait til I get home. I'm going to talk much crap to him—

[The teacher walks in and interrupts the conversation by passing out a quiz.] Mrs. Faulk: OK, class, (passing out the quiz) this quiz should take the rest of the period. Hope you studied. (she walks to her desk and sits down reading a book)

Ashlyn: I know I did.

Tamara: (looks at the quiz) I didn't. Corey: I know I did, too.

Tamara: Say what? A person who skips class all the time?

Corey: That's because I get something taken care of. (he pops his collar) Ashlyn: (writing her answers down) You so nasty. (she laughs softly) [They take their exam.]

*The scene fades away.*

**Scene 31**

When: The end of the school day Where: School parking lot

*The hours pass; the school bell rings; everybody goes to their cars or catches the bus. Ashlyn is walking by herself to her car. She waves at Deniece and Tamara while they drive to the gym and park in front of it. Brandon passes by while Ashlyn throws her backpack in the backseat of her car and shuts the door. Brandon runs to Ashlyn's car.*

Brandon: Hey, Ashlyn, did you read my note?
Ashlyn: (sits in her car and shuts the door) Yes, I did. And the answer is no. I don't date out of my race, especially friends of the enemy.
Brandon: Who, Chris? Aw, man, Ashly, baby, I'm not like him; I want to— Ashlyn: You want to (she turns on the ignition to start the car) fuck me. And it's not going to happen, white boy. So, play that music somewhere else 'cause this brick house door entrance is locked up, you know? (she drives off) Brandon: (looks down and kicks the dirt) Damn, I really do like her. Shit! (he walks off and gets in his car)
[Brandon follows Ashlyn to her house and watches her.]
Brandon: Damn, look at that ass. Damn, I'm hard. Shit! (pauses and shouts loudly) Yo', Ashly!
Ashlyn: (opens her door and whispers to herself) Did I hear? (she turns back and sighs)
Brandon: C'mon, Ashlyn, let me just touch it 'cause I really do like you! Just don't tell nobody I said that. I always liked you when you first came here!
Ashlyn: (smiles) Really? (she walks toward his car) You want some of this? (she spins around for Brandon)
Brandon: Yeah. (grabs himself) Oh, Ashlyn. (he licks his lips)
Ashlyn: Um, Brandon, I would but NOT. (she walks off) And you betta not (turns around and talks loudly) come here again, or else I would put cap in your ass!


[Carlton runs out half-dressed and Leslie, too. Brandon drives off.]
Ashlyn: (turns around and sees Carlton and Leslie) What the hell?
Carlton: Who was that? (fixing his clothes)
Leslie: Um, Ashlyn, you got a white boyfriend?
Ashlyn: Look, you don't know me, ho! Leslie: Say what? I *know* you . . .!
Carlton: Say? Ash, was that a *white* boy?

Ashlyn: Yep! And that's not (points at Leslie) Darnesia.

Carlton: Ash, don't start. You know Darnesia is not being faithful to me. But you and white boy? C'mon, Ash.

Ashlyn: Naw, he just want to get in the bed. That's all. And I told him I will kick his ass if he don't leave me alone. (she rolls her eyes at Carlton, then smirks at him) Oh, and another thing. Corey told me (she looks at Leslie with a grin on her face) what happened. You got some explaining to do.

Carlton: She already knows.

Ashlyn: (she looks at Leslie) Really? What does she know about you and Lyn?

Leslie: (walks up to Carlton) Say what? What is she talking about, Carlton? Carlton: What I already told you!

Leslie: Uh-huh. That's why you worked so hard on me, 'cause you really did fuck my li'l sista.

Carlton: Baby, give me a chance. Goddamn! Woman, listen to me!

Leslie: (walks to her car) Whatever! (she gets in and drives off)

Carlton: (looks at Ashlyn) See what you did? You always cock blocking! Ashlyn: Yep, because she's no good, and you need to be with Darnesia. [Carlton and Ashlyn walk into the house and stop in the kitchen.]

Carlton: In case you didn't know, your girl broke up with me last month because she found out by one of her cousins that goes to school with Leslie at HCC that I was with Leslie intimately. And I didn't deny it, so she moved on, even though we still talk.

Ashlyn: Ooops, I didn't know. I guess you got what you deserve. (pauses) Anyways . . . (she pats him on the shoulder and walks upstairs)

[Carlton mean mugs her as she walks upstairs.]

*The scene fades away.*


**Scene 32**

When: Two weeks later Where: School

*The doctor now permits Ashlyn to play basketball. Class is dismissed. Ashlyn walks to her car to drive it to the gym so she can practice with the team to get ready for the district games next week. She goes into the gym.*

*Brandon and all the football players are in the stands eyeballing Ashlyn as she walks into the gym to go to the locker room. Tamara, Amanda, and Deniece greet Ashlyn as she puts down her gym bag and begins to put on her practice uniform.*

Deniece: What's up, Ashlyn? You ready for next week?
Ashlyn: (putting on her socks and shoes) Yep. Just need to practice the offense and the D-drills a little bit more since I've been out, you know?
Tamara: Yeah, I heard you. Just can't wait. You heard me?
Coach Matthews: (comes in) All right, ladies, let's go! (she walks back out) Amanda: Welcome back, Ashlyn! (she runs out of the locker room) Deniece: Let's go, playettes!
[Ashlyn, Tamara, and Deniece run out; Coach Matthews blows her whistle for them to start stretching. Brandon is just smiling at Ashlyn as she's stretching.] Brandon: Damn, gotta get a dose.
Corey: (looks back at Brandon) Say, white boy, watch it. (he comes down the stands to greet Coach Matthews)
Brandon: (looks at Corey) He just jealous 'cause she looked at me. (he laughs with his friends)
[Corey waves at Ashlyn; Ashlyn waves back. The team begins to do their drills while the entire football team watches. After practice, Ashlyn is walking to her car by herself 'cause Deniece, Tamara, and Corey left early to go to work. Brandon says good-bye to his crew, then walks behind Ashlyn.] Brandon: Hey, Ashlyn! Ready for next week?
Ashlyn: Yes. And I would like you to stop following me. (she walks to her car and opens the trunk to put her bag in it)
Brandon: (grabs Ashlyn around the waist and turns her around) Damn, you feel good.
Ashlyn: Brandon! Get your hands off of me! (pushes his hands away)
Brandon: (grips her tightly) No. I want you bad, Ashlyn! (he grabs her face and holds her tightly to his body) Stop! Stop pushing away! 'Cause I *know* you *want* this good vanilla stick.
Ashlyn: (start crying) Brandon, don't do this! You will regret it for the rest of your life.
Brandon: (he start pulling out his privates and start hunching and kissing her) Just relax, baby. I want to make you feel better after all you've been through. Let me mend your broken heart.
(Ashlyn is pushing away and tugging even though he is the start DE and weighs 270 lbs.) C'mon, Ashlyn, let me tap that ass just one time. Please, (he starts tugging at her privates, but Ashlyn pushes his

hands back) Ash, let me put it in. (he start hunching her) Oh, Ash, please let me in. (holds her and kisses her)

Ashlyn: (stops fighting) OK. (pauses) I'll let you. (speaks nervously) Just loosen your grip around my neck, and I'll let you rock my world. (she grabs his ass and kisses him)

Brandon: (loosens his grip and lets her lead) Oh, Ash, I love you so much! Ashlyn: (opens the car door) Say what? (looks puzzled)

Brandon: (pushes Ashlyn in her backseat and lies on top of her, humping her) Let's do this!

Ashlyn: (stops kissing him) Oh, Brandon, (he kisses her and tries to pull her pants down) OK. (she's nervous and almost panics) Oh, God, help me. (she's struggles to push his hand away from her crotch, but he sticks his fingers in her pants) Brandon! Stop!

Brandon: Stop moving! You got me in the mood! (he tries to force his privates in Ashlyn)

Ashlyn: (kicks Brandon in his privates, then kicks him out of her car) You're never gonna get this. (she kicks him in the nose outside of her car, then shuts the back door) You never gonna get this (crying and opens her front car door and gets in) caramel punani. (she starts the car and drives off while Brandon is on the ground in a fetus position)

*The scene fades away.*

### Scene 33

When: The next day
Where: School hallway

*Ashlyn, Tamara, and Deniece are walking down the hallway to their lockers. Brandon passes them, smiling at Ashlyn while he is walking with his friends. Ashlyn rolls her eyes at him as she, Deniece, and Tamara approach their lockers.*

Tamara: Say, Ash, (putting her books up) what's up with Brandon?
Ashlyn: In case you (putting her books up) didn't know, Brandon wants a dose of this, but he never gonna get it.

Deniece: (shuts her locker and walks up to Ashlyn) Fo' real? You can't be serious.
Tamara: (starts laughing and shuts her locker) Damn, Ash.
Ashlyn: (shut her locker) Yep, I'm serious. Would I lie about a white boy liking me out of all people who's a friend with Chris? C'mon,

sistas!

Deniece: I guess so.

[Deniece, Tamara, and Ashlyn are walking to the cafeteria for lunch; Corey and his crew stop them before they get in the lunch line.]

Corey: (walks up to Ashlyn) Say, Ashlyn, is it true about you and Brandon? Ashlyn: What are you talking about? And why are you huffing and puffing like that?

[Deniece and Tamara just look at Corey about how he's pacing back and forth.]

Corey: Brandon said (he whispers in Ashlyn's ear) he boned you last night in the backseat of your car.

Ashlyn: He said *what*? (she shakes her head) Who else did he tell it to? Corey: The athletic squads from first period. I mean, *everybody*.

Ashlyn: Oh, hell, NO!

Deniece and Tamara: OOOOOOOH, somebody is going to get their ass kicked! Sista girl is hot!

Ashlyn: Oh my God, my God! That white bastard! Where is he? (she quickly walks through the lunchroom angry) I'm going to kick his ass!

Corey: (runs after Ashlyn) Say! Slow down.

Deniece and Tamara: (run after Ashlyn, too) Say, Ash, slow down!

[Ashlyn reaches Brandon and his table where all the guys are listening to his lie about him and Ashlyn.]

Ashlyn: (interrupts the entertainment) Excuse me! I'm sorry for interrupting your skin dig, but I want to let your boy know (looking at Brandon) that this body of mine will not allow some trash like him destroy the beauty and elegance I have.

[The guys are laughing and jiving with Brandon.] Friend 1: Damn, she told you!

Brandon: (stands up and talks loudly about what Ashlyn did) Yeah, just like you grabbed my ass and kissed me at the same time. (Ashlyn gets even angrier and balls her fist) Oh, can you deny it? (he puts his hand toward his ear) I don't hear a response, do I?

[Corey, Tamara, and Deniece are standing together watching Ashlyn. Courtney joins them along with other students.]

Ashlyn: You motherf—! (she leaps at Brandon and hits him) Corey: (jumps in to pull Ashlyn off of him) Oh, shit, y'all! Help!

[Ashlyn is stabbing Brandon with a plastic fork and hitting him with his tray. The players are pulling her off of him.]

Ashlyn: (Corey holds her) I can kill you, you white bastard! (jumping up and down as Corey holds her back from Brandon)

[Ashlyn stabs Brandon in the shoulder, his arm, and right side of his stomach with a plastic fork. Brandon leans over on the table while the players are trying to sit him up and keep him up. Principal Berg and the teachers come over to him while Deniece, Tamara, Courtney, and Corey escort Ashlyn to the hallway.]

Ashlyn: Oh, I want to kill him! I am so sick of these white boys! First, they spit at me, then they try to rape me! What else is it going to be? Y'all should have let me kill him!

Deniece: Look, Ash, I know you're upset—

Dr. Berg: (interrupts as he walks by) Ashlyn, come to my office now!

Ashlyn: Excuse me! You don't have to yell at me!

Corey: Ash, we'll walk with you.

Tamara: Yeah, we will.


Courtney: Even though I don't come around as much, I'll walk with you. [Ashlyn walks with Deniece, Tamara, Corey, and Courtney to the office as Dr. Berg holds the door; they walk into the office, then Dr. Berg walks to his personal office and Ashlyn follows.]

Ashlyn: (sits down in his office) OK. Can my friends come in here and sit down, too?

Dr. Berg: (shuts the door and sits down) No! They can't! They didn't stab Mr. Fields.

Ashlyn: (frowns) They are my witnesses.

Dr. Berg: Ashlyn, ever since you got here, there has always been trouble following you. (pauses) By the way, I don't care at this point. Maybe you should transfer out of this school and go to Elsik or Hastings, huh?

Ashlyn: You know what, Dr. Berg? You can kiss my proud black ass. I mean my black *ass*. (she pauses) As a matter of fact, let me call my mother.

Dr. Berg: Oh, your mother has already been notified by the secretary.

Ashlyn: Oh, OK. I guess that's how you white people are; you stick together, even though that individual is in the wrong, huh?

Dr. Berg: That's not true, Ms—

Ashlyn: (interrupts) Berg, you didn't even ask me why I did it, did you? Or didn't you?

Dr. Berg: No, I surely didn't, and I apologize. (sighs) So, Ms. Ashlyn, why did you stab Brandon?

Ashlyn: The reason why I stabbed him is because he's spreading rumors about me and him sleeping together, which is not true. Mr. Fields has been harassing me and even tried to force himself on me yesterday evening when I was leaving from practice. I had to pretend I wanted to engage in sexual activity, but I kicked him in his privates and his nose, got him out of my car, then I drove off.

Dr. Berg: So, you caught him off guard yesterday. You didn't go through with it?

Ashlyn: No! I didn't engage in any sexual activity with him.

Dr. Berg: OK. (sighs) Umm, Ms. Richardson, I apologize for his behavior, but your reaction to the rumor was out of control. You can go to jail for that.

Ashlyn: I know it. And I'll tell them what I told you. Brandon had sexually harassed and stalked me for a while. If they don't believe it, they can kiss my natural—

Debbie: (walks in) You betta not say it! You have a lot of explaining to do, Ms. Thang! (she turns to Dr. Berg) What is the problem now, Dr. Berg? (she sits down beside Ashlyn)

Ashlyn: (interrupts) The problem is—

Debbie: Ashlyn, don't say one word! Do you hear me? Ashlyn Renee Richardson, do you *hear* me?

[Ashlyn nods yes and rolls her eyes at Dr. Berg.]

Dr. Berg: Well, Mrs. Richardson, Ashlyn stabbed a student because he had disrespected her in public by spreading rumors that they had engaged in sexual activity which Ashlyn says is not true. She also said he had been sexually harassing her and stalking her for a while. So when she confronted him about the rumor, he showed no denial but disregarded how she felt about the situation. And that's all I can tell you.

Ashlyn: (crying) That's what I was trying to tell you last night, but you told me to handle the situation if it happens again, Mom!

Debbie: Ashlyn! I didn't tell you to stab him, especially if he's just talking to his peers! C'mon, Ashlyn, what's the problem? Girl, you can go to jail and get freakin' charges on your black behind!

Ashlyn: Well, Momma, I'm tired of trying to fit in! Every time I feel like things are getting better, it gets worse!

I want to transfer to Yates and stay with Vanessa and Darnell to finish my senior year 'cause this school here is in denial of racial discrimination. I mean, ever since I got here I have been pounded by racial slurs and almost raped by a white guy. Where is the justice in that? Huh? Tell me 'cause if Brandon was black, I wouldn't be receiving transfer papers! And you know that! (she gets out of her seat) Mom, just sign the damn papers because I don't need this! (she storms out of the office)

Debbie: (looks at Dr. Berg) Well, Dr. Berg, you got what you wanted. Another black, intelligent, and athletic student is leaving the school 'cause you can't control these white kids' attitude toward the blacks. (pauses) Just give me the papers so I can sign my child out of this racist school. (she grabs the form and signs it) I just can't believe this. Out of all the blacks here, my child, who just got here, has to suffer like this!

Dr. Berg: That's easy. She's sassy and a smart aleck. She doesn't understand what could happen if she reacts a certain way.

Debbie: Excuse me? I don't believe you called my child a smart aleck after she had to defend herself time after time cause of the color of her skin. (sighs with rage) Huh? I think you need to (stands up and throws the papers at Dr. Berg) check yourself before you wreck yourself and this so-called educational institution! And may God help you 'cause you gonna need it when I get through with you! Oh, you betta pray, even if you don't believe in him! [Debbie walks out of the office, and Ashlyn is outside of the office talking to Corey, Deniece, and Tamara.]

Ashlyn: Well, you guys, it's been real, but they gave my mom the transfer papers to send me out of this racist school. Hopefully, I'll go to Yates and finish there. I'll keep in touch.

Corey: No doubt! (he hugs her) We'll keep in touch. Deniece: Damn, Ash, I told you to chill.

Tamara: Yo', Ash, I probably would have done the same thang 'cause back in the Quarters, he would have been killed.

Corey: Word!

[Debbie walks to Ashlyn, Corey, Tamara, and Deniece.]

Debbie: (speaks) Hello, everyone. In case, you don't know, Ashlyn will not attend Kemptner High anymore, but you all are always welcome to visit her. Corey: Thanx, Mrs. Richardson. You know I got to see my li'l sis.

Deniece: Yeah. We gonna to miss this ol' heifer. Ashlyn: A'ight. Don't push it.

Tamara: Sista girl, keep in touch, you heard me? (she gives her a phone number) Call me when you need me.

[They all hug her, including Corey.] Debbie: Oh, y'all gonna make me cry.

Corey: (hugs Debbie) Don't cry, Mrs. Richardson, don't cry.

[They all laugh, then Debbie and Ashlyn exit out of the school; Ashlyn looks back and waves at Deniece, Tamara, and Corey. She goes to her car while Debbie gets in hers. Debbie waits for Ashlyn on

the side street of the school; Ashlyn drives off, and Debbie follows.]
*The scene fades away.*

**Scene 34**

When: Moments later
Where: The Richardson's home

*Debbie and Ashlyn arrive home. They walk in together going through the kitchen to get to the den; Jeff gets out of the recliner to greet them while Carlton is entertaining his new friend, Iman.*

Jeff: (Debbie sits beside Jeff) What happened, Debbie, at the school?
Debbie: (looks at Ashlyn, then at Jeff) Well, our daughter got kicked out of school for stabbing a white boy. (she sighs, then pulls her shoes off) Carlton: (interrupts) I *know* I just didn't hear that.
Debbie: Yes, you did.
Jeff: Why, Ash? Tell me why. You just got here, baby girl.
Ashlyn: (sits down and begins to cry) I did it because he kept harassing me, and he tried to rape me on the school campus. Then today, he spread rumors about me sleeping with him and even challenged me about it at the school in front of everybody. So, how else was I supposed to act? You tell me!
Jeff: (he runs to Ashlyn and holds her as she cries on his shoulder) Oh, baby girl, Daddy didn't know. Why didn't you tell me?
Carlton: (jumps up) Yeah . . . why didn't you tell us, Ashlyn? We could'a filed charges against this ol—
Debbie: All right, Carlton, watch your mouth. We have company. (she looks at Iman) I'm sorry you had to witness this drama.
Iman: Oh, that's OK. She's the one that needs to be taken care of. Especially with what she's gone through.
Carlton: (jumps up and down) Tell me, Ashlyn. That is not the boy that's been following you home! Please tell me that is not him! 'Cause if it is, I will find—
Jeff: (hugs Ashlyn and yells at Carlton) Carlton, your sister has already defended herself enough! She don't need anything else to happen! You are not the only one upset! (turns and looks at Debbie) Did you know about the incident? If you did, why you didn't you tell me? Huh? Answer me right now! Debbie: Look, you don't ever raise your voice at me whenever you want an answer. For your information, Ashlyn had told me that she had seduced him enough to

defend herself. She didn't want you and Carlton to get involved 'cause she was afraid of losing someone else she loves. So, I told her to tell the principal about it and make sure she tells everything so the boy won't deny it. I didn't tell her to try to kill the li'l white boy, but if he put his hands on her again, to whoop his ass to the ground. Then pray for him.

Carlton: Well, Mom, is the boy gonna to press charges?

Debbie: I don't know. All I know is Ashlyn has been involuntarily transferred out of Kemptner. Hopefully, he won't file charges. (sighs) I just pray he doesn't.

Ashlyn: (wipes her tears and gets up from her dad's arms) If he does, I will tell the truth 'cause I know the school got everything on camera. So, if he does, he'll be charged for sexual assault.

Jeff: (gets up and stands still) In that case, we leave this in God's hands. We'll just call Vanessa and Darnell to see if you can (talks to Ashlyn) stay with them while you go to Yates.

Debbie: Yep. (reaches for the phone) Let's call them.

[Debbie dials Vanessa's cell number, then the doorbell rings. Jeff gets the door while Debbie is waiting for someone to answer Vanessa's cell phone.] Jeff: (opens the door) Well, well, look who we have here.

Vanessa: (walks in) Hey, what's going on? I received a phone call from the school.

Debbie: (gets out of her seat to greet Vanessa) Girl, I was calling you. Why didn't you let me know you were at the doorstep?

Vanessa: Oh, the phone is on vibrator. Debbie: Where's Darnell?

Vanessa: He's at the school tutoring one of his students that's an outstanding basketball player.

Debbie: Really? How old is he? (she smiles at Ashlyn)

Vanessa: He's about 20 or 21; he's a junior.

Debbie: Oh, he's out of the question.

Vanessa: Say what? (she pauses, then looks at Ashlyn) Mom, I know you're not trying to—

Jeff: (interrupts) All right, ladies, that's not our concern. Ashlyn has too much on her plate right now. She needs to get her education first. (pauses and sighs) Vanessa, we were wondering if you and Darnell would allow Ashlyn to stay with you two so she can enroll at Yates High School. (They walk in the kitchen and sit at the table)

Vanessa: Well, uh, I don't mind, but I have to discuss that with

Darnell. (she takes her cell phone and calls Darnell)

[The scene switches to Darnell's office at U of H, where he's talking to Raymond Tillman and grading his paper; his cell phone rings; it's Vanessa, who's at her family's house in the kitchen talking to Debbie and Jeff about Ashlyn's moving arrangements.]

Darnell: (picks up his cell phone) Hey, baby, what's up?

Vanessa: Baby, Mom and Dad want to know if it's OK for Ash to stay with us and graduate from Yates since there's been another occurrence at the school. Darnell: Well, baby, I'm OK if she stays, but she has to respect you and abide by our rules. Let them know it's fine 'cause we are family and we love Ash.

And we did promise her we will be here for her since she's been going through the tragedy of losing Omar and the baby. So I don't mind at all. She just got to do her part, OK?

Vanessa: (smiles at Ashlyn) Okay, baby, I'll tell them.

Darnell: All right, shorty, I have to finish up with this NBA prospect's grades, and I'll be waiting on you and Ashlyn at the house, OK?

Vanessa: All right, baby, I love you. Darnell: I love you, too. Bye-bye.

Vanessa: Bye. (she hangs up the phone and turns to Ashlyn) Well, Ash, get your clothes, li'l sis. You're moving in with me.

Debbie: I guess (sighs) we have to enroll her in school now before next week so she can participate in extracurricular activities for the following semester. Vanessa: Yep. So get all of her records together so I can take them up there (she looks at her watch) right now since it's just 3 o'clock.

Debbie: OK. Let me go in the office and get her birth certificate and immunization records. (she leaves the kitchen)

Ashlyn: (gets up) Thanks, sis. I need to get away from this environment. (she goes upstairs to get her clothes and other items)

Vanessa: You're welcome!

Jeff: Well, Nessa, you make sure Ash does her homework and stays out of trouble. I don't want to hear any negative reports regarding her.

Vanessa: I'll make sure. You know me. I'll get dead in her you know what. Carlton: Shoot, you betta 'cause otherwise, it'll be vice versa. (he laughs) Ashlyn: (runs downstairs with her suitcases) All right, Nessa, I'm ready!

Vanessa: (walks out of the kitchen to the end of the stairs where Ashlyn is standing) Dang, girl, those suitcases look heavy! Should you leave some stuff here?

Ashlyn: I did. This (pats her suitcase) stuff is just for 2 weeks.

Carlton: (grabs the suitcase) Damn, girl. Are you sure this is only for 2 weeks? Ashlyn: Oh, you just weak, that's all. (she laughs) Need a li'l muscle.

Carlton: Shut up. (pick ups the suitcases and walks out the door with his girlfriend on his side)

Vanessa: (talks to Ashlyn as they walk out) He's just showing out in front of his new friend. (they laugh)

Debbie: (comes behind them with the birth certificate and shot records) Here you go, Ashlyn. (she hands the documents to Ashlyn) There's your documents.

Ashlyn: OK, Momma, thank you. (she gives her a hug)

Jeff: (comes out of the house to join everybody else) You're gonna leave me behind him, huh?

Vanessa: Nay, we love you. (she hugs him)

Ashlyn: Yep, we love you, old kryptonite. (she laughs and hugs him)

Debbie: (laughs) All right, leave my sugar bear alone. (she walks toward him and kisses Jeff on his lips)

Vanessa: Well, Ash, let's go before the school closes. (she gets into the car) Ashlyn: (walks to the car and looks back at her parents and Carlton) I'll miss y'all. (she acts like she's crying as she opens the car door)

Carlton: You're just going to Vanessa's and probably be over here every day! Ashlyn: Well, I guess, (she gets in the car and rolls down the window to talk to Carlton) excluding you . . . you ol' dried-up bag of dog food. (she laughs) Carlton: Oh, you got jokes! All right, I'm gonna let you make it!


[Everybody laughs; Vanessa backs up the car while Ashlyn buckles her seat belt; Debbie and Jeff are hugging and waving at Ashlyn and Vanessa while Iman and Carlton sit in Iman's car.]

*The scene fades away.*

# ACT 7

## Scene 35

When: Thirty minutes later
Where: Yates High School

*Ashlyn and Vanessa pull up to Yates High School in the third ward in between U of H and TSU. They see students coming out of class getting in their cars or walking to Burger King. Students are driving and riding in their cars with their loud music playing Lil Keke and DJ Screw. Ashlyn smiles and undoes her seat belt. Vanessa shakes her head. They park and get out of the car, then walk into the school building. Students are looking at them, trying to see who they are. Then a female walks up to Ashlyn and Vanessa.*

Tameka: (touches Ashlyn's shoulder) Hey, cuz! What y'all doing here? Ashlyn: (turns around and looks at Tameka) Tam, you betta be careful creepin' behind people. Girl, you was about to catch a beat down. [Tameka, Vanessa, and Ashlyn laugh out loud.]

Vanessa: Your cuz is going to school here.

Tameka: Fa' real? Oh, oh, oh, we're going have a track team now. (pauses) Look out, Gail Devers!

Ashlyn: You know it!

Vanessa: Tameka. Where's the administration office?

Tameka: Oh, it's down the hall to the left. (pauses) You want me to show ya? Ashlyn: Yeah. That's cool.

Tameka: A'ight. (Tameka, Ashlyn, and Vanessa walk down the hall; guys are checking out Ashlyn and Vanessa)

Guy 1: Hey, Tameka! (looks at Ashlyn and smiles)

Tameka: What's up, Slim? (she opens the administration door, and Ashlyn and Vanessa walk in.)


[The principal, Dr. Phillips, is talking to his secretary, Miss Davidson, when Ashlyn, Vanessa, and Tameka walk into the office.]

Miss Davidson: OK, Dr. Phillips, I'll make sure that is taken care of.

Dr. Phillips: OK. (he looks and sees Tameka, Ashlyn, and Vanessa) Hey, Miss Tameka Richardson, who do you have with you?

Tameka: Oh, these two women are my cousins. (she points at Ashlyn) This my cousin, Ashlyn. She wants to enroll and join the track team, and (she points at Vanessa) this is her sister. She teaches at U of H.

Vanessa and Ashlyn: (speak) Hi.

Dr. Phillips: Hello, ladies. (he shakes their hand) Nice to meet you.

(he talks to Ashlyn) So, Ashlyn, you want to join the Jungle, huh?

Ashlyn: Yep. (she gives him the papers) Here's my birth certificate, shot records, transcript, and transfer documents.

Dr. Phillips: (looks over the documents) OK. Won't you two follow me to my office so we can get Ms. Ashlyn started? Follow me. (he walks to his office and Ashlyn and Vanessa follow)

Tameka: Say, I'll see y'all later. (she walks out of the office) [Now, Dr. Phillips, Ashlyn, and Vanessa are sitting in his office.]

Dr. Phillips: (sitting down at the desk) Ashlyn Richardson, you want to join the Jungle? (looking at the transfer documents) These transfer documents state it was a mandatory release due to a violent act toward another student, and why is that?

Ashlyn: Well, uh, (she clears her throat) I was disrespected and discriminated against ever since I came to Kemptner this semester.

Dr. Phillips: Hmmm . . . Well, Ms. Richardson, you will not have that problem here. It seems you have to do unto others as you want them to do unto you. I don't have a problem accepting you here because you are not the only young, black, intelligent student that has transferred from Kemptner. I know personally because my daughter had the same problem.

So, I understand how you and your family feel. (pauses) Enough being said, Ms. Richardson, I see you're an outstanding student academically (looking over her grades and accomplishments from Kemptner and Inglewood) and athletically. You're a natural-born leader and a scholar.

Ashlyn: Well, I try to do the best I can be at anything I choose to have an interest in and subjects that will help me to succeed in life.

Dr. Phillips: (smiles) I like that response. Hopefully, you can influence others at this school to be the best they can be in everything that helps them succeed in life. (sighs) Well, Vanessa, since you are here, I need you (he goes into his files in his desk to pull out registration forms) to fill these forms on Ashlyn's behalf. (gives the forms to her) You can fill them out right now.

Vanessa: OK. (she grabs the forms and fills them out)

Dr. Phillips: While your sister filling out the forms, let's take a tour, shall we? (he gets up and opens the door)

Ashlyn: A'ight. (she gets up and walks through the door)

[Ashlyn and Dr. Phillips take a tour around Yates Sr. High School campus; she's being introduced to the basketball and track and field coach, also the athletic director in the gym.]

Dr. Phillips: Mr. Johnston, Dr. Rusk, Mrs. Love, this is Ashlyn

Richardson from Kemptner High School. Of course, you know she is a basketball standout, but she's also good in track.

Mr. Johnston: (shakes Ashlyn's hand) Welcome to the Jungle. I'm the track and field coach. I'd love to see your potential on the track. (he smiles at Ashlyn)

Dr. Rusk: (shakes Ashlyn's hand) Ashlyn, it's honor to have such a scholar like you to join the Jungle. I hope you're interested in athletic scholarships just as well.

Mrs. Love: (shakes Ashlyn's hand) Well, I finally get to meet the superstar that the entire 4A District is so amazed about. Now, we got ya. (she laughs) Dr. Phillips: Yep. I hope they will allow her to play in January.

Dr. Rusk: They will. 'Cause we have two weeks of school left before Christmas break. All she needs to do is enroll right now, Dr. Phillips.

Dr. Phillips: OK. I guess that part is already taken care of since her sister, Vanessa, is filling out the papers right now as we speak.

Mrs. Love: Good. She just has to take the exams to test out of the classes. Dr. Phillips: Oh, she won't have a problem. (turns to Ashlyn) Isn't that right? Ashlyn: Yes. That is correct. I'll make sure I study.

Dr. Rusk: All right, Ms. Thang. See you next week on the court. (he walks out of the gym)

Dr. Phillip: Well, Ashlyn, let's go enroll you in the classes you took this semester at Kemptner. (speaks to Ms. Love and Mr. Johnston) And Ms. Love and Mr. Johnston, I'll see you later.

Ms. Love and Mr. Johnston: (respond) All right! (walk away speaking to Ashlyn) See you later, Ashlyn!

[Ashlyn waves at them, then she and Dr. Phillips walk back to the administration office to finish the enrollment process. Ashlyn is finally happy and comfortable.]

*The scene fades away.*

**Scene 36**

When: A week later on a Friday afternoon Where: Classroom at Yates High School

*Ashlyn has finished reviewing for her final exams and now takes the exams to test out of the classes. She's in her last class, government AP.*

Ashlyn: (watching the clock and silently talking to herself) *Damn, this exam is easy.* (bubbling in the answers) *I'm almost halfway through and there's still 25 minutes more.*

[Ashlyn continues to bubble her answers. Ten minutes later she is done. Ashlyn gets up and turns in her exam. People are still taking their exam and some of them look up at Ashlyn. Ashlyn smiles and takes her seat. While she is sitting in her seat she writes a poem regarding what she has been through and how she overcame it. Before she can give it a title the bell rings. She exits the classroom and goes to the gym for basketball practice. When she goes into the gym, the team is already dressed for practice because they just had athletics. One of the players comes up to Ashlyn and introduces herself as Ashlyn walks across the basketball court to get to the locker room.]

Angie: Hey, Ashlyn. My name is Angie Wilson. I'm the captain on the squad. I'm glad you here to help a sista out. (she laughs)

Ashlyn: I accept the welcome, Angie. I'm pretty sure these girls are all right. You just have to regroup and lead them, that's all, even though I know there are more queen bees than you can bargain for. (pauses and begins to walk inside of the locker room) Let me go so I can come back and show you what I'm made of. (she winks)

Angie: A'ight, Queen Bee! (she laughs and shakes her head, then walks to the center of the court with the rest of the team to stretch as Ashlyn goes into the locker room)

[Within 8 minutes, Ashlyn comes out of the locker room, dressed and ready to go.]

Ashlyn: Angie! Where's coach? (she walks to the center)

Angie: In her office, (stretching) Champ, or should I call you Queen Bee? [The girls laugh along with her.]

Ashlyn: Oh, you got jokes. (she sarcastically grins) A'ight, keep it up.

Mrs. Love: (comes out of her office jogging to the center of the court and blowing her whistle) All right, ladies! Are we ready?

The team: (responds) Yeah!

Ms. Love: Our first district game is January 6, 1997! We gotta come with it! (she turns to Ashlyn) Are you ready, Ashlyn?

Ashlyn: Yeah! I'm ready! Let's get it going!

Mrs. Love: You heard her! Our new addition says let's get it going! All right? (pauses)

The team: A'ight!

Mrs. Love: Ladies, let's join together and pray the Lord's Prayer in silence! [The team bows their heads and prays; 2 minutes later, they are chanting in the circle.]

The team: (chants) We ready! We ready! We ready! We ready!

Mrs. Love: All right, ladies. Let's run the 3-man weave and 2 defenders on offensive players! Let's go! Hustle! Hustle!

[The team runs the three-man weave. Ten minutes later, they run other offense and defense drills. An hour and half pass. Vanessa stands at the entrance door waiting on Ashlyn to come out of the locker room; Ashlyn runs across the court to greet her sister.]

Vanessa: (smiling) Damn, you sho' is happy! (walking out of the gym with Ashlyn to her car)

Ashlyn: I feel so relieved here, even though some of the girls are hating already because of my skillz and beauty.

Vanessa: (gets into the car laughing) All right, this ain't Kemptner.

Ashlyn: I guess you forgot I came from the I-wood. (sits in the car and puts her bags on the backseat of the car)

Vanessa: I know but still keep your temper in control and the B-mode in check.

[Vanessa drives out of the parking lot.]


Ashlyn: Excuse me! I *know* you didn't have the enough to place me like you. (sarcastically laughs) I'ma let that ride, sis. I'm goin' to be good.

Vanessa: (driving to U of H entrance to go to Darnell's office.) You betta. Hum.

Ashlyn: (laughs) Girl, you just don't know. UMMMMM . . . Humph.

[Vanessa pulls into the parking out. She parks, then she and Ashlyn go into the engineering department.

They walk into Darnell's office where he is tutoring the NBA prospect, Raymond Tillman. Darnell and Raymond look up; Vanessa walks to Darnell.] Darnell: (gets out of his seat) Hey! Baby, (kisses Vanessa on her forehead) have a seat. (he pulls a chair close to his behind the desk)

Ashlyn: Hi, Darnell.

Darnell: Oh, hey, Ash. I didn't forget ya.


Raymond: (smiles) Hi. (waves at Ashlyn) I'm Raymond. You can call me    R.T. since somebody couldn't introduce us properly. (he looks at Darnell with a devilish grin)

Darnell: I apologize. Forgive me, you two. It's just that . . .

Ashlyn: You hypnotize whenever you see my sis. (grins) I guess I know who gets their way all the time.

Darnell: (looks at Vanessa) Baby, did you hear that?

Vanessa: Yep. (pauses and sighs) I surely do. (she kisses Darnell on the forehead)

Darnell: (puzzled) OK? (pauses) Anyways, Raymond is the NBA prospect. I've been tutoring in mathematical-linear equations so he can graduate this May and be eligible for the NBA draft.

Ashlyn: Oh, I'm impressed. (she smiles)

Vanessa: OK, Ashlyn, I think it's time to go so Raymond can finish his tutoring session.

(Ashlyn smiles at Raymond, and Raymond smiles back) Ash, let's go, girl. You can talk later.

Ashlyn: (flirts with her eyes at Raymond) Oh, I surely will. (speaks to Raymond) It was nice meeting you. (then she picks up a pen off of Darnell's desk and tears a sticky tab to write her number) Here's (she hands the number to R. T.) my number. Call me sometime. (she walks out of the office)

Vanessa: Um, that girl is too hot for her own good.

Raymond: You got that right. (smiling) I sho' will call her. Darnell: All right, bro, that's my li'l sis. She's too young for you. Vanessa: Surely is. (she leans over and kisses Darnell)

I'll see you later. (she walks out of the office)

*The scene fades away.*

**Scene 37**

When: It's Saturday morning 11:30 A.M. Where: Vanessa and Darnell's house

*Ashlyn is up watching cartoons in her silk pj's while Vanessa and Darnell are still in bed. The phone rings; its R. T.*

Ashlyn: (answers) Hello.

R. T.: Hello, Ashlyn, this is R. T. Ashlyn: (sits up) Oh, hey.

R. T.: (sitting in his dormitory room watching the recap of the high school football game) I was wondering if I can come by and pick you up so we can go to the movies.

Ashlyn: Sure. (smiling from ear to ear) I just have to get dressed, but before I do, I have to let my sis and bro know.

R. T.: A'ight. (pauses) You can call me back to let me know what they say. You got the number, I hope?

Ashlyn: Yeah. It's (713) 362-3875.

R. T.: Yep. Call me now. Don't have me waiting or else come by unannounced.

Ashlyn: A'ight, I'll call ya.

R. T.: OK. Bye-bye.

Ashlyn: (hangs up the phone and screams) Yes! Finally got a man to love again. (she runs upstairs; knocks on Darnell and Vanessa's door) Yo', Nessa. Nessa, can you hear me?

[A lot of moans and groans comes from the bedroom; Ashlyn puts her ear to the door.]

Darnell: Aw, Nessa, that feels good. Vanessa: Oh, baby, I'm almost there.

Ashlyn: Damn, they making out. (she bites her lip, then knocks hard on the door) Vanessa, could I go out with R. T.?

Darnell: (wraps up in a blanket and swings the door open) Say what? I did *not*
hear that, did I?

Ashlyn: Yes, (frowning and fanning) you did! I didn't st-urrr-da!

Vanessa: (puts a T-shirt on and walks to the door) Ash, he's too mature for you. He'll use you. I don't want you to go with him. He's nothing but trouble. Ashlyn: Say what? Vanessa, Omar was a licensed carpenter with his own crib. Tell me something I don't know about older men. (pauses) I'm waiting.

Darnell: (speaks in anger) I don't believe this. I told him not to call here for you! He can call for help for his assignments, not for young ass! (he walks into the master bathroom and slams the door)

Vanessa: (looks back, then turns to Ashlyn) Ash, I know you're trying to move on, but this guy is bad news. He's a womanizer, for God's sake. He's not the right one for you.

Ashlyn: (speaks loudly) You know what? Let me be the judge of that, big sis! Let me be a woman not a little girl! I have to live and learn, Vanessa! So, whether you like it or not, I'm going out with him today! (she walks off into her bedroom)

Vanessa: (opens Ashlyn's door) Ash, you betta not go with him! He's no good!

Ashlyn: (picking out her outfit and laying it on her bed) You know what? Vanessa: What?

Ashlyn: You can kiss my black ass!

Vanessa: Oh, no, I won't! I'm going to kick your ass 'cause this is *my* house and you abide by *my* and Darnell's rules! Do you understand me? Ashlyn, I'm talking to you!

Ashlyn: You know what, Nessa? Words cannot explain your hypocritical ways! Let me go out with him! I know it so hard for you not to be a BITCH but try to be open-minded. I'm a senior in high school, getting ready for college! So, let me live my life, OK?

Vanessa: All right! Fine. Do your thang but don't come telling me he raped you or impregnated your ass! (she walks out and slams the door)

Ashlyn: I know she . . . (pauses) I know (points at herself), I know she didn't 'cause she can't talk. She and Darnell slept in Mama and Dad's bed when they were in school, while Darnell was with another broad. (shakes her head) Oh, well, let me call him and tell his fine ass to get over here.

[One hour later, Darnell and Vanessa are upset, fully dressed, sitting in the den watching *Nutty Professor* on cable. Ashlyn runs downstairs dressed in a long dress with a split on the side. The doorbell rings. Ashlyn runs to the door; Darnell and Vanessa follow.]

Ashlyn: (opens the door) Hey, R. T., I'm ready to go.

R. T.: (smiling and checking out Ashlyn from head to toe) A'ight.

[Ashlyn and R. T. walk to R. T.'s car while Vanessa and Darnell stand in the doorway.]

Darnell: (speaks straightforward) Make sure she's back home before midnight! Did you hear me, R. T.?

R. T.: Yeah. She'll be back here at a decent hour since its just 2 P.M. (opens the door for Ashlyn)

Vanessa: Take care of her—

Darnell: Or else you will be behind bars! (slams the door)

R. T.: (shakes his head as he gets in the car) Damn, Ash, what's his problem? You got a surveillance on ya? (starts the car up)

Ashlyn: Naw, they just trippin' on our age difference.

R. T.: Oh.

[R. T. and Ashlyn drive off from the house to go on their first date.]

*The scene fades away.*

**Scene 38**

When: Later that afternoon Where: Tinseltown

*Ashlyn and Raymond are on their first date. Raymond takes Ashlyn to see* Vampire in Brooklyn, *starring Eddie Murphy. While they are standing in line to get their tickets, girls and women are staring at Raymond. Ashlyn smiles to herself and grabs R. T.'s arm. Then the females roll their eyes at her and whisper but smile at R. T.*

R. T.: (smiles as he approaches the ticket booth) You all right, Ashlyn. (digging in his pocket to give the ticket agent the money for two) You sho' got a handle on me.
Ticket agent: What movie would you like to see?
R. T.: *Vampire in Brooklyn* and for two in case you didn't notice. (he smiles) Ticket agent: Oh, I noticed. (she gives him the tickets and his money change) Here's your change. Enjoy your show.
Ashlyn: (holds on to R. T.) What's that all about?
R. T.: Nothing. Just hating, that's all.
Ashlyn: Uh-huh. I guess . . . (she looks back at the ticket agent)
[Ashlyn and R. T. walk inside the theatre and go straight to the concession stand.]
R. T.: Ma'am, (he talks to the cashier) I would like two large popcorns and two . . . (he looks back at Ashlyn) what kind of drink you want?
Ashlyn: Coke. Cherry Coke.
R. T. (speaks to the cashier) Two large cherry cokes. (pauses and grabs his wallet out of his pocket)
Cashier: (adds up the items and tells R. T.) That will be $11, sir.
R. T.: OK. (hands the $11 to the cashier)
[The cashier gets the popcorn and drinks together, then hands the items to   R.
T. and Ashlyn. R. T. holds his soda and popcorn while Ashlyn holds hers; they go to the complimentary bar to get the salt, butter, and cheese for the popcorn and straws for their sodas. Afterward, they walk to Screen 15. The movie is already playing. The audience is laughing at Kadeem Hardison. Ashlyn and R. T sit down at the front.]
*An hour passes and Ashlyn and R. T. are still looking at* Vampire in Brooklyn
*while finishing up their popcorn.*
R. T.: (asks) So, Ashlyn, do you want to hang out here and watch

another movie for free or go out to eat, then later go hang out at my place? (stuffing his mouth with popcorn)

Ashlyn: We can go out to eat for a while, then take a walk in the park for a while, and maybe go to your place.

R. T.: OK. We can do that since its just 4:09.

Ashlyn: (talking about the movie) Oh, that's nasty. (pauses) That's a deal.

*The scene fades away.*

## Scene 39

When: Forty-five minutes later Where: Bennigans

*Ashlyn and R. T. are eating dinner.*

R. T.: So, Ashlyn, have enjoyed my company so far? Ashlyn: Yes. But I feel you holding back on your true self.

R. T.: Really? (chewing his food and then takes a sip out of his glass) Why do you say that?

Ashlyn: Well, in the car, I was the one telling what I've been through and what I plan to do with my life. Now, I do know you are 21 and a NBA prospect majoring in computer engineering at U of H. You also graduated from Alief Elsik in '93. What else is there, R. T.?

R. T.: Well, Ashlyn, I'm the youngest boy out five children. Ashlyn: Uh-huh.

R. T.: Born and raised by two civil rights attorneys in Alief, Fort Bend County. I love basketball, computer graphics, poetry, and playing the piano. My favorite rapper is Rakim. My favorite R&B female singer is Mary J. Blige and male is R. Kelly. My favorite athlete is MJ, Michael Jordan. (pauses) Anything else?

Ashlyn: Yes. Um, what type of females have you dated in the past? And how was your relationship with those females?

R. T.: (laughs softly) Drama . . . Drama . . . Drama.

Ashlyn: (has a serious look) I don't see that as funny at all because I told you what happened to my previous relationship, and I'm still recovering from that.

R. T.: I'm sorry, Ashlyn. I'm very sorry. It's just that . . . that the females I dated were ghetto, but when I met them they were like you . . . until the truth came out. (pauses) The last girlfriend was a track star at Rice University. We were compatible. She loved poetry.

She was musically inclined. Somewhat spiritual but an undercover ho. She cheated on me constantly with all kinds of men. I found numbers in her drawers.

You know, dresser drawers. Couple of the guys called while I was there until one day I finally left her alone. She cried, slashed my tires, scratched my car, and even tried to fight one of the girls I was seeing.

Ashlyn: Damn, she *was* ghetto. (pauses) So, how long was the relationship and when did it end?

R. T.: Well, it lasted for 2 years. By the way, she was 3 years older than me. We started dating at the beginning of my sophomore year. And we broke up around last year. (pauses) No, this year, in February, I broke up with her and started playing the field and focusing on basketball and my education.

Ashlyn: Um. So, that explains why my sister and brother-in-law told me not to get involved with you.

R. T.: I don't know. It could be.

Ashlyn: Well, R. T. I'm sorry you got played but don't do that to others 'cause it could happen again.

R. T.: Oh, I make sure I tell the females I see other people and I'm not ready to commit. I got so much going on in my life right now.

Ashlyn: At least you are straightforward. (smiles) I like that.

R. T.: Really? (shouts) Yes! Finally a woman can accept it.

Ashlyn: (laughs) What time is it? 'Cause I really would like to go to the park. Especially to burn this food off. (rubbing her stomach, then drinks her tea)

R. T.: Well, (looks at his plate which is empty) I'm done. We can go now. It's up to you.

Ashlyn: (stands up) Let's go.

R. T.: All right. (he gets up and places a tip on the table with the money)

[Ashlyn and R. T. walk out of the restaurant holding hands; 25 minutes later, they are playing at the Memorial Park for about an hour and half; then they leave to go to R. T.'s apartment not his dormitory in Rice Village.]

R. T.: (gets out of the car) Ashlyn, this is my apartment.

Ashlyn: (gets out of the car) Oh, I thought you meant the dorm was the apartment.

R. T.: (walks to the door) The dorm is paid for. I already had this apartment since I graduated from high school. (he opens the door)

Ashlyn: Oh, okay. (she walks into the house) Wow, this is tight. (she looks at the African artwork on the wall, the vase, and statue)

R. T.: (walks through the apartment) Yeah, it's just a one bedroom, 1.5 bath, and a study, but it will do. (he looks at Ashlyn's behind while she turns looking at the pictures)

Oh, Ash, do you want something to drink before we go and sit down to watch some ol' school?

Ashlyn: Yeah. (still looking at the artwork) I'll drink a wine cooler.

R. T.: (walks in the kitchen) Wine cooler? You drink alcohol?

Ashlyn: Yeah. Sometimes, but it has to be fruity.

R. T.: (smiles) OK. Tell me some more 'cause I don't drink or smoke. (pauses) So, how about Canadian ginger ale?

Ashlyn: (sits down on sofa) That's fine. So, what are we watching?

R. T.: (puts ice in the cups and pours the ginger ale) *School Daze, Boomerang, Do The Right Thing*, and *Foxy Brown* with Pam Grier in her younger years. (he comes out of the kitchen) OK, baby girl, (hands the drink to Ashlyn) here you go. (he sits beside her, takes a sip, then gets up and puts the Foxy Brown movie on) Now, we are set.

Ashlyn: What did you put in?

R. T.: I put in Foxy Brown. (pauses and props his feet on the coffee table, then stretches his arm on the back of the couch behind Ashlyn) I hope that's OK with you.

Ashlyn: That's fine. (she slides closer to R. T. and props her head on his chest, then crosses her legs) You know, R. T., I feel very (she pauses and kisses him on the lips) vulnerable. I want to . . . (she kisses him more) . . .

R. T.: (he kisses her back) Are you sure? You just met me.

Ashlyn: So? (she keeps kissing him) There's something about you that got me hooked on you already. I guess you display a real man that is dominant, ambitious, affectionate, and wants a woman to be satisfied with who she is.

R. T.: OK. (he kisses and caresses her) How would you feel if I told you I want to take it slow 'cause I don't want any trouble from your brother-in-law and sister. He's already threatened me. I mean, when I first saw you, I was drawn to you. I guess I found out that you are one in a million. (pauses) I would not mind . . .

Ashlyn: (stops kissing him) So, you don't want to? OK. I guess I have to calm down. (she moves away from him)

R. T.: Ash, don't be mad. I just don't want to disrespect your—

Ashlyn: I know. You are being good so far. I guess I'm like the rest of the women you bring home. (she folds her arm and rolls her eyes at him)

R. T.: No. Because I would have been slept with you at a cheap hotel.

I don't bring women to this apartment unless I'm considering settling down with that person. (pauses and grabs Ashlyn's face)

Ash, I want to sleep with you so bad 'cause I'm attracted to you, not just your body, (he smiles) but I can't. You're so young. I don't want to hurt you in any way, then your bro hunts me down and kills me.

Ashlyn: R. T., I'm a senior in high school and not a virgin. I can take care myself. Trust me.

R. T.: Girl, you making it hard. (fans himself with his shirt) Damn, Ash. (he stands up) Oh, Ash, you look so good, but I promised your bro that I'd just take you out, not have sex and not bog you down in a committed relationship. Ashlyn: What? Darnell made you promise? I don't believe this! R. T., I don't care what they say. All I know is I really need to be loved tonight and if . . . (pauses) and if it does happen, it's up to us to keep it on a down low or take it to another level.

R. T.: Yeah, you right, but I'm not sure if that's a good idea.

Ashlyn: R. T., I'm telling you I need this. I've been through so much. I need to be free.

R. T.: I hear you but—

Ashlyn: No buts. Just come over here and relax. I won't bite you. (she laughs)

R. T.: (sits down by Ashlyn) OK, but I told you already. So, you can't get mad.

Ashlyn: (climbs on his lap and hands him a condom) Uh-huh. Just relax. (she kisses him on his ears and nibbles on his neck)

R. T.: Damn, you sho' you just 17?

Ashlyn: I'll be 18 next month. (kisses on his lips)

R. T.: Uh, Ashlyn, why are you doing this? (speaks nervously)

Ashlyn: 'Cause I need it, and you need it. (she undoes his pants and rocks back and forth in his lap) C'mon, R. T., relax.

R.T.: OK. Oh, boy. (he start kissing Ash, then picks her up, walks to the bedroom, and falls in the bed) Oh, Ashlyn, I hope ya ready. (kisses her) Ashlyn: I'm ready.


[Ashlyn is lying in the bed on her back while R. T. is on top of her kissing and nibbling on her. Then he puts the condom on and begins to grind.]

*The scene fades away.*

## Scene 40

When: It's 10 P.M.
Where: Darnell and Vanessa's driveway

*Three hours later R.T. and Ashlyn drive up to Darnell and Vanessa's driveway. The front lights are on, but no lights are on at all in the house.*
*The cars are out front. They sit in the car for a minute.*

R. T.: Ashlyn, oh, Ashlyn, you made me say some things I never thought I would say. Please don't tell nobody what I said. I'm serious. It's between me and you. I want you to scream my name. I even want to be your man and your only man, if that's OK with you, but if you don't want that, I'll be persistent because tonight your body felt so damn good to me. I mean, you hit the G- spot. I mean, you made me feel like a man. Um, girl, you just don't know.
Ashlyn: Damn, R. T., are you sure this is what—?
R. T.: (he grabs her left cheek and kisses it) Baby, I (hesitates) want you to be mine. Eweee, girl, damn, you make a nigga feel good! Damn, I could go another round, which would be the fourth.
Ashlyn: The fourth? I thought it was the fifth.
R. T.: Whatever. Just be mine. I don't care what Darnell says. All I know is I admit I'm sprung, Ash. I'm sprung. (pauses and sighs) Please, don't tell nobody. Just keep that to yourself.
Ashlyn: (leans over) You want to come in and go for another round?
R. T.: Girl! You gonna get me killed! Girl, are you crazy?
Ashlyn: I want to satisfy my new man. (she smiles and gets out of the car, then walks to the house)
R. T.: (looks up at the sky) Lord, forgive me, but I need this. (he gets out of the car and runs behind Ashlyn; he grabs her around her waist, then grinds on her behind) Damn, I can't wait.
Ashlyn: (opens the door; she hears bumping coming from upstairs as she walks into the house) Damn, Darnell wants a baby. They are at it again.
R. T.: Yep, just like we are. (starts kissing Ashlyn's ears) Where's your room? Ashlyn: Upstairs. (whispers) But we're going to the basement.
[They walk down to the basement which is laid out as an extra bedroom.] Ashlyn: Are you ready? (she lies down on the bed)

R. T.: You ain't said nothing but a word. (crawls on top of her) Let me get my condom on. (he gets it and puts it on over Ashlyn)

Ashlyn: (moans) Oh, R. T., go faster this time.

R. T.: Oh, baby, I will. Hold on to me.

[While they are having sex, Vanessa and Darnell open the basement door and run down the steps because they hear voices; it's R. T. having an orgasm.]

R. T.: (closes his eyes and shakes) Oh, yeah.

Ashlyn: (moans) Oh my. (she looks up and sees Vanessa looking down) Oh,

R. T., baby, get up. I think we are caught.

R. T.: Oh, shit! Damn, Lord. (he gets off of Ashlyn, pulling his pants up) [Next thing you know Darnell hits R. T. with his fist; R. T. falls down, holding his jaw.]

Darnell: Get the fuck out of my goddamn house!

Ashlyn: You did not have to do that! I *wanted* to sleep with him!

Darnell: Ash, I know you've been through a lot, but you got to respect me and your sister in this household! I don't care if Jesus Christ wanted to sleep with you! I will not deal with this shit at all! (he looks at R. T. tucking his shirt in) You gave me your word, you dirty bastard, if you decided to date Ash! But you didn't, you son of a bitch! I can kick your ass some more until your python will be out of order through the rest of your future NBA seasons! Man, I can just blow a goddamn blunt through your ass so your head can't think straight!

Ashlyn: (puts on her dress and jumps in between Darnell and R. T.) Darnell, you betta not hit him, Darnell! Or else, (she takes off her earrings, watch, and bracelet) I will kick your (she points at Darnell) ass!

Vanessa: (comes up to Ashlyn) You betta not 'cause *you* are the one that's in the wrong! Boning someone under our roof! You li'l ho! I outta beat the shit out of you, just to let you know who the queen bee is!

Ashlyn: Fuck you! I'm not a child. I'm a woman now, bitch! So, shove that in your ass! Plus, you are not Momma or my elder! So leave me the fuck alone!

R. T., let's go! I don't need this! (she walks upstairs)

Vanessa: I *know* she didn't. (looks at R. T.) You betta not follow her!

Darnell: You betta stay away from my house, R. T., I know that much!

R.T.: I'll stay away from ya crib, but Ashlyn I *will* see each other. (he walks off)

[Vanessa and Darnell follow him to his car. Ashlyn waits for him beside his car, all frowned up and rolling her eyes at Darnell and Vanessa.]

Vanessa: You betta not leave with him, or else I will let Mom and Dad know that you are acting like a tramp with no caution tape!

Ashlyn: (gets in the car with R. T. and leans out the window) Tell it! And kiss my natural black ass!

Darnell: Ashlyn, don't do this!

[R. T. backs out of the driveway. Darnell throws a fit while Vanessa is yelling Ashlyn's name until she can't see the car any more.]

Darnell: Damn! How could this be! She's just so . . . so hardheaded! Goddamn! (he walks into the house and slams the door)

Vanessa: (stands in the driveway crying and speaks to herself) I never thought I would see the reflection of me. Now I see what Mom and Pop were going through. (she walks into the house and shuts the door)

[Twenty minutes later, Ashlyn and R. T. pull up at R. T.'s apartment; R. T. gets out of the car, then opens the door for Ashlyn to get out; they walk elbow to elbow to the apartment and go in, then shut the door.]

*The scene fades away.*

# ACT 8

***Scene 41***

When: A week has passed
Where: The Richardsons' house

*School is out, but basketball is on the agenda. Ashlyn is staying with R .T.; she and Vanessa rarely talk since that night. Somehow, Vanessa and Darnell have not told Jeff and Debbie what happened. R. T. passes his exam with an A, which gives him a B+ in his engineering computation course so he doesn't see Darnell for a while. R. T. goes to watch Ashlyn play at the Booker T. Washington tournament the following week on Monday, Tuesday, and Wednesday.*
*On Christmas, Jeff and Debbie finally meet up with Darnell and Vanessa, along with Ashlyn, at the Richardsons' house. They all are sitting in the den watching* The Birth of Jesus, *a documentary on a VHS. Carlton has his new girlfriend, Iman, over there too. During the gathering, Ashlyn is very quiet and keeps to herself while everybody else is talking and laughing. Jeff and Debbie are on the phone giving directions to Speedy and his fiancée on how to get to the house. Darnell and Vanessa leave the den to fix their plates.*

Iman: (talks to Ashlyn) So, Ash, how you like Yates? Ashlyn: Oh, it's cool, just like I-wood High.
Carlton: Ash, you sho' is quiet. What's going through your thick head of yours?
Ashlyn: (she smiles) I'll tell you later. Jeff: (interrupts) Tell what later?
Vanessa: (sits down with her plate) Yeah, Ash, tell what is. (she stuffs some ham and potato salad in her mouth)
Ashlyn: (rolls her eyes at Vanessa) I hope you choke. Iman: (laughs softly) Ash, girl, you give your sista hell.
Ashlyn: She's always instigating when she needs to back off.
Vanessa: (wipes her mouth with a napkin) Don't start with me 'cause I will let the cat out of the bag.
Debbie: (looks puzzled) What are you talking about, Vanessa? Jeff: Yeah, Vanessa, tell us what's happening.
Darnell: (looks at Vanessa, then Ashlyn) Well, your daughter has a serious problem. She does not respect our household at all.
Debbie: Really? (looks at Ashlyn) Is that true, Ash?
Ashlyn: Look, Mom, I'd rather not discuss it right now. This is a time to enjoy ourselves as a family with no (rolls her eyes at Darnell and

Vanessa) DRAMA! Do I make myself clear?

Jeff: Ash, I don't care what you say, Ash. Your mother and I call the shots here!

(The doorbell rings; Jeff and Debbie get up together to greet the visitor, but Jeff turns back and looks at Ashlyn) We'll discuss it in a minute.

[Jeff walks to the door and opens it along with Debbie; it's Speedy and his fiancée, Teresa.]

Speedy: What's up, Pop? (gives him a hug) Hey, Mom. (kisses her on the forehead)

Debbie: I'm so glad you're here. You look so good. (she smiles) So, come on in. (speaks to Teresa) You too, baby.

[Speedy and Teresa walk in the house and follow Debbie and Jeff to the den.] Carlton: (gets up and gives Speedy a hug) What's up, bro?

Speedy: 'Bout to take that step. (smiles and grabs Teresa around her waist) Jeff: (sits down beside Debbie) You two lovebirds have a seat.

[Speedy and Teresa sit down next to each other.]

Vanessa: So, Teresa, shall I say welcome to the family? (she gets up and hugs her, then sits back down)

Darnell: Congrats, bro. (smiles and shakes his hand, then sits back down by Vanessa)

Speedy: Thanx, man. Uh, I just can't wait. (leans over and kisses Teresa, then turns to Ashlyn) Ash, you mighty quiet. What's wrong, li'l sis? You can't give your ol' bro a hug?

Ashlyn: (gets up and gives Speedy a hug) What's up, man? I see you brought ya girl. (speaks to Teresa) Teresa, welcome to this crazy family. (she laughs) Teresa: Thank you, Ashlyn.

Carlton: Oh, Speedy and Teresa, this is my (looks and grabs Iman's hand) beautiful woman, Iman.

Iman: Hi. I heard a lot about ya. Your brother looks up to ya, Speedy. Congrats to both of you.

Teresa and Speedy: Thank you.

Speedy: Well, back to Ashlyn, li'l sis; what's up, superstar? You're normally running at the mouth. You must got a man on the DL.

Ashlyn: (shakes her head from side to side) You see, you are trying to start something.

Darnell: I think you hit the jackpot, bro.

Ashlyn: Did anybody ask your input? (pauses) I think not, Darnell. (rolls her eyes at him)

Speedy: OK? Moving along.

Jeff: So, Ash, do you have a boyfriend on the DL?

Ashlyn: (sighs) Yes, I do. He's an athlete at U of H. He's the one that had the tutorial sessions with Darnell. Anything else you want to know?

Debbie: Yeah. How old is he?

Vanessa: Too old for her. (sipping on her soda)

Ashlyn: That's exactly why I can't stand you. You always jump in on somebody's conversation. So, will just shut up and let me respond? Your name is *not* Ashlyn.

Speedy: I guess she told you. Iman: (laughs) Sho' did.

Carlton: Ash, don't start. Please, don't start.

Ashlyn: Well, she always do that. She needs to stop before her feelings get tormented!

Vanessa: Oh, I'm scared, you li'l ho!

Debbie: Vanessa, chill out. Vanessa, (points her finger at her) you hear me? (turns to Ashlyn) Ash, go ahead and answer my question.

Ashlyn: He's 21 and a senior in college. He'll be graduating this year in computer engineering. (pauses) He's also a NBA prospect.

Debbie: That's not bad. So what are (points at Darnell and Vanessa) you talking about? 'Cause I don't see a problem with her dating with someone that's a scholar like that.

Vanessa: That's not it. R. T., her boyfriend, is a womanizer. He's got women lined up at his doorsteps, and he's playing Ashlyn.

Ashlyn: That is *not* true. He's very straightforward! He let me know, Vanessa and Darnell, that he just got out of a relationship 8 months ago. The woman was 3 years older, and she used him as play toy for 2 years. Then, when he broke up with her, she became hostile and psychotic toward him, even though she had phone numbers of other men and had some call the house while he was there, trying to make him think it was her study group, until he found the letters and men's underwear in her dresser drawers that were either too big or too small for him. She was an undercover ho.

Carlton: Damn, he got played! (laughs)

Ashlyn: That's not funny, Carlton. (rolls her eyes at Carlton) Anyway, so after they separated, he began playin' the field and he let those women know he was not interested in a committed relationship.

He even told me the same thang, but he said these (points at Darnell and Vanessa) two had a problem with it because of what they saw of him for the li'l time they knew him.

Vanessa: I can't believe you believe that crap he dished out to you.

Darnell: Well, Vanessa, he did tell me about the female who he used be involved with had damaged his cars and even jumped on a female he was currently dating. I can recall the conversation we had about his ex and why he was seeing a lot of women because of her inconsideration and disloyalty for their relationship. He even told me those women were out for his money and also for his future fortune. So, he's playing for what it's worth as long as he tells them he's not ready for a relationship. So, Ash is right. I didn't expect him to tell her about his ex. He never does that.

Vanessa: Really? Um, I guess so.

Ashlyn: Thanx, bro. You're back to normal. Jeff: So, Ash, when are we going to meet him? Ashlyn: Soon. I mean real soon.

Vanessa: You know, Ashlyn, you still did not disclose why we said you disrespected the household! Now did you or did you not?

Ashlyn: Vanessa, you just won't let it rest. Go ahead. I don't care.

Debbie: Tell us what?

Vanessa: Me and Darnell caught them in the basement having sex!

Darnell: (shakes his head) Oh, Nessa. Why?

Vanessa: It needs to be told. (Ashlyn bites her lips while staring at Vanessa) And she moved in with him after we confronted them. How disrespectful is that? Tell me!

Jeff: Ashlyn! I don't believe this! You're not even in college yet! Didn't you learn your lesson dealing with Omar, may he rest in peace? Damn, Ashlyn, we didn't send you across town to lie in the bed shacking up with a grown man! You were to go there to finish high school and get into college! Not to— Debbie: (interrupts)

Ashlyn, I'm very disappointed in you. It's OK to see him, not to live with him! We did not raise you that way!

Ashlyn: I know you didn't, but I still go to school and play ball! I'm a grown woman now! I have to make my own choices and suffer the consequences and/or accept my blessings. That's what you don't recognize! I'm no longer a child! I should be treated as an adult! Yes, I apologize for having sex under Vanessa and Darnell's roof. That's why I left, 'cause it is time for me to make my own rules.

Carlton: She does have a point. I agree. Iman: I agree, too.

Teresa: I disagree because he's more mature than you are, Ashlyn, and he's bound to hurt you. If you want to be recognized as a woman, get a job and live in your own apartment, not his.

Speedy: Naw, she needs to get her education first before taking any man that seriously.

Ashlyn: Now, you (points at Vanessa) see what you started. That's why we do not get along. She's always pointing out what other people do, but I remember when Mom and Dad caught you and

Darnell having sex in their bed when you were a junior in high school and he was a freshman in college. So, how come it's a crime when you already broke the seal? Now, come up with something else. (pauses) I thought not. You ol' hypocrite. (rolls her eyes at Vanessa) Debbie: Ashlyn, you need to move back with your sister until you graduate. I'm your mother, and you are going to respect me. Do you understand me?

Ashlyn: Yeah, I understand, but I'm going to visit him every day.

Jeff: And where would that be? Not in the bedroom. It betta be school campus, and that's it or else you will go to Alief Hastings or commute back and forth. (pauses and thinks) You know what? You need to stay here until you finish school to make sure that certain incidents will not occur again. (he turns to Debbie) What do you think?

Debbie: It's (shrugs her shoulder) OK because Carlton goes to U of H every day. She can ride with (turns to Carlton) him. Carlton doesn't mind.

Carlton: It's fine with me, you know. I don't have a problem with that.

Ashlyn: (frowns up) Mom and Dad, I am practically grown! (she stands up) I might as well stay with R. T. until I can get my own apartment!

Jeff: You will *not* stay with a man, not being married! You understand me? I will not tolerate your trifling attitude any longer! As a matter of fact, you will not receive any phone calls from him and you betta not go see him! I don't care what he's got going for himself! I care about you and your well-being, young lady! Therefore, the rule is you are staying *here* and you are grounded! No more driving! No more dates! Not until you learn how to respect others and their household! Do I make myself clear? Ashlyn, I don't hear you!

Ashlyn: (start crying) Why do you have to continue to see me as a child? I am not a child anymore! This is my last semester in high school! I think I deserve to be respected as an adult! (she storms out of the house and jumps into her car, then leaves)

Jeff: Goddamn you! If she doesn't act like you, Vanessa, I can kiss my own behind!

Speedy: Oh boy, here we go again. (he gets up and goes to fix his plate; Teresa follows)

Carlton: Man, Nessa, you just *had* to start some shit when everybody is here enjoying the family affair! I'm like Ash. You are a bitch that used to be a ho. So how can you call the kettle black? You can't. Not when it's black, too. C'mon, Iman, let's go. (Carlton walks out of the room)

Iman: (gets up) Well, everybody, it was nice meeting you. (she follows Carlton out of the house)

Speedy: Well, Nessa caused it.

Darnell: Look, everybody, just leave my wife alone! She pointed out what needed to be pointed out about Ashlyn! And if she didn't, she would have been held responsible for whatever happened to Ashlyn! Everybody would blame her! So just chill. (he puts his arm around Vanessa)

Vanessa: (softly speaks) Everybody, I'm sorry. I just want Ashlyn to be better than me. I'm not picking on her. I'm just trying to steer her the right way to do things, that's all. (sighs) I guess Darnell and I should leave. (turns to Speedy) I'm sorry you came home in the middle of drama but call me whenever you get a chance. (she gets up and turns to Teresa) Oh, Teresa, I'm a little embarrassed, and I apologize. Don't judge me today. Please don't. (she hugs Teresa) Call me if you need someone to talk to while he's gone out of state to play ball. (smiles)

Teresa: I will. (she smiles)

Darnell: All right, everybody, (he gets up) I'll see you later. Debbie and Jeff, we'll keep an eye on Ash still.

Jeff: Thank you. Just let her experience life on her own. Don't intervene unless she really needs your help. I admit I'm very upset right now, but she wants to be an adult, so she has to live as one. I mean, pay her car notes and rent by getting a job. That's all I have to say. I'm celebrating the rest of the evening with Speedy, Teresa, and Debbie, and I'll keep in touch. (he hugs Vanessa and Darnell)

Debbie: Ashlyn is in God's hands. (hugs Darnell and Vanessa) We just have to pray, OK?

Darnell: All right. (Darnell and Vanessa walk out of the house)

Debbie: (leans out the door) We'll see you later.


[Vanessa and Darnell leave the Richardsons' house while Speedy and Teresa are still there talking to Debbie and Jeff.]

*The scene fades away.*

**Scene 42**

When: Two months later Where: Yates High School track

*Ashlyn is running track. She receives many honors at Yates High School and broke three school records in the 100, 200, and the long jump. She was also ranked #1 in state and #4 in the nation in the long jump and 100 meter dash. Now, she is at track practice with Coach Johnston, one-on-one, at Yates High School; she's already broken the school record there and in the Houston area for all three events.*

Coach Johnston: (walks and talks to Ashlyn on the track) Take a deep breath, Ashlyn. Let me know when you need to stop, OK?
Ashlyn: Yeah. Coach, I hear you. (breathes hard) Uh-wee, this is a task to try to break my own record. (pauses) Damn, it's hard.
Coach Johnston: Yep. (he looks at Ashlyn as she stops and bends over) You all right?
Ashlyn: (she stands straight with her hands on top of her head) Yeah. I'm fine. (she breathes slowly)
Coach Johnston: (looks around the track and field) Well, everybody has run their last run and left like OJ did. (he laughs)
Ashlyn: (laughs) See, you are wrong.
Coach Johnston: What do you mean I'm wrong? It's the truth.
Ashlyn: Coach, you are wrong, wrong.
Coach Johnston: (walks with Ashlyn to her car) No, I'm not. (pauses) Just make sure Mr. R. T. takes care of you when ya get home so you will be ready for tomorrow at TSU relays.
Ashlyn: (tosses her bag into the backseat) I surely will. (she gets in the car; buckles her seat belt, then starts the car) Trust me. (she smiles and backs up the car, then drives off)
Coach Johnston: (talks to himself as he walks to his car) Man, man, I wouldn't mind being with her. She's the right kind of woman, just six years younger than me. Damn! (pauses) Um, ummmph, oh well, have to keep my feelings for her on the DL.

[Coach Johnston gets in his car and drives off.]
*The scene fades away.*

## Scene 43

*Ashlyn pulls up at the apartment, and she notices there is another car in the driveway; she gets out of the car. She goes to the door to unlock it, but as she unlocks it, she hears noises from the bedroom.*

Ashlyn: (runs to the bedroom and yells) R. T.! R. T.! (the music gets louder and louder as she enters the bedroom; she sees R. T. having sex with another woman. She screams with anger) R. T.! How could you do this to me? You motherfucker! (she balls her fists and grits her teeth, staring him down)

R. T.: (jumps off the woman) Ash! Baby! Ash, (put on his boxers) baby. I'm sorry! (Ashlyn looks at him with rage, tears falling from her eyes) Baby, she's nothing to me! It just happened! (he grabs Ashlyn) Baby, don't leave me! Please! (he start crying)

[The woman is his ex-girlfriend, Tonya; she gets up and puts on her clothes like nothing ever happened.]

Tonya: (speaks with authority and boastfulness) Well, R. T., looks like I still got it. (she smiles and kisses him) Don't I? (turns to Ashlyn and walks out of the room)

Ashlyn: (runs behind Tonya and grabs her hair to pull her back) Oh, no, you don't, bitch! (Tonya falls back)

R. T.: (grabs Ashlyn, trying to pull her away from Tonya) Baby! Baby, stop! Ashlyn: (she punches Tonya in her face and stomach) Bitch, he's mine! You no-good ho! (Tonya runs out and R. T. catches Ashlyn and picks her up as Tonya leaves the house) Let go of me! I want to kill that bitch! Let me go,   R. T. (steadily fighting R. T.) Let me go!

R. T.: (holds on tightly) Baby, stop! Please, baby, stop! Don't be mad at her! Be mad at me!

Ashlyn: (stops and turns toward R. T.) You're right. I should kick your ass, you tired, broad-ass nigga. That's what you are. You're not a black man! A black man respects and is loyal to his black woman!

R. T.: (grabs Ashlyn's arm) Baby, I'm sorry! (he cries out) I made a mistake, a'ight? It just happened. My ol' feelings just came out! I'm sorry, baby! Please, forgive me! I won't do it again . . . I promise! Just listen to me! Ashlyn: (yanks away) Really? (tears fall down her face) So, do you love me, or am I your toy like you were to her? Huh? (she slaps him) Answer me!

R. T.: (rubs his face) I love you . . . but you betta not hit me ever again like I'm your damn child, a'ight? Even though I deserve it! Two wrongs don't make a right! We're adults here, so act like one!

Ashlyn: *Excuse me?* So what are you saying, tired broad-ass nigga? (she paces back and forth) Tell me!

R. T.: Don't you hit me, woman! I didn't hit you! All I know is, Ashlyn, I want you to forgive me! You are the one woman for me! Just forgive me! (he grabs his jaw)

Ashlyn: (cries) I need some air. (she runs out)

R. T.: (tries to grab her) Ashlyn! Ashlyn! (he stumps his foot as he runs after her) Goddamn it. (he stops and grabs his foot while Ashlyn jumps in her car and drives off) Goddamn it; shit, that hurts. (he looks up and she's gone so he limps back to his apartment in pain and slams the door)

[Ashlyn drives to Memorial Park to get some fresh air. As she's sitting on her car, Coach Johnston runs past her and turns back to talk to her.]

Coach Johnston: Ashlyn? What are you doing here? (jogs in place by her car) Ashlyn: (wipes her tears) Me and R. T. had a falling out.
Johnston: (stops and sits on the car beside Ashlyn) Oh, Ash, (puts his arm around her) it's going to be okay.
Ashlyn: Yeah. I hope (sniffles) so. (pauses) All I know is my sister told me so, and *bam*, I found him in the bedroom with his ex all naked having hot sex.
Johnston: Whoa! That's some shit. Damn. (pauses and sighs) Um . . . Umm . .
. Humph . . . Uh . . .
Ashlyn: (she looks into his eyes) You're speechless? Aren't you . . .
Johnston: Damn, Ashlyn. I'm this close . . .
Ashlyn: (leans over) This close to do what, Coach?
Johnston: This. (he French-kisses her and grabs her waist to pull her close to him)
[Next thing you know, Coach Johnston and Ashlyn are in the backseat kissing and grinding each other.]
Johnston: (caught in a moment) Oh, Ashlyn, I've been wanting to do this for the longest. Too bad we can't have sex.
Ashlyn: (sits up while Coach gets off of her) Yeah. That will not be good. Even though I know you would be good in the bedroom, but I can't do it.
Johnston: Yep. You are right. (he kisses her) You want me to follow you home?
Ashlyn: No. (she gets in the front seat while the coach gets out of the car; he stands by her front door) I have to do this by myself.
I really need to handle this situation with the man I love. Even though I wouldn't mind being with you tonight, it's not going to happen.
Johnston: Yep. (sighs and steps back from the car) I guess I'll see you tomorrow.
Ashlyn: OK. (she smiles and drives off)

[Ashlyn pulls up in the driveway and gets out of the car. R. T. opens the door; she walks to the door and looks at him, then R. T. grabs her and kisses her. They go into the apartment and close the door.]

*The scene fades away.*

# ACT 9

## Scene 44

When: The next day Where: Robertson Stadium

*Ashlyn is at the Robertson Stadium for the TSU relays. R. T., Debbie, Vanessa, Darnell, Jeff, Carlton, and Iman are in the stands cheering for Ashlyn.*

The announcer: All right, Ladies and Gentlemen, this is the 2nd heat of the high school girls 100m dash!
[The crowd cheers.]
R. T.: C'mon, Ash! Show them what you working with! Jeff: Let's go, Ash!
Ashlyn: (gets on her block) God be with me. [The seven other girls get on their blocks.]
The announcer: On your mark; get set . . . (the ref shoots the gun) *POW!* [Ashlyn pulls off so quickly with a long strive that she finishes first with a set record 10.99; she puts her hands on her head to take breather; Coach Johnston comes up to her in the field area.]
Coach Johnston: Dang, Ash, you were blazing! Great job, Sista Souljah! Queen Bee! (he hugs her)
Ashlyn: Thank you. (catching her breath) Hard work pays off. Now, I have to run in the semifinals.
Coach Johnston: Yep. (grabs her waist) You got to stretch before you run the 200m dash next.
Ashlyn: (bends over and touches her toes) OK. (takes a deep breath) Oh, boy. (she stands up straight)
[Eight minutes later, Ashlyn is on the blocks again but for the 200m dash.]
R. T.: Damn, my baby can run!
Vanessa: (looks at R. T. and rolls her eyes) Baby? Uh-huh, whatever.
Carlton: Vanessa, chill. (pauses and turns the camera on Ashlyn) A'ight, Ashlyn, let's go!

The announcer: On your mark; get set, and (the ref shoots the gun) *POW!* [Ashlyn takes off leading the pack all the way. She crosses the finish line at 22.43; Coach greets her at the finish line.]
Coach Johnston: A'ight, Ashlyn! You doing good! (hands the water bottle to her) Drink some, then we'll stretch so you won't cramp up.
Ashlyn: (drinks the water) Coach, that was slow. I hope I can

run better tomorrow. (sips some of the water)

Coach Johnston: (sits down on the field) All right, Ash, let's stretch you out. Ashlyn: (lies on her back while Coach pushes her legs toward her) Dang, Coach, you tryin' to kill me?

Coach Johnston: Well, tell me when to stop. Ashlyn: Stop! Right now!

Coach Johnston: (stops and get up) All right, that's it.

Ashlyn: Are you sure that's it and nothing else? (she has a devilish grin)

Coach Johnston: Go on, girl! You know I cut for ya; just can't expose it in public. (he grins)

[R. T. notices the chemistry between Ashlyn and Coach Johnston. Ashlyn walks off the field to the stands where R. T., Debbie, Jeff, Vanessa, Darnell, Carlton, and Iman are.]

Ashlyn: (reaches to grab R. T.'s leg) Hey, baby! I thought you weren't coming 'cause you had a conference with the GM of the Rockets.

R. T.: (leans over the rail) You know I had to be here for my boo. (he jumps over the rail)

Ashlyn: Oh my God. (smiles) Baby . . .

R. T.: (picks her up and spins her around) Give me a kiss, girl!

Ashlyn: OK. (she kisses him)

Jeff: OK. (grunts) That's enough, you two.

R. T.: Oh, we sorry. (puts Ashlyn down)

Ashlyn: Sorry, Dad. (pauses) By the way, thanks for coming; you too, Mom, Vanessa, Darnell, Carlton, and Iman.

Debbie: Of course, we had to see our baby run. I wouldn't miss it.

Carlton: You did damn good, sis!

Iman: (nods –yes‖) Sho' did. I didn't know you can run like that, girl!

Ashlyn: Oh, it takes practice. (she smiles)

Vanessa: Yep, you did well. Keep it up. (she smiles at her) Darnell: You go, girl; that's all I have to say!

Ashlyn: Thanx.

Debbie: Well, I guess we can go to Golden Corral for dinner or Frenchy's. Everybody: Frenchy's!

[The entire group left with Ashlyn to go across the street to Frenchy's.]

*The scene fades away.*

**Scene 45**

When: The next day Where: IHOP

*Ashlyn won the 100, 200, and placed 2nd in the long jump. She set the record in the 100m dash at 10.88 nationally. The family celebrates with the Yates track team at IHOP. The team overall placed in second. Coach Johnston sits at the table with the team while Ashlyn sits by R. T. surrounded by her family, including big brother, Speedy, and his fiancée, Teresa.*

Coach Johnston: (stands up to give cheers) May I have everyone's attention (everybody faces him) please! (pauses) I thank God for allowing us to be here on this earth to accomplish what we have accomplished this weekend. I told you work without faith is in vain and faith without work is in vain, too. However, I saw work and faith in each individual here tonight. That's how we were able to place in the top five out of all the 35 schools that participated. I give a special recognition to Ms. Ashlyn Richardson for setting a record in the 100m dash at 10.88. She was second slowest from collegiate women's record in this event. Dang, girl, you can run! You go, girl. (he smiles and winks at her)
Ashlyn: (smiles) Thanks. (R. T. stares at Coach Johnston)
Coach Johnston: OK, team, our next big challenge is Texas Relays in Austin. Yeah, baby, may God be with us, and I thank the support from the family and may God bless you!

[Coach Johnston sits down and stares at Ashlyn as she's kissing and talking to
R. T.; everybody else is talking and eating.]

*The scene fades away.*

### Scene 46

When: Two weeks later at 10 P.M. on a Wednesday Where: R. T.'s home

*Ashlyn is at home with R. T. preparing for the big meet at the Texas Relays in Austin, Texas.*

Ashlyn: (takes her wind suit of the dryer) R. T.!

R. T.: (sits in the living room watching *Def Comedy Jam* hosted Martin Lawrence) What?

Ashlyn: (comes out of the utility room and walks into the living room) Baby, are you coming with my family tomorrow night? (she sits down beside him and kisses him) Huh, baby?

R. T.: I don't know. I might have a meeting with the GM at Dallas. This Saturday, I have a meeting with the GM with the Rockets. So, I don't know if I'll be able to see you run. I'm sorry, but you have your dreams and I have mine, too. Not all the time the support is physical; (pauses and grabs her chin) it can be spiritual, too.

Ashlyn: (has a sad look as she looks into R. T.'s eyes) Baby, I want you to try to be there, at least Saturday (pauses) if I make the finals.

R. T.: (he hugs and kisses her) I'll try, OK? 'Cause I love you.

Ashlyn: (speaks softly) OK, baby.

[Ashlyn feels down and out as she sits down in R. T.'s lap watching *Def Comedy Jam*.]

*The scene fades away.*

**Scene 47**

When: Thursday night
Where: Austin, Texas at the Texas Relays

*The best of the best are at this meet. Ashlyn is on the track getting ready to run the 100m dash. She looks up at the stands to see if R. T. is there, and he is not, but Vanessa, Darnell, Speedy, Teresa, Iman, Carlton, Jeff, and Debbie are there cheering for her.*

Ashlyn: (stretches and talks to her cousin, Tameka, who's helping her to stretch) Girl, (she grunts as Tameka pushes her back forward) that's enough. (she stands up) Ew, ewwweee, that feels good! (jumps up and down)

Tameka: Cuz, you betta run hard 'cause ol' girl on the side of you can run a 10.6.

Ashlyn: Fa' real? Oh, shit, my 10.88 ain't nothing then.

Tameka: It is, but hers is a national record. She's trying for the Junior Olympics.

Ashlyn: (gets paranoid) Damn! She that good?

Tameka: (nods her head) Yep!

The announcer: May all the runners get in their lane and blocks for high school girls 100m dash! Please report to your lane!

Tameka: (runs off) Good luck, Ash!

Ashlyn: (gets on the block) Oh, boy, God help me through this. (closes her eyes and prays, then looks at the stands)

Vanessa: Come on, Ash!

Carlton: Bring it home, Ash. (records Ashlyn's every movement)

Jeff: Let's go, Ash!

Iman: C'mon, Ash!

Speedy: Put your foot to the pedal! Teresa: Go, Ashlyn!

Debbie: Come on, baby! Sho' them what ya made of! [Ashlyn turns ahead and gets in position.]

The announcer: On your mark! Get set! (the ref shoots the gun) *POW!* [Ashlyn and the soon-to-be Olympian are neck-to-neck all the way to the finish line. Ashlyn drops her head into the tape; she stops and drops to the track; the girl does too. The crowd cheers and screams loudly. Ashlyn lies on her back, knees bent with hands on her face, rocking side to side. The girl is standing but bends over. Coach Johnston runs to Ashlyn and picks her up. Tameka follows him along with the relay team.]

Tameka: Damn, Ash, you ran a 10.58! Goddamn, you were blazin'!

Coach Johnston: (stands Ashlyn up) You a'ight?

Ashlyn: Yeah. (she grabs her head) I'm just a li'l light-headed.

Coach Johnston: (grabs a bottle of water from one of the athletes and gives it to Ashlyn) Here you go, baby. Drink it.

Ashlyn: (looks at him with amazement) Coach, you called me . . . (pauses and looks around with an *oh* expression)

Tameka: (grins) Oh . . . I smell trouble, but I won't tell nobody.

Coach Johnston: Tell what? (acts surprised)

Ashlyn: You know (drinks her water) what you said. Uh-huh. (smiles) [Ashlyn, Coach Johnston, and Tameka walk in the middle of the field.]

Coach Johnston: (laughs) A'ight, a'ight, you got me. (Tameka walks away and laughs) Ash, I'm proud of ya. (he smiles) I hope you run like that Saturday morning in the finals. Ashlyn: (speaks with confidence) Oh, I will.

Coach Johnston: Ash, are you still going to run the 200 tonight?

Ashlyn: Yep. It's almost time after two more races.

Coach Johnston: Naw. Four more. And you need to stretch. (he smiles at her) Ashlyn: (smiles back) OK. (sits down and lies on her back)

Coach Johnston: (grabs her legs and pushes them toward her) Tell me when to stop.

Ashlyn: Stop!

Coach Johnston: (he holds it) 1 1,000; 2 2,000; 3 3,000; 4 4,000. (then he grabs one leg and pushes toward her, and lays the other leg down)

[Ashlyn is stretched out and ready to go. Fifteen minutes later, Ashlyn is on the block ready to run 200m dash. She looks at the stands to see if R. T. is there. Apparently, she sees only her family.]

The announcer: On your mark! Get set! (the ref shoots the gun) *POW!* [Ashlyn is in third around the curve but within half of a step she stretches into the lead during the straightaway all the way to the finish line. She puts her hands on top of her head. Coach Johnston and Tameka run to Ashlyn to greet her and help her off the track; they all walk onto the field.]

Tameka: Girl! You pull off like a pro! Damn, cuz, you got juice!

Ashlyn: Damn, I'm tired! I hope I don't have to (taking a breath) run anymore tonight!

Coach Johnston: Ash, your time was better than the one at the TSU relay! It was 22.41! You go, shorty! (he hugs her) I knew you could do it!

Tameka: Yeah, I bet. (smiles)

Coach Johnston: (gives Ashlyn a bottle of water) Here you go. You need that so you can cool off.

Ashlyn: (drinks the water) Thanx. (sips the water) I guess I can now, huh? Coach Johnston: You can, but I prefer that we all stay at the hotel together as a team.

Ashlyn: Well, I was planning to go with my family 'cause R. T. might come. Coach Johnston: Ash, I know you want to be with your family, but as a team we need to stick together 'cause we all need to stay focused, including you.

Tameka: (grins) Look at Coach trying to be serious. Coach Johnston: Say what?

Ashlyn: Are you sure that's why and not something else? Coach Johnston: I'm positive. (he smiles)

Tameka: OK. (sighs) I think it's time to go so I can rest up for tomorrow morning's 400 relay semifinal.

Ashlyn: (walks up to coach) You are lying. (she walks away to greet her family)

[The Richardsons are on the field talking and hugging Ashlyn; R. T. still isn't there.]

*The scene fades away.*

## Scene 48

When: Friday, the next morning Where: On the field

*Ashlyn is on the field doing the long jump. Her first attempt is 17. Then her second is 18¾. Her final attempt, she takes a deep breath and runs down the straightaway like she's running in the 100 m; she flies in the air jumping her best, 20½. Coach Johnston jumps up and down. Tameka had done the long jump, too; she got 4th place with a 18¾ jump. Ashlyn received 1st place. After she receives recognition, she looks at the stands to see if R. T. is there; he is not. She looks down and walks toward the opposite side of the stand; Coach Johnston follows her.*

Coach Johnston: Hey, Ash! You a'ight? Ashlyn: (wipes her tears off her face) No.

Coach Johnston: (stands in front of her) It's R. T.? (shakes his head) Look, Ash, you have to live for the moment. You don't need a man to motivate you or support you. You are a strong, beautiful, talented, independent woman. You don't need him. (he turns and points at the stands across the way) Look what you have accomplished here. Tomorrow, you will be in the finals in all three events and will probably place at least 1st in two. C'mon, shorty. (he grabs her hand and looks at her) You have support here: me, the team, and your family. You don't need to get emotional over him. I know you've been through a lot. Just meditate for a while and focus on you. Let go and let God. Do it for yourself. (he leans over and kisses her on the forehead)

[Vanessa sees the kiss and hits Darnell with her elbow; Darnell shakes his head.]

*The scene fades away.*

## Scene 49

When: The next morning, Saturday Where: The hotel

*Night came and went; Ashlyn tries to call R. T., but all she can get is the answer machine all through the morning. It's time for her to go to the field. Tameka notices Ashlyn is not focused on her events but on R. T.*

*The team leaves the hotel and arrives at the stadium with all their luggage packed on the charter bus. Fifteen minutes later, Ashlyn is on the track ready to run the 200m dash; she's jumping around; Coach Johnston and Tameka are standing in the field while Vanessa, Darnell, Carlton, Iman, Jeff, and Debbie are cheering in the stands for Ashlyn.*

Debbie: C'mon, Ash! You can do it, baby!

Carlton: (focuses the camcorder on Ashlyn) Sho' ya skillz, sis! You got more to go!

Jeff: Let's go, baby girl!

The announcer: On your mark! Get set! (ref shoots the gun) *POW!*

[Ashlyn takes off full speed; no one can catch her. She crosses the finish line breaking the national record for high school and collegiate at 22.05. She looks at the stands and smiles. Everybody is cheering. She looks around the stands and notices she doesn't need R. T. to accomplish her goals; all she needs is God, with the support of her family. She smiles and waves her hand to the crowd, especially to the Yates fans. The 400 relay is next. The relay gets on the track ready to go; Tameka is the last leg; she jumps up and down, shakes her head from side to side. Ashlyn sits down with the team, along with Coach Johnston and the managers who were close to the finish line waiting for the gun to shoot. Coach Johnston looks back at Ashlyn and smiles at her.]

Ashlyn: (smiles and speaks softly) Thank you.

[The gun goes off. Yates is in the lead; the baton finally gets to Tameka. Tameka runs so fast; Ashlyn stands up and runs to the finish line.]

Ashlyn: Go, Tameka! (jumps up and down cheering)

[Tameka crosses the finish line; Ashlyn runs to her and hugs her cousin; the whole team joins in screaming and yelling. Coach Johnston hugs all girls on the relay team.]

Coach Johnston: Well, team, you set a new record! You were blazing! You ran a 42.5!

Tameka: Damn! We did! Ashlyn: You heard him!

Tameka: Ew--wee, I got the juice, too! Baby, ba---ab--bae!

[Tameka dances beside Ashlyn. That night the relay team won 1st place. At 10:40 A.M., Ashlyn runs the 100m dash with no problem. The contenders fall short, and she runs a 10.79 like a pro. Ashlyn crosses the finish line with grace. Coach Johnston picks her up again and the team joins him.

She won 1st place in the 100, 200, and the long jump without the support from

R. T. with God's grace and with the support from her family and team; she accomplishes and reinforces the Ashlyn everyone knows as the independent, intelligent, aggressive, athletic, ambitious, and spiritual woman. She  stands tall at the ceremony with her medals around her neck waving at her family.]

[It is definitely a night to remember. After the ceremony, the team decides to attend Ashlyn's church for the celebration. They left Austin and went  straight to H-Town, eating on the way back. Carlton and Iman take Ashlyn home; they drop her off; R. T.'s car is there; Ashlyn walks in the apartment; she sees R. T. on the couch hugging her picture, and she smiles.]

Ashlyn: (leans over and kisses him) Hey, baby. (she puts her picture down  on the table) Hey, wake up. (she sits down above his head, picking it up to place his head in her lap) Baby, I'm here.

R. T.: (opens his eyes) Hey, baby. (perks his lips up; she leans down to kiss him) I missed you. I'm sorry I didn't make it. I had to meet the GM for the Rockets again. (pauses) They told me they want me to play for the team on  a three-year contract worth 18 million and 1.5 million signing bonus. I was like, damn! It don't get no better! So how, (he sits up and kisses Ashlyn) so how did you do?

Ashlyn: (she leans over and goes into her bag) I placed (she pulls out the gold medals) first, baby!

R. T.: Damn! (he grabs the medals) Holy shit! Baby, in three events! Damn, girl! Did you set any records? I know you did!

Ashlyn: (gives him the scorecard) Here are my times and measurements. (she grabs the tape) Oh, Carlton taped the whole track meet (she gives him the tape) so I can have it for . . . bragging rights!

R. T.: Damn, (looking at the record and Ashlyn) Ash! You beat the guys. I mean, the collegiate men on 100m dash except one of the winners; he ran a 9.99! (pauses) Damn, baby! Man, if we ever have kids, man, they will be world-class athletes!

 Man! My baby! Aw, man, I can't wait to see the tape! (he gets up with tape in his hand to put it in the VCR)

Ashlyn: (stands up and grabs his butt) Watch the tape later. (she holds on to it) I want you to watch me right now. (she takes her clothes off as she walks backward to the bedroom using her finger to tell R. T. to follow her)

R. T.: (looks at the tape and puts it down) All right, baby. (he runs to the room) Let's make a baby! Oh yea!

*The scene fades away.*

**Scene 50**

When: Sunday, the next day
Where: St. Mark United Methodist Church

*Everybody is at church, including the Yates track team and fans. R. T. sits by Debbie and rest of the family. Ashlyn is in the choir. Jeff approaches the pulpit again.*

Jeff: Today is the day for all of us to say we are proud of our children. The Yates track team brought home a total of 19 medals. I know three of those medals (looks back at Ashlyn; she smiles) came from my own flesh and blood, my baby girl!

The church: Amen! Praise the Lord!

Jeff: I feel like shouting some more! Even though there are things she does I disagree with, she showed me she is her own woman! She can do it no matter what comes in her pathway! She is not a child anymore! She's grown to be a woman that can hold her own, no matter what! This year she will be a freshman at Texas Southern University!

Sister 1: All right! Praise the Lord!

Jeff: I'm a proud father! And the track team came to church to celebrate and praise God for giving them the ability to accomplish their goals to be winners on the track at Austin, Texas! So stand up, track team, and come to the front! I want everyone to greet you with love!

(Coach Johnston, Tameka, and the rest of the team, including Ashlyn, come up to the altar; some of them were crying, wearing their medals and ribbons) Congratulations! Congregation, I want you to stand up and come to the future of tomorrow with love and support! They need it, my sisters and brothers in church! Come on!

[The congregation gets in line to greet, hug, and kiss the Yates track team with lots of love. The choir sings ‒We're Going to Make It‖;

they also greet the team.]

*The scene fades away.*
**Scene 51**

When: 4:30 in the afternoon, Sunday Where: At R. T.'s home

*After church, Ashlyn and R. T. go home. R. T. sits down watching the track meet tape; he notices Coach Johnston is very close to Ashlyn. Meanwhile, Ashlyn is in the utility room washing clothes while R. T. is seeing nothing but red as he sits at edge of the couch watching the tape; R. T. rewinds the tape to the part where Coach Johnston kisses Ashlyn on the field; he pauses the tape and gets up with rage.*

R. T.: (yells with anger at Ashlyn) Ash! Ash! Come here, right now!
Ashlyn: (drops her clothes on the floor and peeps around corner) What?
R.T.: (walks to her and pulls her in the living room) What the hell is *that?* (he picks up the remote control and rewinds the part where the coach is kissing Ashlyn over and over again) What is that shit? (he continues to rewind and play and points it out to Ashlyn) Look at that shit! Ash, do you see that shit? (he paces back forth with the remote control in his hand pushing rewind, stop, and play) Do you see that? You see that! What the hell is that shit? Huh? Answer me, woman! I can't hear ya! Speak louder! (holds his hand against his ear toward Ashlyn)
Ashlyn: (a tear falls down her face) Baby, it's not what you think! I promise! (she cries out) I love you! I'd never betray you!
R. T.: (he paces back and forth) I can't believe this shit!!! How could you lie to me about this? Huh? How could you lie to me in my face? Huh? Hell, you probably fuck'em! Huh? Answer me, goddamn it!
Ashlyn: No! I didn't!
R. T.: Really? (pauses and stares at the TV and presses rewind, stop, and play again.) Well, why is it on this tape this damn asshole always helping your ass and not the others? Explain that, Ms. Ashlyn Renee Richardson! It seems like this fo' is all up and under your ass since day one I meet him! You can't tell me this shit's not what I'm seeing! I know you boning this motherfucker! Look at the damn tape! (he rewinds and plays the kissing scene)
Ashlyn: (gets mad) *Say what?* I know you didn't . . . You tired broad-ass nigga, I caught your ass in the bed with your ex! How I know

you don't have feelings for her? (she pauses and grabs her keys) So, how can you act like you're a fucking angel when you are not? Tell me that, son of bitch!

R. T.: Uh-huh . . . Hmm . . . You women . . . are just the same. Always got to throw in what the man has done . . . Hmm . . .

I guess somebody is being spiteful . . . Just like I figured! So, you *did* bone that motherfucker! Tell the truth, Ash! Tell the goddamn truth!

Ashlyn: (she shakes her head and walks out of the house) I don't need this shit! I told you I didn't fuck him! I've only slept with your sorry ass! (she gets in her car) I don't know why I'm with you! I deserve better!

R. T.: (runs to the car) Hold up, Ash! Where are you going? (leans in the car; Ashlyn starts the car) Ash, get out of the car!

Get outta tha damn car, woman! (she pushes his hands back and rolls the window up) A'ight, go head. That proves I'm right! You fuck'em!

Ashlyn: (backs up the car fast; R. T. runs with the car; she rolls her window down) R. T.! I didn't! And you can take it, leave it, or just shove it up your goddamn Blue Chip ass!

[Ashlyn drives off at full speed; R. T. lets go and stands on the corner of the driveway.]

R. T.: (yells) Fine! Leave! I don't need you! I hope you get your goddamn clothes and get the fuck outta my life! (he walks into the house and slams the door.)

[Ashlyn goes to Iman's house where Carlton is; she gets out of the car with the tape in her hand; she runs to door and bangs real hard, like she's the police.]

Ashlyn: Carlton! Bring ya ass out here, *now!*

Carlton: (peeps out of the window and comes out) Damn, Ash! (fastens his pants with no shirt on) What's your problem?

Ashlyn: Carlton! Why did you tape everything that happened at the Texas Relay?

Carlton: Ash, I wanted you to have it so you can keep it for your bragging rights! Why?

Ashlyn: Well, you taped Coach Johnston kissing me and spending time with me throughout the whole tape. I mean, the whole 3 days! Now, R. T. and I are no longer together!

Carlton: Damn, fa' real? Oh, shit, sis. I didn't mean to. I mean I wanted to help ya, not hurt ya.

Ashlyn: (put her hands on her hips) Well, you somewhat hurt me. But maybe it's best for me and R. T.

Iman: (runs out and interrupts) Ash, R. T. called! He said he wants you to come and get your clothes 'cause he can't trust you like he thought he could. (pauses) In my opinion, it's best for you to be separated. I'm sorry, Ash.

He wasn't good enough for you anyway. I think you should be with somebody that will support you.

Far as I know, I heard he's been seeing his ex.

Carlton: Say what? I oughta beat that son of a bitch's ass! My sis don't deserve that shit at all!

Man, he got a nerve to call her with that shit! (he walks in the house to get his shirt and keys) Let's go get your shit! You can stay here with us! You don't need fu! (he walks to the car, opens the door, and gets in)

Ashlyn: Naw, Carlton! That's all right! I'll get it myself! (she runs to her car and jumps in, then drives off)

Carlton: (sits in the car and starts it) Iman, baby, let's go!

Iman: OK! (goes into the house to get her keys and purse; comes out of the house; shuts and locks the door; then gets in the car)

[Carlton drives off at a high speed; he gets to the apartment and sees R. T. throwing Ashlyn's clothes outside; Ashlyn is outside crying and picking her clothes off the ground. Carlton parks the car and jumps out like a madman; Iman tries to grab him.]

Carlton: (runs up to R. T. and pushes him down) Motherfucker! I'm gonna kick your ass! How could you (he pushes him down again as R. T. tries to get up) do my sis like this? (he punches and kicks him, then R. T. grabs Carlton's legs and flips him over on his back, then body slams him; Iman is helping Ashlyn pick up her things. Then Ashlyn jumps in the fight. Carlton and R. T. are still fighting)

[Iman grabs Ashlyn; she tries to pull her away before she gets hurt; Ashlyn pushes away from Iman.]

Iman: Ashlyn! Girl, you gonna get hurt! Let them fight!

Ashlyn: I can't! Let me go! (she yanks away again and runs to them; R. T. has Carlton in a headlock; Carlton has R. T. around his leg while he's bent over gasping for air)

R. T: Nigga, you don't know me! (squeezes Carlton's neck tighter)

Ashlyn: (jumps on R. T.'s back and start choking him) Let him go!

Carlton: Ash! (coughs) Ash! (coughs) Get off of him! I got him! Let him go!

R. T.: (gasping for air as Ashlyn squeezes his neck while on his back) Ash! You choking me! I can't breathe!

[Ashlyn jumps off of his back, then Carlton tackles him; he punches R. T. in his face twice with a Muhammad Ali combination; R. T. catches his breath, then jabs Carlton in the jaw, knocking him down. All of a sudden, the police arrive and people gather around the fight; the police jump in to break up Carlton and R. T. Ashlyn runs to the police officer (male, black 6'2).]

Ashlyn: Officer, my brother is innocent. He was just trying to defend me, that's all.

My ex-boyfriend and I were having an altercation; he was throwing all of my stuff at me. (she points out her items on the ground) As you can see, some  of it is still on the ground.

Police Officer 1: OK, I can definitely see that, ma'am. Do you know who hit whom first?

Ashlyn: No. All I know is that both of them were rolling in the grass fighting. [While one police officer is talking to Ashlyn, Iman comforts Carlton while the other police officer is talking to Carlton and R. T. regarding their conduct in public.]

Officer 1: (writes down the info that is given by Ashlyn) OK, let's go over there and talk to your brother and ex. (they all walk over to where the other officer, R. T., and Carlton are)

R. T.: All I know is C. pushed me down first, then I retaliated! Especially when this is my property!

Carlton: I wouldn't have pushed you if you hadn't thrown my sister's belongings at her while she was outside! Now what? Try again! (shakes his head and turns to the officers) Officers, all I know is my sister didn't deserve (points at the items on the ground) this!

Iman: (holds on to Carlton's arm) Baby, calm down. Carlton: Can't calm down! He could've hit her, Iman! Iman: I know, baby. Baby, just calm down.

Ashlyn: (hugs her brother) It's OK. I'm fine. I just have to move and stay with you and Iman.

Carlton: That's cool. (he rolls his eyes at R. T. and walks to his car and gets in it; Iman follows)

Police Officer 2: I guess everything's OK now. Unless, (looks at R. T.) Mr. Raymond Tillman, you want to press charges?

R. T.: No! I just want them gone! (he walks off, goes into the house, and slams door)

[Ashlyn picks up the rest of her belongings, then puts them in the car. When Ashlyn gets in her car, tears roll from eyes as she signals Carlton to go ahead; they pull off from the driveway; the cops leave right behind them.]

*The scene fades away.*

## Scene 52

When: Two months later Where: U of H Pavilion

*Ashlyn is graduating from Jack Yates High School. She just doesn't realize that the hurdles she jumped over to get there are just the beginning of life itself. The whole family is there watching baby girl graduate from high school. She is officially a grown woman.*

Principal Phillips: It is a great honor to stand before the Class of 1997 to acknowledge one of the most gifted, talented, and ambitious scholars who has made a huge transition and took no time to adapt, to achieve, and to go beyond her goals. That young woman will receive a NCAA full scholarship to any university she chooses. She has a 4.5 GPA on a 5.0 scale, is a member of the National Honor Society, is an active member of the Journalism Club, is the assistant editor for the yearbook and newspaper for the short period of time that she's been here, received 18 gold medals, 1 silver in track and field, is All-American in basketball, and, of course,

she broke numerous records in the school, city, state, and at national level in both sports. She also has a hidden talent, which is singing at her father's church. Let's hear it for Miss Ashlyn Richardson!

[Ashlyn gets up and walks to the stage to accept her scholarship; cameras are flashing as she poses with Dr. Phillips holding her scholarship.]

Vanessa: Go, Ashlyn! (takes pictures of Ashlyn) Carlton: A'ight, Ash! (tapes the graduation)

Jeff: That's my baby girl!

Debbie: A'ight! Show them how beautiful you are!

[Ashlyn sits down and exhales with her eyes and mouth closed as flashbacks of what she's been through in her senior year come to mind; she opens her eyes and smiles; she finally graduates into womanhood.]

*The scene fades away.*

**End of Part I**

# Part II
## (Womanhood)

*[Ashlyn Richardson is now a grow woman with more responsibilities aligned in her path that were either planned and unplanned. She also endure more hatred and betrayal within her path as she gets closer to achieving her ultimate goal as a executive producer at a television station.]*

# ACT 10

**Scene 53**

When: It's 9:30 in the morning
Where: Carlton and Iman's house

*Summer begins; Ashlyn is no longer with R. T. She's staying with Iman and Carlton just for the summer and is making preparations to attend Texas Southern University for the fall of '97 and working at KBXX 97.9 as a part- time account specialist assistant. Carlton and Iman have already gone to work. Ashlyn rolls over and feels pain in her stomach. She gets up and runs to the bathroom; she leans over the toilet and vomits. She stays in the bathroom for at least 30 minutes. Then the doorbell rings (ring . . . ring . . .). Ashlyn gets up and wipes her face. She leaves the bathroom to answer the door. First, she looks into the peephole in the door and sees her best friend, Darnesia.*

Ashlyn: (opens the door) Oh my God! (she hugs Darnesia) Darnesia: Hey, girl! What's up?
Ashlyn: What's the damn deal?
Darnesia: (she walks into the house looking around) Girl, starting summer school at U of H.
Ashlyn: Fa' real? (closes the door, then leads Darnesia to the living room) Come on in and have a sit down.
Darnesia: (sits down when they reach the living room) Where's Carlton? Ashlyn: Oh, he's (sits down in the recliner across from Darnesia) at work. (grabs and rubs her stomach)
Darnesia: Girl, why are you rubbing your stomach? Ashlyn: (frowns up) Oh, I got to . . . (jumps up and runs) Darnesia: Damn, Ash. Who got you knocked up?
[Ashlyn is in the bathroom hanging over the toilet, throwing up. Darnesia walks in.]
Ashlyn: Darnesia! (gags and throws up)
Darnesia: (frowns and fans Ashlyn with a towel) My, my, girlfriend, your ass is pregnant because if it was the flu you'd have a (touches Ashlyn's forehead) fever. Which you don't.


Ashlyn: (stands up and goes to the sink to wash her face and hands) I can't believe this. I'm pregnant again? (grabs her stomach; runs the water and soap over her washcloth)
Darnesia: Whose the daddy?

Ashlyn: R. T. (wipes her face) He's the only one after Omar.

Darnesia: Really? Are you still with him?

Ashlyn: (grabs her toothbrush and toothpaste; begins to brush her teeth) Nope. We broke up 3 months ago. (spits out the toothpaste) I mean 2 and a half months ago. (wipes her face again and grabs the mouthwash to rinse her mouth, then she spits it out)

Darnesia: So how are you going to convince him it's his?

Ashlyn: I don't know. (she get a dry towel to wipe her face) I guess I can call him to let him know, but I got to go to the doctor first.

[Darnesia and Ashlyn walk out of the bathroom into the living room. Ashlyn lies on the couch while Darnesia sits in the recliner.]

Darnesia: So, do you want to go now to get it over with? 'Cause, girl, you need to.

Ashlyn: I can't. I gotta work late tonight at the radio station.

Darnesia: What radio station? Girl, you got a job?

Ashlyn: I've been working there since I graduated. It's been about 3–4 weeks. I assist the producer and the account executive with writing the format and the commercial ads. They pay me $8/hour, and I work 20 hours a week.

Darnesia: That's a good start. So, what time do you go in? Ashlyn: At 8 P.M.

Darnesia: Ah, girl, you got time.

Ashlyn: I guess so. It's only (looks at the clock above the TV; it shows 11:30 A.M., then reaches for the phone) 11:30. Dee, hand me the phone, please. (Darnesia gives her the phone) I hope this doctor (dialing the number) is there. (grabs her stomach as she waits for someone to pick up)

[Someone answers the phone.]

Ashlyn: (responds) Hi. I want to make an appointment today with Dr. Welch ASAP. (pauses) OK, it's for a pregnancy test. (pauses to listen to the person on the other end of the phone) At 3 P.M.? That's fine. I'll be there. Bye-bye. (she hangs up the phone)

Darnesia: I guess you can go and get ready while I chill.

Ashlyn: A'ight, girl. (she gets up and goes to her room)

Darnesia: (changes channels with the remote) OK, I need to find something good to watch.

[Forty-five minutes pass; Iman and Carlton walk in; Carlton stops dead in his tracks when he sees Darnesia; Iman is mad to see his ex in her house.] Carlton: Say, what are you doing here?

Darnesia: To see Ash. You know she's my best friend since we were in diapers.

Iman: (walks in front of Darnesia and stands there) Is *that* the real reason? Or are you here to see Carlton?

Darnesia: Yes. And no, I'm seeing someone else. He's a good friend of Ashlyn's. He goes to U of H and plays football.

[Ashlyn walks in; Carlton mean mugs Ashlyn.]

Ashlyn: Oh, Iman, this is my best friend, Darnesia. We grew up together in I- wood. And yes, she is Carlton's ex, but that's history. Trust me.

Carlton: Yep.

Darnesia: Anyways, Ashlyn, do you know a guy name Corey from Kemptner? If so, that's my new man.

Ashlyn: Say what? Big C is yours? How did you two meet again?

Darnesia: We met at the block party. And boy, he's a good man.

Carlton: I bet.

Iman: Uh-huh, you betta watch it, Carlton. (she walks off)

Carlton: Ash, I can't get you for this one. (pauses) You look different, Ash. Are you pregnant?

Ashlyn: I don't know. That's why I'm getting ready to go to the doctor. (she grabs her keys and purse, then walks toward the door) Bye, Iman!

Iman: (comes back into the living room) Bye, Ash!

Carlton: Damn, Ash! I hope you are not, but if, so you got us.

[Ashlyn smiles and hugs Carlton; she opens the door and Darnesia walks out the door, then Ashlyn follows her.]

*The scene fades away.*

**Scene 54**

When: 1:47 P.M.
Where: The doctor's office

*Ashlyn drives all the way to Sugarland to see Dr. Welch. It takes 45 minutes to get there. Ashlyn and Darnesia enter the doctor's office at 1:47 P.M.; Ashlyn walks up to the receptionist's desk to get the form to fill out while Darnesia takes a seat observing the area that is filled with pregnant women. Ashlyn sits down beside Darnesia.*

Darnesia: Damn, this place gives me the creeps. Looks like a bunch fat women 'bout to burst, creating a nuclear wipeout.

Ashlyn: Darnesia, that's not nice. (fills out the form)

Darnesia: They do. Shoot, move over, cows, we got milk here. (Ashlyn laughs) And they don't take pride in themselves; I mean they look like— Ashlyn: That's enough, Dee. (speaks seriously and under eyed) That's enough, I'm not joking. (she gets up to turn her form in, then sits back down) Darnesia: I'm sorry, Ash. I just hope you don't let yourself go like them.

Ashlyn: Don't worry. You still going to hang with me even if I do (laughs) look like a baboon in a drag queen parade, all greasy and overcooked. Hell, I might have a bunion that smells like onions that'll make your ass cry, (Darnesia laughs) not by sight but by smell. (Ashlyn and Darnesia laugh out loud) Damn, I still got it.

Darnesia: Girl, you stupid. (shoves Ashlyn)

[Two minutes later, Dr. Welch comes out of her office.]

Dr. Welch: (stands by the entrance of the sitting area) Ashlyn Richardson! (she looks around the room holding her clipboard) Ashlyn Richardson! [Ashlyn and Darnesia get up and walk to Dr. Welch.]

Dr. Welch: Hi, Ashlyn. (holds the door open for Ashlyn and Darnesia to walk in; they go into Dr. Welch's office)

Ashlyn: (sits down) Dr. Welch, I need to do a pregnancy test right now and get the results ASAP.

Dr. Welch: (sits down) OK, we'll do a urine test. Then I'll get the results within 1 hour and 30 minutes. Is that too long? 'Cause you are really early for your appointment. It's just 1:58 P.M.

[Darnesia looks at Ashlyn.]

Ashlyn: I can do that. (pauses) So, where's the cup?

Dr. Welch: (reaches into her drawer behind her to get it) Here you go. (she hands the cup to Ashlyn) You (pauses) know where the bathroom is, right?

Ashlyn: (she gets up) Yeah. (she walks out of the room to take the test) [Several minutes later, Ashlyn comes back and hands Dr. Welch the cup in a ziplock bag.]

Dr. Welch: OK, Miss Richardson, (takes the cup) let me run the test so (she gets up and walks out toward the doorway) you can get your results ASAP. (she exits from the office)

[Darnesia and Ashlyn wait in the Dr. Welch's office.] Darnesia: Well, Ash, the truth will be told in another hour.

Ashlyn: Yep. I hope R. T. doesn't deny the baby if I am pregnant. (takes a deep breath) If he does, I would raise the child on my own.

Darnesia: Girl, don't worry. (hugs Ashlyn) I got ya, then you got ya fam, you know?

Ashlyn: Yeah. I know. It's just that . . . I wish I would'a had Omar's instead, you know? 'Cause he was the love of my life. He was always there. (a tear drops from her eyes) I mean, (she wipes her face) he loved me (Darnesia rubs her back) for who I am, I was, and what I'll become. He was very supportive and loving. I mean, a damn good lover. But he's not here anymore. (she cries out loud)

Darnesia: (hugs Ashlyn) It's okay. He's still here in spirit, and he will always be with you. You just have (looks at Ashlyn in the eye) to live, Ash, like Omar would have wanted you to. A woman that carries herself with grace, confidence, and independence; who has enough aggression, intelligence, and ambition to overcome and go beyond whatever obstacles have been placed before her. You can do this, Ashlyn. I know you can. Just keep God first and work, along with faith in him, to live your destiny.

Ashlyn: (wipes her tears away and smiles) Damn, girl, you've been talking to Mrs. Jones, haven't ya?

Darnesia: Uh, yeah, I have. That's why I'm here. (she smiles)

Ashlyn: Well, thanx fir being here with me. You like a twin sister I wish I had. (she laughs)

Darnesia: Oh, girl. You do. Ashlyn: Who?

Darnesia: Vanessa.


Ashlyn: (shakes her head no) Don't go there. (pauses) I love her, but I can't stand her, and you know that. (Darnesia laughs)

[Ashlyn laughs along with Darnesia. Twenty-five minutes later, Dr. Welch walks into the office with the results and shuts the door.]


Dr. Welch: (sits down at her desk) Well, Miss Ashlyn Richardson, you are a mother-to-be.

Darnesia: (grabs Ashlyn's arm and looks at her) You can do this, Ash. You got me and your family.

Ashlyn: I know I can. (turns to Dr. Welch) Dr. Welch, can I do an ultrasound? Dr. Welch: (gets up) Sure. (walks to the door) Follow me. [Ashlyn and Darnesia follow Dr. Welch to the ultrasound room; they go in; Dr. Welch turns on the machine.] Ashlyn, I need you to sit on the table without your shirt and pull down your pants away from the bikini line. (she grabs a hospital gown and gives it to Ashlyn to put on; Ashlyn takes her shirt off and puts on the gown, then sits down)

Ashlyn: (pulls down her pants) OK, I'm ready.

Dr. Welch: (puts on her gloves) This is going to be (puts gel in her hands) cold. (rubs it on Ashlyn's stomach) Now, since I rubbed it in, (pulls out the scope) I'm going to use this to see the baby and how far along you are.

Darnesia: (looks at the monitor) I see the baby. It looks like a tadpole.

Ashlyn: Ah, that's my li'l one. (she smiles) I'm going to love ya no matter what 'cause you are mine.

[Darnesia smiles along with Dr. Welch.]

*The scene fades away.*

### Scene 55

When: The next day
Where: In Carlton and Iman's house

*Ashlyn calls R. T. to tell him she's expecting.*

Ashlyn: (holds the phone to her ear) C'mon, R. T., answer the phone. (the phone rings) C'mon, c'mon.

[R. T. still doesn't pick up so Ashlyn leaves the house to go tell him in person. Ten minutes later, she drives up in the driveway. She notices his ex's car is parked in the driveway; she shakes her head and gets out of the car; she walks to the door, and Tonya comes out of the house smiling at Ashlyn as she walks to her car.]

Ashlyn: (puts her hands up) What's up?

Tonya: (gets in her car and rolls down her window) Nothin'! Just lookin' at a li'l girl that is not ready to play in a woman's game! (she laughs and drives off)

R. T.: (comes to door with his shirt off) What the hell you want? Didn't I tell you it's over between me and you?

Ashlyn: Look, jackass, I came over here to tell you, since you don't answer your phone, that I'm . . . that we are having a child, and I know the child is yours!

R. T.: You pregnant? (laughs) You gots to be kidding me! All the times we had sex you took birth control pills, and sometimes I used a condom. So, I know the baby is not mine.

Ashlyn: How could you say that? We lived together!

R. T.: Yeah, and you slept with your track coach, even though you deny it! Ashlyn: For your information, I just kissed him and that was it! It was the day I caught your sorry ass having sex with Tonya and her ol' trifling ass!

R. T.: Really? And you had enough nerve to fuck my brains out that night! After you were being spiteful! (he steps back into the house, and Ashlyn follows him in) I don't believe this, Ash!

Ashlyn: I told you I didn't sleep with him! This child is yours!

R. T.: How I know that? You might be trying to trap me since you know I'm a millionaire now, huh? Can you answer that?

Ashlyn: I don't believe you! I don't want your damn money! Hell, I'll be making just as much as you in one year after I graduate! Watch me, 'cause I'm all about mine, baby! I don't need a man to take care of me! I'm going to use what God has given me to succeed and to make sure this baby is taken care of with or without your sorry ass!

(she throws the copies of the sonograms at his feet, then runs out of the house to her car and drives off)

[Ashlyn goes back to the house around 4 P.M. Vanessa's SUV is parked behind Iman's car. Ashlyn pulls up in the driveway and gets out of the car; she walks into the house using her keys. Vanessa is sitting down talking to Iman about Ashlyn.]

Vanessa: (speaks with sarcasm) Well, hello, Ash, where did you go?

Ashlyn: (speaks with an attitude) None of your business!

Iman: Oh, boy. (sighs and gets up) You two need to chill, OK?

Ashlyn: Stay out of it, Iman!

Vanessa: Look, Ms. Thang! You don't listen! Now your ass is pregnant with a full scholarship in both basketball and track! Now, how ya going to keep that intact? (pauses) You remember the last time, don't ya?

Ashlyn: You know what? I don't need you here giving me a fucking lecture! I know I made a bad decision, so I don't need you to cram it down my goddamn throat! What I need you to do is to leave me and my baby alone! (she jumps in Vanessa's face) You got that, bitch, 'cause you just too damn negative for me? All you want to do is tear people down so you can be on top!

Vanessa: Excuse me, you li'l ho. (Carlton walks in) I've been trying to keep your ass from doing the things I did when I was your age! But somehow, your trifling ass wouldn't listen! Now your ass is pregnant again, and the nigga probably denies the baby! Especially

R. T.'s trifling hoish ass!

Ashlyn: You didn't have to go there, Nessa! Now, I . . . (she jumps closer to Vanessa's face)

Carlton: (interrupts the altercation) Okay, my sistas, that's enough! (sighs and looks at Vanessa) You really truly—

Vanessa: (interrupts) Well, it is the damn truth! That's all—

Carlton: (yells at Vanessa) Vanessa, shut up! Ashlyn needs us right now! She don't need to hear you bitchin' about the decision she made! It's the past! She has to live for right now!

Ashlyn: Thank you, Carlton! At least someday knows—

Carlton: And Ashlyn, this is not your house. You have to respect Iman by walking away from Vanessa's shit. Also . . .

Vanessa: Say what? I *know*—

Carlton: Damn, Vanessa! Shut up! (looks at Ashlyn) Ashlyn, Vanessa's just being overbearing and protective. She doesn't want you to detour from your goals and to make mistakes like she did. Evidently, you learn the hard way. And me and Iman will always be there for you, no matter what 'cause we know how strong you are. Just chill for minute, OK? (walks up to Ashlyn and put his arm around her) You're not alone.

Ashlyn: (smiles) Thanx, Carlton. (she hugs him)


Iman: (goes to Ashlyn and hugs her) Girl, you are tough to handle, but you stand sturdy and tall against anything that comes your way. I admire that, (she sighs) and I can't wait to see the li'l one. (she laughs)

Vanessa: (rolls her eyes) That's her problem. You constantly pat her on the back! And kiss her ass! She's going to keep running into trouble! She needs someone to let her know the truth and drill it in her head that it's wrong when it's wrong! Damn, you're sickening! Stop babying her! She's never going to learn from her mistakes! You see she got pregnant again! (pauses) You know what? I'm going to let you deal with it 'cause when Mom and Dad find out, they are going to trip out on (she points at Ashlyn) you! And you know it, Ash!

[Vanessa grabs her purse and walks out of the house.]

Iman: I didn't know Vanessa is such a bitch! I mean, she's telling the truth, but Ashlyn understands she has to learn from her mistakes and live with the consequences that follow.

Ashlyn: Now you see why we don't get along? I think she's jealous of me 'cause Dad and Mom rode her ass to the T. but eased up on me.

Carlton: So, did you tell R. T. about the baby?

Ashlyn: Yes, I did. He denies it, but I told him I don't need him anyway. I'll raise this child on my own.

Iman: (looks at the clock) Ash, it's 5 o'clock.

Carlton: R. T., R. T., he's just bad news. (shakes his head) You did the right thing, sis. That's all I got to say.

Ashlyn: Yep, it's 5. I guess I need to get ready so I can get to work early. Carlton: Say, Ash, how are you going to tell Mom and Dad?

Ashlyn: I don't know. I'll probably tell them tomorrow.

Iman: What about your basketball scholarship?

Ashlyn: I'll just run track and continue to work during this semester. Hopefully, the school won't trip.

Carlton: They won't. Iman: Yeah.

Ashlyn: (sighs) OK. (looks at the clock and walks out of the living room) So much drama but I'll make it! (walks out the door)

Carlton: Yep. (sits down on the couch, and Iman sits in his lap watching TV)

*The scene fades away.*

## Scene 56

When: The next day at 3 P.M.
Where: The church where Ashlyn's father works

*Ashlyn visits her mom and dad at the church. Vanessa and Darnell are already there. Ashlyn pulls up in the church driveway ready for the lecture, even though she doesn't want to hear it. She gets out of the car and walks into the church. Darnell greets her.*

Darnell: Hey, li'l sis, how's it going? (he hugs her)

Ashlyn: Fine. (she walks to her dad's office where Jeff, Debbie, and Vanessa are discussing her situation) Well, (she walks in) well, somebody has already spread the icing on the cake before it cools off.

Debbie: (stands up) Ashlyn, don't come here with an attitude toward Vanessa because she told us about ya. (pauses and walks to Ashlyn) I can't believe you allowed him to do this to you. That's why I did not approve you staying with him.

Ashlyn: (looks down) I know it, Mom. I don't need (she looks at Debbie) you to chastise me on this matter. It was unplanned. It just happened, whether you like it or not. So be it.

Jeff: (stands up, then sits on his desk with his arms folded in disappointment) Ash, baby girl, I am very, very upset. I thought you could show me that you would not allow yourself to be caught up in this mess again. Last time it was a tragedy. This time, your accomplishments from high school have all been in vain and meaningless because you chose to do what you wanted to do.

So, those scholarships will be invalid because you will not be able to play the sport until next year.

Ashlyn: Dad, I know. I already talked to the TSU athletic department today— Jeff: (interrupts) Really? What did they say?

Ashlyn: They told me I could use the scholarship for track only and enroll in the Honors program to get the scholarship so my schooling will be paid for in full. Since the scholarship was for both basketball and track as a scholar, I can substitute the Fredrick Douglass Honors Scholarship to get the same amount. All I have to do is write a personal statement and attach my transcript with the TASP and SAT scores. So, I thank (sighs) God for that.

Debbie: And what about R. T.? Does he know? Vanessa: Um, I asked the same thang.

Ashlyn: (rolls her eyes at Vanessa) Anyways, (pauses and takes a deep breath) he does know, but he denies the child is his so I gave him a piece of my mind. I told him I don't need him, I don't need his help, and I can do it all by myself. Jeff: (stands up) Oh, Ash, baby girl, why? Why did you say that? That child needs to know the father.

Debbie: Well, Jeff, if he denies the child, the only way to determine paternity is by a DNA test which he probably would decline. Shoot, I don't blame you, Ashlyn. I'd probably do the same thing.

Ashlyn: Thank you, Mom. I appreciate your understanding on why I will raise my child on my own.

Vanessa: It's not going to be easy. Trust me, I've witnessed it. My classmates back in Inglewood did the same thing as you're going to do now. I just hope that no-good trifling a—man will man up to his responsibility.

Jeff: Yep. I sure hope so, or else he will regret it. (he sighs then walks up to Ashlyn with open arms) Baby girl, next time, listen to us 'cause we know more than what you think. Hopefully, this time you'll be more cautious and not act on spitefulness 'cause it will haunt you even if it doesn't hinder you. Just remember that. Also, we are here if you need us or (he hugs her) don't. We will be here, no matter what.

Debbie: (hugs her) Yeah, my baby, we will be here for you and our first grandchild. (she smiles) Just keep your head up like 2Pac said. (Ashlyn and Vanessa laughs)

Jeff: (looks at Ashlyn) My baby girl having a baby.

Vanessa: Yep, but she's not the only one. (she smiles) Me and Darnell are expecting. Hopefully, this time, my body will let nature take its course.

Ashlyn: Say what? You're pregnant? How many . . .?

Vanessa: Three months. (she rubs her li'l pouch) Yep, Darnell is a daddy, and I'm a mommy, too. (she grabs Ashlyn's hand)

Sis, I might have been a, (looks at Debbie and Jeff) excuse my language, a bitch, but I'm just trying to protect you, that's all. I look at you, and I see me all over again. I want you to do better than me, even though I got married and I have a career. In my life, it wasn't always peaches and cream, you know. (she sighs) Ash, I love you with all my heart. If you need anything, let me know.

Ashlyn: OK. (she hugs Vanessa) [Darnell walks in.]

Darnell: Well, I see everything is fine.

Vanessa: Yep. (she turns to Darnell and walks to him) I told them.

Darnell: OK. That's good. (he smiles) I guess we can—

Jeff: Let's celebrate! My girls are having babies! Debbie: Did you tell Carlton and Iman, Vanessa?

Vanessa: Yeah. I did yesterday. (Vanessa continues to talk to Debbie and Jeff while Darnell talks to Ashlyn)

Darnell: (turns to Ashlyn) So, how long are you? Ashlyn: A month and a half. Almost 2.

Darnell: Yep. It's R. T.'s, huh? (Ashlyn nods yes) I hope he stops denying and just be the man that he proclaims he is.

Ashlyn: I'm not worried. I got this, you know?

Darnell: You are one strong but stubborn cookie. (he chuckles) Jeff: (interrupts) Ashlyn, are you coming to the house tonight? Ashlyn: I have to work.

Jeff: Oh, that's right. I guess we can (looks at everybody) go out to eat to celebrate right now. Let's call (he pick up the phone to call Carlton and Iman) Carlton and Iman. (he talks to Carlton on the phone) Hey, son . . .

Debbie: (walks to Darnell, Vanessa, and Ashlyn while Jeff talks to Carlton over the phone) I guess we can go to Golden Corral or Pappadeaux's.

Ashlyn: Pappadeaux's would be better. (looks at Vanessa and Darnell) Do you think the same?

Darnell and Vanessa: Yeah.

Jeff: (hangs up the phone) They're on their way. (cleans off his desk) So where are we going?

Debbie: Pappadeaux's off of 610. (turns to Ashlyn, Vanessa, and

Darnell) Right, y'all?

Ashlyn: Yes.

Debbie: (goes to the phone) Let me call them back so they can meet us there. (she picks up the phone and calls Carlton and Iman; she talks to Iman) Hey, Iman, meet us at Pappadeaux's on 610 by the Astrodome, not the downtown one, OK? (she nods) Bye-bye. (she hangs up then turns to everyone) They're going to meet us there, so let's go.

[Ashlyn leads the way out of the office while Vanessa, Darnell, Jeff, and Debbie follow her.]

*The scene fades away.*

Part B

When: Forty minutes later Where: Pappadeaux Restaurant

[Music plays in the background; the Richardson family is laughing, talking, and eating at Pappadeaux's.]

*The scene fades away.*

# ACT 11

## Scene 57

When: Five months later
Where: Classroom at TSU in Houston, Texas

*Winter is approaching in Houston and Ashlyn is now seven months pregnant living on her own; she is still working at the radio station and attending Texas Southern University; she is sitting in her English 244 African American literature class taking an exam under Professor Kyle.*

Prof. Kyle: Class, you have 10 minutes to finish.
Ashlyn: (looks at her test and talks to herself) I hope I pass this exam. The answers are correct, I think. I guess I can go ahead and turn it in. (she gets up and turns in the test to Prof. Kyle) Here you go.
Prof. Kyle: Ash, I need to speak to you after class, so don't leave.
Ashlyn: OK. (she goes back to her desk and sits down)
Prof. Kyle: Five minutes, everyone. Remember, if you pass the exam with 80 or above, you will not have to take the final exam next week.
Ashlyn: Good. I get to stay at home. (she talks to Tameka's sister, Trina) Trina: You know you pass, Ash. 'Cause, cuz, you got it like that.
Ashlyn: Anyways. I struggle, too. Trina: Uh-huh.
Ashlyn: Oh, (rubs her stomach) the baby kicked pretty hard. Did you see his elbow sticking out?
Trina: Nope. But I tell you what, you're gonna have that baby next month not January.
Prof. Kyle: Time is up. You are dismissed except you, Ashlyn.
[Ashlyn nods and keeps talking to Trina.]
Ashlyn: I sure hope so. (rubs her stomach then pauses and takes a deep breath) How do you do it with five kids, Tre? Tell me that.
Trina: (she gets up and puts her books in her bag) Motivation and God are the two primary keys. I know I have responsibilities. (everybody leaves the class room except Ashlyn and Trina, along with Prof. Kyle) So, I have to care what I got 'cause nobody else will. They didn't lie down and have my kids for me. So when I look into their eyes, it motivates me to be a provider to establish a foundation that is stable and secure for them. And that's what I have to do as a parent; do whatever it takes to help my child, not hinder or cause harm, but to make sure all of his or her needs are taken care of, even if I'm lacking

what I want and need. You have to sacrifice and put them first.

In my situation, the father of my children is in their lives, even though we are not together. It helps. And hopefully, R. T. will come around, and if he doesn't, someone will consider your child to be his. It always happens. Watch and see. Once the new man comes in your life, he will come around. Trust me. (she laughs) I'm serious.

Ashlyn: (laughs) Girl, you crazy. Right now, my concern is my baby not another man. I'm just gonna be me. If someone comes around, I'm going to be hard to get, you know?

Trina: (sighs) Well, you do you. Don't let nobody take your dreams away. And your child is going to motivate you to do so. Just know that. (she starts walking off) Ash, I'ma let you talk to Professor now. I got to go handle some business. You know what I'm saying? I'll talk to you later. Come by (she leaves the class) if you can.

Ashlyn: (shouts) I will!

Prof. Kyle: Well, well, Mrs. Richardson. I wanted to talk to you about your work. I'm extremely impressed.

Ashlyn: Thank you.

Prof. Kyle: I want you to apply at . . . um . . . (she clears her throat) KPRCT Channel 2 television station as an intern in the production department where you can develop hands-on skills which you can use as an executive producer one day. They do have an opening for next semester, if you're interested.

Ashlyn: OK. That sounds promising. Do they pay?

Prof. Kyle: They will pay $12 an hour, which is better than what you're making at the radio station.

Ashlyn: Hmm. I guess I can apply now. Do you have the application?

Prof. Kyle: (goes to her desk and gets the application, then hands it to Ashlyn) There you go. Fill it out and turn it in ASAP and use me as a reference since I know the human resources and production department very well. I used to work there full time, but now, I'm part time in the production department because I want to educate others like you to work in that field. And I know you are very intelligent and ambitious to accept the challenge to better yourself.

Ashlyn: You got that right. I'll fill it out right now. (she starts filling out the application) How long will it take for them to contact me?

Prof. Kyle: If you turn it in today, which is Thursday and it's 1 P.M., they'll probably call you tomorrow and interview you on Monday.

Ashlyn: (filling out the application) OK. That's cool. I need this breakthrough.

Prof. Kyle: Another thing, Ashlyn. I just realized you went to school in Inglewood, where my cousin was your teacher. Her name is Ms. Jones. I remember when I talked to her she mentioned ya. She was letting me know you were very good in producing, editing, and writing at the school-based network. You even received honors doing that. Why didn't you let me know? I would have given this application to you a long time ago.

Ashlyn: Well, I didn't know you knew Ms. Jones, who happens to be my former mentor. (she smiles) And plus, I'm not the type that brags. I just do.

Prof. Kyle: She said you were going to say that. Ashlyn: (laughs) So when is she coming to visit ya? Prof. Kyle: New Year's.

Ashlyn: Well, give her (she writes her phone number and address down) my number and address. (she hands the piece of paper to Prof. Kyle) Tell her to call me.

Prof. Kyle: OK. I'll give it to her.

Ashlyn: (looks at her watch) Oh, it's time for me to go to work. I'll study for the exams and definitely turn in the application.

Prof. Kyle: I'll turn in the application for you. It's no big deal.

Ashlyn: OK. I appreciate that. (she hands the application to Prof. Kyle) I'll talk (she gets up and walks to the door) to you later and don't forget to tell Ms. Jones to call me.

Prof. Kyle: OK.

[Ashlyn exits the classroom.]

*The scene fades away.*


## Scene 58

When: Friday morning
Where: In Ashlyn's home

*Ashlyn is getting ready for school, and the phone rings while she is in the bathroom doing her hair.*

Ashlyn: (picks up the phone and answers it) Hello.
[On the other end of the phone line is Donna Vicks at KPRCT-Channel 2; she's sitting in her office looking at Ashlyn's application and recommendation letter from Prof. Kyle.]

Donna Vicks: Good morning, Ashlyn. This is Donna Vicks from KPRCT- Channel 2 television broadcasting network. I want to see you today at 12 P.M., if that's OK.

Ashlyn: Sure. I'll make it there by 11:30, ready to talk to you, if that's all right with you.

Donna Vicks: OK, Miss Ashlyn. (she pauses and puts a paper clip on Ashlyn's application and letter) I just want you to know, I already talked to Prof. Kyle to see if it is okay for you to miss her journalism class. And she's fine with it since she referred you to me.

Ashlyn: Oh, okay. Well, I'll be there sharp and on time. Donna Vicks: All right I'll see you later. Bye-bye. [Donna and Ashlyn hang up the phone.]

Ashlyn: (pumps her fist) Yes! (continues to curl her hair, making sure it's decent for the interview) I guess I got to change outfits since I'm not going to my 10 o'clock class.

[The phone rings again.] Damn, who is this? (she leaves her hair alone and picks up the phone) Hello.

[The person on the other line is Mrs. Jones; she's at Inglewood High sitting in the Teacher's Lounge using her cell phone.]

Mrs. Jones: Hey, stranger. How are you? Ashlyn: Mrs. Jones?

Mrs. Jones: How are ya, Ms. Thang?

Ashlyn: Fine. Experiencing some drama, but I'm doing better. Just carrying a load of my own, too. (she smiles and rubs her stomach in the mirror)

Mrs. Jones: Yeah, I heard what's been happening to ya. That's why I called right away to let you know I'm here for ya, li'l sista. Ashlyn: Thanx.

Mrs. Jones: So, when is the baby due?

Ashlyn: January the 10th. But I hope I have him or her this month.

Mrs. Jones: Have ya sista had her baby?

Ashlyn: Dang, how you know she's . . . she was . . .?

Mrs. Jones: Darnesia told me. So, when did she have the baby?

Ashlyn: Last month on Nov. 1st at 2 A.M. in the morning. Damn, she was in pain . . . much pain. I was there the whole time. You know she was due in October on the 20th, but the baby came when she wanted to come.

Mrs. Jones: Yeah, that's how it is. Trust me, I know, I have two li'l ones. Ashlyn: I heard. What're their name?

Mrs. Jones: Kenwin Jaleel and Keira Jonel. They're going to be 1 on January the 18th. So, what's your sista's baby's name?

Ashlyn: Darlesia Voniq. She was 8 lbs and 10 oz. She's bigger than that now. And boy, she can eat. Dang, that girl can eat. (Ashlyn goes into her bedroom and takes out her black maternity suit) Hold on, Mrs. Jones. (she puts the phone on speaker) All right, Mrs. Jones, I'm back. I had to put you on the speakerphone 'cause I have to get ready for the interview your con Stacey hooked me up with. (puts on her suit, stockings, shoes, and jewelry)

Mrs. Jones: Oh, OK. Well, let me talk to you later. I was just calling to check up on ya. You do good and stay out of trouble as much as you can.

Ashlyn: All right. Bye-bye. (she hangs up the phone) OK, I'm (she looks at herself in the mirror) ready to go. (she looks at her watch; it's 10:39 A.M.) [Ashlyn grabs her black purse and a folder with her résumé, then she walks out the door.]

*The scene fades away.*

### Scene 59

When: It is 11:19 A.M.
Where: KPRCT Channel 2 TV Station

*Ashlyn arrives at the TV station; she walks in the building and everybody is just staring at her. The percentage of minorities here is very low, so Ashlyn has an eerie feeling about that. She walks to the receptionist to let her know she is here for an interview with Donna Vicks.*

Receptionist: Ma'am, may I help you?

Ashlyn: (talks to receptionist) Yes. I have an interview with Donna Vicks in the production department. I'm Ashlyn Richardson. I was supposed to be here (she looks at her watch) at 11:30, but I'm early. Could you notify her?

Receptionist: OK. (she picks up the phone to call Donna Vicks)

Ashlyn: (sits down in the lobby area) Oh boy. (sighs) Receptionist: Ms. Vicks will meet you in a minute.

Ashlyn: OK. (she looks around and see a majority of white people) Umm . . . umm. (she sees a brown-skinned brother sitting down at a table talking to white men; he wears a two-piece black suit with a blue-collared dress shirt and a black, gray, and blue tie)

[Ashlyn is hypnotized at how good looking the guy is, but she's not there to get a man. She is there to get a head start on her career.

She turns her head away from him, then he stares at her and smiles. She knows he is looking at her so she stands up and walks toward the desk. He walks quickly to the desk to approach her.]

Trevon: Hi, my name is Trevon Lewis. What's your name? Ashlyn: Ashlyn Richardson. (she shakes his hand)

Trevon: So, Ashlyn, who are you here to see?

Donna Vicks: (walks behind Trevon) She's here to see me. (she turns to Ashlyn) Hi, Ashlyn. (shakes her hand) I'm Donna Vicks.

Ashlyn: Nice to meet you.

Donna Vicks: Same here. (turns to Trevon) Excuse me, sir. (walks) Follow me, Ashlyn.

Ashlyn: OK. (Ashlyn walks behind Donna and smiles at Trevon; Trevon smiles back and waves at her)

[Donna and Ashlyn walk into Donna's office. Ashlyn sits down while Donna closes the door, then sits down in her seat; she picks up and reviews Ashlyn's application.]

Donna: OK, Miss Richardson, I want you to give me three personality traits of yourself that people will describe you as.

Ashlyn: (she clears her throat and sits up straight) They would say I'm ambitious, aggressive, and intelligent.

Donna: Those are good qualities. Now, I want to know what your career goals are.

Ashlyn: I want to be an executive producer for a television network.

Donna: Does it matter what type of network? Such as sports, music, news, movies, or a combination of all.

Ashlyn: It doesn't matter, because I am very attentive to all matters that are influential in our society. I've learned that media television broadcasting is an open door for people to see what's going on within the community, city, state, nation, or world. It's a tool to address what has been left out from the literary works that cannot be seen.

Donna: Good response. (sighs) Now, tell me your weaknesses and strengths. Ashlyn: My weakness is being too blunt and straightforward. My strength is . .

. ambition. I'm a go-getter and a self-starter.

Donna: Um . . . You're also very honest. No one has ever told me in an interview their weakness is being too blunt. I personally don't see that as a weakness. I see that as one of your strengths because that shows how confident you are with such a strong will.

You're not easily influenced by anybody. To me, that's good in this type of business. You won't allow anyone to push you around or advise you to write something that doesn't have historical facts behind it. You even said how straightforward, aggressive, and intelligent you are. That's why you are here, Miss Richardson. (she smiles) And I would like you to come in tomorrow if you can, you and the little one.

Ashlyn: (smiles) OK, Ms. Vicks. I should be here at . . .?

Donna: Ash, call me Donna, okay, (she smiles) and be here at 8 A.M.

Ashlyn: All right, I'll be here at 8 A.M. tomorrow. Do you need me to bring anything like breakfast, extra copy paper, or . . .?

Donna: No. I'm here to train you to become an executive producer not to cater to my ego. (she laughs)

Ashlyn: Um . . . I understand that. So what's next for today?

Donna: (she gets up and walks to the door) Let me give you a tour and introduce you to the staff.

Ashlyn: (looks at her watch and gets up to follow Donna) OK.

[Donna and Ashlyn walk out of Donna's office; she takes Ashlyn to the media room and introduces her to Steve Romanoski.]

Donna: Ashlyn, this is Steve Romanoski. He's the head of the multimedia department. He makes sure the VHS are in sequential order to be played on air. (turns to Steve) And Steve, this is my assistant, Ashlyn Richardson.

Steve: (shakes Ashlyn's hand) Hi, Ashlyn, welcome aboard. Ashlyn: Thank you.

[Donna shows Ashlyn the computers and the equipment Steve has to use. Then they walk out of the multimedia room and go into the writing clinic where she sees Trevon using a laptop typing his report for the anchorman to read off the teleprompt; she looks at him and smiles.]

Donna: (notices Ashlyn looking at Trevon) Ashlyn . . . Ashlyn.

Ashlyn: (turns to Donna) Yes.

Donna: He's good looking, isn't he? (she laughs, and Ashlyn just looks) Just make sure you know he's mine. So don't cross that line.

Ashlyn: Oh, I'm sorry. I didn't mean any harm. I didn't know.

Donna: I forgive you 'cause you didn't know. (sighs) Anyways, let's introduce you to the journalist that is present. (she walks over to Bob Hancock) Hi, Bob. (she points at Ashlyn) This is Ashlyn Richardson. She's my new assistant. (she turns to Ashlyn) Ashlyn, this is Bob Hancock, the sports anchor.

Bob: Hi, Ashlyn, I hope you enjoy working here with us. Ashlyn: Oh, I will. (she glances at Trevon)

Donna: (sees her) Ashlyn?

Ashlyn: What?

Donna: (walks with her to introduce to Kellie Wright) Ms. Kellie Wright. This is Ashlyn Richardson. She's my new assistant. (she turns to Ashlyn) This is Kellie Wright, the weather girl.

Ashlyn: Hi, Kellie, nice meeting you. (shakes her hand)

Kellie: Nice meeting you too, Ashlyn. Welcome to the Jungle. (she laughs) [Donna and Ashlyn walk out of the writing clinic without Donna introducing Trevon. Donna walks Ashlyn to the production room to meet her staff.] Donna: Now, Ashlyn, this is where you're going to work alongside with these people, including Trevon. He's the supervisor. I'm the executive producer. I tell him what needs to be done so he will tell them (points out the staff) how I want it to be run. (she grins with sarcasm)

Ashlyn: OK.


Donna: As you can see, they are busy for tomorrow. (Trevon walks in, and Donna turns to him with a smile) Mr. Lewis, Ashlyn is going to be working with you tomorrow.

Trevon: OK, Ashlyn, welcome aboard. (turns around to the staff) Hey, staff, we have a new member. Her name is Ashlyn.

Ashlyn: Richardson.

Trevon: Ashlyn Richardson. The guy over there to your right is Heath Tolliver. (Heath waves, and Trevon points to next person) That's Kent Joseph. Kent: Hi, Ashlyn.

Trevon: (points at Mandy Dansby) That's Mandy Dansby. (Mandy waves; he turns around and points to Jessica Schafer on the far left) Ashlyn, that's Ms. Jessica Schafer.

Jessica: (gets up from her seat to shake Ashlyn's hand) Hi, Ashlyn. I heard a lot about ya.

Ashlyn: What did you hear? (she laughs) And from whom?

Jessica: I heard you were a knockout on the basketball court and on the track. And also, about your journalism skills at Inglewood High School. By the way, your brother, Carlton told me. He was in my business class last semester. All he talked about was you.

Ashlyn: Really? Hmm. I guess. Did you date my brother?

Jessica: No. We were just in a group together. You know, in a study group. Ashlyn: Oh, okay. (pauses) Well, it's nice to know you know of me. (she says it in a sarcastic way)

Trevon: (interrupts) Well, it's good to see that you two somewhat know each other. (turns to Ashlyn)

Ashlyn, if you want, you can stay with us for about an hour to observe what we do here. (turns to Donna) If that's OK?

Donna: (sighs and scratches her head) It's fine. Ashlyn, just remember what I told you. (she walks out)

Trevon: What was that all about?

Ashlyn: (shrugs her shoulders) I don't know.

Jessica: (whispers in Kent's ear as she gives him written format) I told you Tre and Don were sleeping around. I told you. (she walks away, and Trevon stares at her)

Trevon: OK, everyone. Let's continue; make sure everything is in proper order and well scripted. (turns to Ashlyn) Ashlyn, let's go to my office and have a one-on-one talk, OK?

Ashlyn: (smiles) Sure.

[Ashlyn and Trevon walk out of the room. Then everybody laughs out loud as they leave.]


Kent: Somebody is in trouble now. Boy, Donna's gonna whop Ashlyn's ass over Tre. You know that's her boy toy.

Donna: (walks in and everybody stops talking and continues working; she looks around) Where's Trevon and Ashlyn?

Jessica: (writes and smiles) In Trevon's office, having a one-on-one interview. [Donna walks out mad; Ashlyn and Trevon are in his office sitting down and talking; Trevon is at his desk while Ashlyn is on the opposite side of the desk.]

Trevon: So, Ashlyn, what year are you in at TSU? Ashlyn: Freshman.

Trevon: Freshman. Naw. (pauses) Really?

Ashlyn: Yes. I have nine more hours to be a sophomore. Trevon: Oh, you took an overload, huh?

Ashlyn: Yes. I did it because of my li'l one. (she rubs her stomach)

Trevon: So, when is the baby due? (he looks at his tablet to write down the discussion)

Ashlyn: January the 10th. I hope that's not a problem.

Trevon: No. I just need to know so the staff won't be shorthanded. (sighs) By the way, what we discuss—

Donna: (bursts through the door) Mr. Lewis, I need to speak with you, right now.

[Trevon and Ashlyn look shocked at how Donna burst in the office.]

Trevon: OK, Donna. (he gets up and walks out with Donna) Ashlyn: Damn, she's a bitch and a ho. (she laughs)

[Trevon and Donna are standing on the outside of the door having an altercation.]

Donna: (upset) What's up, Tre? You wanna bone her, too?

Trevon: Look, Donna, don't go there. You and I are not a couple, remember? Donna: So, that means you like the li'l bitch? Huh?

Trevon: Donna, I told you, you're too old for me. Our age difference is not cool. I feel like I'm your sex toy. I'm tired of being that. I want a woman who loves a man not uses him for his you-know-what. And that's what you're doing to me. (pauses and turns to her) And yes, I like her, and no, she's not a bitch like you. (he turns to the door to go in)

Donna: (pulls his arm) Tre, (she start crying) I'm sorry for making you feel that way.

Trevon: Oh, God. (shakes his head)

Donna: I love you, Trevon, but business and pleasure doesn't mix. If I decide to let everyone know we're a couple, my job is on the line, baby.

Trevon: Donna, that's all you worry about—you. Whenever you want to fuck, I fuck, but when I suggest to make love to ya, it's, hell, no, instead of hell, yes.

[People are looking at Trevon as they walk by.]

Donna: Baby, I thought you love a woman that takes charge. That's why I did it.

Trevon: Donna, I don't believe you 'cause you did Ramon the same way. That's why he left the company, because he knew me and you were intimate. And you just had to have him, but oh, when Ashlyn comes in the picture showing interest in me, you wanna claim me. It doesn't work that way. It is not her fault. It's yours, 'cause of the way you treat people.

Donna: For your information, Ramon was fired by me. He didn't leave on his own.

Trevon: And why did you fire him? Because you knew he was going to tell me you fucked him so hard that he couldn't walk? Tell me that.

Donna: Tre, that's not true.

Trevon: Yes, it is. Far as I know, I don't want you no more. It's over, so find another sex toy. And fire me if you want to. (he walks back in the office with Ashlyn, and Donna walks off mad) Sorry about that. (he pauses as he sits down) Where were we?

Ashlyn: You were asking a question about a discussion I had with Donna before she walked in.

Trevon: Oh, I wanted to know what Donna's problem was for her to say what she said in the production room.

Ashlyn: Oh, she told me you were hers so don't cross the line.

Trevon: Really? (pauses) Well, I'm not hers. We were just intimate.

Ashlyn: Oh, oh, oh, okay. That's enough information.

Trevon: OK, Miss Ashlyn, I guess you've seen and heard enough. I would love to see ya tomorrow, if you don't change your mind about working with me.

Ashlyn: I'll be here at 8 A.M., if that's OK. (she stands up)

Trevon: That's fine. I'll be here at 6:30 A.M. in the production room so meet me there. (stands up and walks to Ashlyn) You want me to walk with you to your car?

Ashlyn: I don't mind. (she smiles)

[Trevon opens the door for Ashlyn, and they walk out together. Donna passes by and mean mugs them. Trevon walks Ashlyn to her car; Ashlyn gets in her car and shuts her car door.]

Ashlyn: (rolls down her window) Thank you, Trevon.

Trevon: (steps back) No problem.

[Ashlyn drives off, and Trevon waves at her. Donna is outside of the building smoking a cigarette, staring at Trevon watching Ashlyn leave the premises.]

*The scene fades away.*

### Scene 60

When: The next day at 8 A.M. Where: KPRCT Channel 2 studio

*Ashlyn reports to KPRCT Channel 2 studio. She walks in the building very concerned about what will happen between her and Donna. She bypasses the receptionist; the receptionist just looks at her as Ashlyn walks to the production room. Kent, Jessica, and Trevon are laughing and joking while they are sitting down at their station.*

Ashlyn: Good morning, everybody! How is everyone?

Kent: All right so far. We just know how boss lady is going act today. (he laughs)

Jessica: (laughing) Yep.

Trevon: Ashlyn, you can sit by me so I can train ya. Ashlyn: (she walks over to Trevon) OK. (she sits down)

Trevon: (points to the switchboard) This button rewinds the tape for you to analyze the picture and determine what needs to be edited out or stay in. You take note of what needs to be done.

Ashlyn: All right.

Trevon: I'm going to advise you what needs to be included or not. And give you a list to show what you need.

Donna: (walks in) Good morning, everyone! There is coffee, doughnuts, bagels, and fruit salad in the conference room, if you would like some. Don't be afraid to go get it. (she walks to Ashlyn) Ashlyn, you were supposed to report to me first to pick up your employment package, then come here.

Ashlyn: Oh, I thought I was supposed to report to the supervisor, which is Trevon. That's what Trevon had said.

[Jessica, Kent, and Heath are laughing to themselves. Donna faces them  with a mean frown on her face.]

Donna: Oh, Trevon told you to come here instead of you, a new employee,  to meet in my office, the person that has control over him? (she smiles hard) Trevon: Look, Donna, you've allowed everyone else to report to me when they were hired. She is no different than them. You even gave me  her employment package to give to Miss Ashlyn, but I forgot to give it to her. So, don't get all upset over this. This is the normal way you and I have handled new employees. (he looks at her under eyed) *Comprendéis*?

Donna: (has a smirk on her face) Sí, señor! I guess I'll let you continue  to train her. (she smiles at Ashlyn, then rolls her eyes at Trevon)

[Mandy walks in late as Donna leaves the room.] Mandy: Did I miss something here?

Heath: Yep, you surely did.

Trevon: Heath, mind your business and do your work.

Kent: Man, man, drama, drama. (writing his format for his project)

Ashlyn: (shakes her head) Trevon, do you think Donna and I are going to bump heads sooner than I think? 'Cause if we are, you need to put her in check. Let her know it's not me and you 'cause I don't need any more  drama in my life.

Trevon: (smiles) I already have, but I would love to talk to you about you and your drama.

Ashlyn: (smiles) See, you don't get it. I don't need you to be my boss and friend. That's going to cause conflict after conflict, especially with Donna. I just got this gig.

I need it to boost my career, not to hinder it with drama. I don't need it. (she sighs and pauses) Your best bet is to train me and continue to be  my supervisor. That's all I ask and to understand my position as a pregnant employee. Can you do that for me? (she touches his hand gently)

Trevon: (looks at Kent and the entire staff) Were y'all listening?

Kent, Jessica, Mandy, Heath: (respond) No.

Trevon: (looks at Ashlyn) I can do that for you, but if you need someone to talk to, come to me.

Ashlyn: OK. That's better.

Trevon: OK. (he starts messing around with the VHS recorder and the monitor) Back to training.

[Ashlyn is watching Trevon demonstrating what she has to do.]

At 12 noon, everyone is taking their lunch. Trevon had brought his staff Chinese food. Jessica, Heath, Kent, Mandy, and Trevon are in the conference room eating; Ashlyn is in the restroom washing her hands so she can join them. Donna walks into the restroom.

Donna: (walks to the sink) Well, hello, Ashlyn. How are you?

Ashlyn: Fine. (she rinses her hands) How are you, Ms. Vicks?

Donna: (goes to the dryer to dry her hands) Okay, so far. It would have been better if you had done what I told you.

Ashlyn: Excuse me, what are talking about?

Donna: Oh, Ashlyn, you know *exactly* what I'm talking about. Don't play stupid.

Ashlyn: Oh, it's about (put her finger on her lip in a thinking mode) Trevon. Someone who I am not with at all but likes me and not you. Hmmmm, I can see why—

Jessica: (walks in looking lost) Hey, Ashlyn, your food is going get cold. You betta go eat. (she walks in the far stall)

Ashlyn: Ms. Vicks, I can't help what has happened to you and Trevon. It's not my fault.

Donna: You li'l bitch. You practically flirted with him yesterday before you even had your interview.

Ashlyn: Did you just called me a bitch? Lady, you don't know like that! Just because you hired me does not mean you can disrespect me!

Donna: Well, if you hadn't crossed the line with Trevon yesterday like I told you not to, I wouldn't call you a bitch, or maybe I should call you a ho! Is *that* better?

Ashlyn: (speaks angrily) You are really pushing it, Donna! (jumps at Donna) I am *this* close of whopping your ass! But I have respect and decency about who I am! I'm a woman that don't stoop to recall trash or clean up shit! (she walks out of the restroom)

[Jessica comes out of the stall laughing quietly; Donna looks at herself in the mirror, then looks at Jessica and walks out; Jessica bursts out laughing. Ashlyn walks into the conference room upset at Trevon.]

Ashlyn: Trevon, I need to speak to you right now. (she walks out of the conference room and Trevon follows)

Trevon: What's wrong?

Ashlyn: You need to talk to Donna. That bitch confronted me in the restroom. She disrespected me, calling me a bitch and ho in my face while Jessica was in there. What type of office manager/executive producer is she? I told her I don't stoop to recall trash and clean up shit.

Trevon: (laughs) I don't mean to laugh, but that was good one. I need to use that one for my damn self. She needed it, but I will talk to her because that was not cool at all just because she's jealous since I've shown interest toward you. So, just go in there enjoy your meal while I handle the trash with shit on it.

Ashlyn: (smiles) Thank you. (she walks into the conference room while Trevon goes to Donna's office)

*The scene fades away.*

**Scene 61**

When: Monday at 8 A.M. Where: History classroom

*Ashlyn goes to class to take her final exam in History 231. She leaves the class at 9:30 to go to KPRCT. She arrives at KPRCT at 10:30 and goes straight to the production department; Donna is talking to Trevon, smiling and rubbing his shoulder; Jessica, Heath, Kent, and Mandy are working together to finalize the taping to format the playlist for next week.*

Trevon: (looks up and gets up to greet Ashlyn) Hey, Ashlyn. How was the exam?

Ashlyn: (sits down by Heath) Fun. (she laughs) I'm just joking. It was easy, though. I passed it with a 95.

Jessica: A 95 in history. Dang, you are smart. History is not easy.

Kent: So, what's your overall average in that class?

Ashlyn: Uh, a 90 . . . 94, I believe.

Heath: How are your other classes?

Ashlyn: Oh, I'm exempt from three classes. I took two final exams already. Both grades were in the 90s. I have two more exams this week, Thursday and Friday, at 11 A.M.

Kent: Very intelligent, I see.

Ashlyn: I try to be. (she looks at her assignment that was given to her by Trevon) Trevon, this is all you want me to do?

Trevon: (Donna massages his neck) Yeah. That's it.

Donna: (gets up) Trevon, I want to see you in my office in about 15 minutes. (she rolls her eyes at Ashlyn and walks out)

Ashlyn: O-Okay. Hmm, seems like someone jumped out of the skillet into the deep fryer.

Jessica: (laughs) You are so right.

Trevon: Ladies, just like I told Heath, mind your business. Ashlyn: With pleasure, honey. (laughs and works on her format) Heath: (whispers to Ashlyn) I guess you got told. (laughs)

Kent just shakes head

[Fifteen minutes pass, then Trevon leaves the room. Everyone looks at him as he walks out, then laughs, including Ashlyn.]

Ashlyn: I can't believe he's kissing Donna's ass. She treats him like a toy. A toy that runs on batteries. She takes the battery out when she doesn't want to use him. And she places the batteries in when she does. What kind of relationship is that? Then she confronts me like I open my legs wide, baby and all, (everybody cracks up) calling him into the end zone. Not so. Shit, I did not know they were a couple until after I met Trevon. So, I left it alone, and he continues to flirt with me from the beginning, you know? Damn, I just got the job, and she hired me. That is crazy. Umm . . . ummmm . . . ummmph, drama; drama after drama. Don't need it. Don't need it.

Heath: I like you. You are so blunt. You tell it like it is. Kent: You surely do.

Mandy: You know what, Ashlyn? Donna is the biggest ho here. She slept with two news anchors back-to-back, then she slept with Trevon on day-to-day basis. She's a ho. She also flipped out on three other girls that worked here last year like she did to you over Trevon. And guess what she did? She fired them.

Ashlyn: No, she didn't. (shakes her head no) I can't believe they allowed her to do that. That's wrongful termination.

Kent: Not only is she a ho, she's a big B-I-T-C-H. (puts in the VHS tape for a test run)

Heath: Don't tell nobody. She slept with me on my first day here. (he laughs)

Kent: You *are* joking, right? (laughs) *Are* you joking? (looks serious)

Heath: Yeah. (laughs) I'm joking. She only prefers black or Latino men.

Jessica: Not so. I've heard her with Michael Leonard one day when I passed his office. And trust me, it was *not* an argument; it was more passion. (she laughs)

[They all laugh.]

Ashlyn: Dang, Donna is a ho. Dang. (she continues to write)

[Everybody continues at their work and laughs at the situation Jessica had mentioned. Five minutes later, Trevon walks in, straightening his tie and clearing his throat.]

Trevon: (sits down by Ashlyn) Everybody through? (turns to Ashlyn) You almost through so I can review your work?

Ashlyn: (finished her format) Yeah. Here's my rough draft. Jessica: Dang, you finished quick.

Ashlyn: (smiles) Oh, I do my job, trust me.

Trevon: (reviews Ashlyn's format) Everything is in place; you did exactly how I had shown you Saturday. I'm impressed. Very impressed. You do handle your business. (he smiles at her)

Ashlyn: Thank you. I appreciate your constructive criticism.

[Donna walks in and sees Trevon smiling at Ashlyn, then walks out. Trevon didn't even notice.]

*The scene fades away*

# ACT 12

## Scene 62

When: Christmas break
Where: Memorial Hermann Hospital

*The first week at KPRCT has passed; Ashlyn quits the radio station. School is out for the Christmas break. The following week, Ashlyn goes into labor; she goes in at 9 P.M. on December 23rd. Darnesia and Corey take her to the hospital. Ashlyn is sitting in the hospital holding both Corey and Darnesia's hands in the delivery room in Memorial Hermann.*

Corey: (bending down almost to his knees) Damn, girl! You got some strength!
Ashlyn: Oh, oh, oh! Ouch, ouch! This is painful! I need a shot to take the pain away! Oh, oh, oh! Damn! Damn you, R. T.! That sorry-ass nigga! Damn that son of a bitch! Got me barefoot and pregnant! May God help him! (she squeezes Cory's hand) Uh, I could kill him! Corey, you betta not leave Darnesia barefoot and pregnant! 'Cause if you do, I'll kick your ass! (she huffs and puffs) R. T. jumping around shooting a goddamn ball while I'm delivering one! Goddamn it! (another contraction hits; she squeezes Darnesia's hand along with Corey's) Oh . . . oh . . . oooh! Goddamn! You goddamn Eve, you just *had* to make Adam eat that damn apple! You selfish bitch! (Jeff, Vanessa, and Debbie run to Ashlyn) Why didn't you tell me this is some hard-core constipation in my damn ass?
[Debbie and Vanessa laugh.]
Debbie: Hey, that's part of womanhood.
Ashlyn: Oh . . . oh . . . oh, I think the baby is coming! (holding onto Corey's and Darnesia's hands tightly)
Corey: Jeff, man, I need your help! She's killing me over here! Help me! Jeff: I can't help you, son! (he laughs) You got it!
Debbie: (looks beneath) Oh my God ! Buzz the doctor. She's ready!
Jeff: (buzzes the doctor) Hold on, Ashlyn! Don't push!
Ashlyn: I ain't holding for no damn body! This baby is coming out *now*!
[The doctor and nurses rush into the room; Carlton and Iman run in after them; Carlton is filming the labor.]

Carlton: Damn, sis! Your stuff is torn! Don't look like it's going back into shape!

Iman: Shut up, Carlton! She's in pain! (she hits him in the back of his head) Carlton: A'ight!

Dr. Welch: Push, push, then take a deep breath, Ashlyn. Count 1 2 3, then push.

Ashlyn: OK. (she breathes 1 2 3, then pushes four times)

[Debbie rubs Ashlyn's hand as she takes Darnesia's spot. The baby is born at 10:30 P.M. on December 23,1997; it's a girl. Dr. Welch gives the baby to Ashlyn; Ashlyn holds the baby. All of the family is there, including Speedy and Teresa, circling around Ashlyn.]

Iman: What's the baby's name, Ashlyn?

Ashlyn: (holds her daughter) Artensia LaShell Richardson. (she kisses her) Teresa: Aw, that's a pretty name for a beautiful baby.

Ashlyn: She's mine. My li'l angel. (sniffles and kisses her daughter's forehead)

*The scene fades away.*

## Scene 63

When: Several months after giving birth Where: TSU track

*Artensia is here; Ashlyn is a mother, a full-time student and a part-time production assistant at KPRCT. Not only does she work, but she also runs track for TSU. After three months of practice, she participates at the Texas Relays in Austin as an anchorman on the 4 X 100 relay and as a sprinter in the 100 meter. This event is held in the first week of April. Coach Robinson is on the track with Ashlyn as she prepares for the 100 meter race. He is constantly mentoring her through the event.*

Coach Robinson: All right, Ashlyn, you need to stay focused. Don't worry about anybody else right now. It's just you, God, and that finish line. Remember that. (he pats her on the back and walks off the track) [This is the 100 meter final; Ashlyn has to break her record when she was in high school. The crowd is cheering—Jeff, Debbie, Speedy, Teresa, Iman, Carlton (holding Artensia), Vanessa (holding Darlesia), and Darnell (taping the event). They were all cheering for Ashlyn. Ashlyn gets on the block.]

The announcer: OK, everybody needs to be on their block. (1 minute later everybody is in their lane on their block) On your mark . . . Get set . . . (the ref shoots the gun) *POW!*

[Ashlyn takes off with no problem; no one catches her. She's 5 yards in the lead. Coach Robinson runs to the finish line shouting and jumping up and down. Ashlyn crosses the finish line at 10.50 seconds, almost tying the record with Flo-Jo. Ashlyn puts her hand over her head smiling.]

Coach Robinson: (runs and picks up Ashlyn) You did it! I knew you could do it in spite of everything!

Ashlyn: (looks around for her family; she finds them) I love you! (she waves and blows kisses)

[Ashlyn wins the 100 meter again but now in college. At the ceremony, she stands with so much confidence and pride that she can conquer all things as long as she has God in the formula.]

*The scene fades away.*

### Scene 64

When: Monday morning at 11 A.M. Where: KPRCT station

*Ashlyn reports to work in a good mood while Artensia is in day care. Ashlyn has just received medals at the Texas Relays, and everyone knew at the job because they were there shooting the sporting event. She walks into the building and sees a banner hanging above the receptionist's desk in the lobby area saying, "Congratulations, Ashlyn Richardson!" She smiles as she walks to the production department; she opens the door and everyone greets her with a pat on the back, handshakes, and hugs except for Donna. She just claps her hands and pretends she's happy for Ashlyn.*

Ashlyn: (smiling) Thank you so much. I appreciate the support and gratitude you all are giving me. I truly appreciate it. Thank you and may God continue to bless you.

Kent: Ms. Richardson, there is cake, ice cream, and all kinds of finger food in the main conference room for ya. So let's go and enjoy it. (he grabs her hand and pulls her to the conference room)

[Everybody is getting their food while Ashlyn is cutting the cake.]

Ashlyn: Wow! I did not expect this.

Trevon: (walks up to Ashlyn) Well, you deserve it, Ash. I'm proud of you. Keep up the good work. (he smiles at Ashlyn)

Ashlyn: Thanx. Boy toy.

Trevon: You didn't have to go there.

Heath: (interrupts; eating his food) It's the truth. Trevon: Did anybody (turns to Heath) ask you, Heath?

Heath: Nope. (licks his fingers) But this is a free country. I do have freedom of speech.

Ashlyn: Heath, (she laughs) you're crazy. Jessica: Congrats, Ash. Keep it up, girl.

Ashlyn: Thanks, Jess.

Trevon: (pulls Ashlyn away by the arm from Heath and Jessica) Ash, those jokes got to stop. Respect me just like you want to be respected. I know you want me, but you decided not to take a dip out of all of (points at this body) this.

Ashlyn: (smiles) Um . . . really. (she grins) Trevon . . . humph . . . humph. Trevon: Huh?

Ashlyn: You're a joke. (she laughs and walks away)

Donna: (walks up to Trevon) What's all that about? (she looks at Ashlyn) I *know* you are not flirting with her right in front of my face. How disrespectful is that?

Trevon: For your info, Donna, I put Ashlyn in her place, so chill out, baby. (he kisses her) You know I love you.

Donna: (laughs softly and shrugs her shoulders) Oh, stop, Tre, stop it. (she glances at Ashlyn)

Ashlyn: (talks to Mandy) I can't believe this bitch is trying her best to—

Kent: All right, Ash. Keep it down. Don't want boss lady to hear ya, even though she is being messy.

Jessica: (walks up to Ashlyn) She is so (looks at Donna) fake.

[Donna and Trevon are being lovey-dovey.]

Heath: (walks over to the circle) Hey, you guys. I heard (she whispers) Donna is going to New York to the KPRCT station this Friday. Bob told me. And when I was walking down the hall passing by her office, she was stacking boxes up in her office.

Jessica: Really?

Mandy: I wonder if Trevon knows.

Heath: He probably does and doesn't care. 'Cause his eye is on (he points at Ashlyn) you.

Ashlyn: Whatever. Don't start no mess. Heath: Oh, I'm just telling the truth.

[Trevon and Donna leave the conference room. Fifteen minutes later, Ashlyn, Jessica, and Mandy are still eating and talking to one another. Trevon walks into the conference room mad and disturbed, followed by Donna. Donna tries to grab him, but he put his hands up to ignore her. Now, Ashlyn, Jessica, Mandy, Heath, and Kent are looking at Trevon and Donna quarrelling.] Ashlyn: He must have just found out.

[Trevon and Donna are still arguing.]

Heath: (stuffing his mouth) This is like the movies. Jessica: You're absolutely right, my friend.

Kent: Well, Ashlyn, looks like Mr. T is going to be all over you.

Ashlyn: Oh, no, he's not. (she walks out of the conference room)

Kent: (watches Ashlyn as she leaves the room) She is nothing but a tease. Heath: You got that right. (he laughs)

[Kent, Jessica, Mandy, and Heath are still eating and talking.]

*The scene fades away.*

## Scene 65

When: Friday
Where: KPRCT station

*Donna has left for New York to work at the KPRCT station there. Trevon is not pleased since he and Donna had established a relationship. He trusted her. Therefore, his attitude has changed toward the staff. Ashlyn walks in at the station at 11 A.M. She goes into the production department and takes her seat at her assigned area. Then Trevon walks in behind her but very quietly; he doesn't speak to Ashlyn. Ashlyn just shrugs her shoulders. Heath, Kent, Jessica, and Mandy are sampling the video format on the monitors. Ashlyn checks her video format. Trevon walks over to Ashlyn and takes a seat beside her.*

Trevon: Ashlyn, how are you today?

Ashlyn: (operating the VHS) Fine. How are you, sir? Trevon: Not so good.

Ashlyn: (she stops and looks at him) Why is that?

Trevon: I feel used and misled by Donna. I can't believe she knew all along she was moving to New York for the past 6 months.

Ashlyn: Really? Hmm. I guess you have to handle it yourself because it doesn't concern me. (pauses) Trevon, I am not biting the bone you are giving me. Like I told you before, I don't need any more drama in my life. And I am not going to be involved in a triangle with Queen Bee and her playboy. That's not me. I'm sorry you had to go through it, but you took that route on your own. And nobody advised you to do it. So deal with it. Be a man.

Trevon: Why are you so heartless toward me, Ashlyn?

[Jessica, Kent, Heath, and Mandy stop working and turn to Ashlyn and Trevon.]

Ashlyn: I'm not. I'm just telling what you need to hear—the truth of the matter. You made that bed and lay in it, so you are the one that has to deal with it.

Trevon: (stands up with an attitude) You right. I admit and respect that. I guess me and you are just colleagues, not associates who listen to each other's problems and comfort each other, huh?

Ashlyn: Whatever, man. You need to grow up and face the circumstances that you created and could have prevented. That's all I got to say. (sighs) Now, uh, I got work to do that has to be finished today.

[Trevon rolls his eyes at Ashlyn. Ashlyn just shake her head.

Trevon walks out of the room in a very bad mood; he even slams the door as he exits.] Heath: Damn, Ash, you really pissed him off.

Jessica: Shoot, I would have told him the same thing.

Mandy: Me, too. He knew Donna was using him, but naw, he wanted to enjoy the moment she acknowledged his presence.

Kent: (stands up and starts joking) Oh . . . oh . . . oh, you guys, I'm the energizer bunny for the bitch that stole my virginity. (laughs)


Ashlyn: You are wrong. You're out of line.

Kent: She did. Trevon was a V when he came here. Ashlyn: I don't believe ya.

Jessica: Ashlyn, he's telling the truth. Donna slept with Trevon when he was an intern.

Ashlyn: So? Trevon is 24. I thought he was older than that.

Jessica: Nope. He graduated from Rice 3 years ago. So, he was 20 when Donna took his precious jewel. (she laughs out loud)

Ashlyn: Humph. That explains why he's tripping over her. Kent: Yep.

Ashlyn: Damn. (she's thinking hard to herself) That means he's still somewhat innocent.

Maybe I will give him a chance. (she thinks hard) Naw, I'll continue to play hard to get. (she laughs within)

*The scene fades away. Scene 66*

When: October, on a Monday morning at 11 A.M. Where: KPRCT station

*Ashlyn leaves school to go to KPRCT. Trevon greets her when she walks into the production room. No one else is there yet.*

Trevon: Hey, Ashlyn. How are ya?

Ashlyn: (sits down at her assigned seat) Fine, and you?

Trevon: Oh, I'm making it. Just aligned the sports clip for the Rockets preseason game. You know it's predicted the former U of H forward, R. T, will lead the Rockets to another championship.

Ashlyn: Really? Whose prediction was that? Trevon: Bob's.

Ashlyn: Hmm. I guess. (she edits her video format)

Trevon: You know, Ashlyn, there's a position for an intern journalist/reporter. Your writing skills and persona matches the requirement. Why don't you apply?

Ashlyn: I'd rather intern at this department because I am able to collate, format, and produce the programs to be on air—which is my preference. Not interviewing people on camera.

Trevon: So, the answer is no?

Ashlyn: That's correct. (she continues to finish her assignment)

Trevon: OK, I tried.

Ashlyn: Yep, you surely did.

Trevon: Ashlyn, would you consider interviewing R. T., just to see if you would like the opportunity as a journalist on Friday before the game?

Ashlyn: I don't think that's a good idea. Me and R. T. are former boyfriend and girlfriend. The relationship ended very ugly. He even denies Artensia is his daughter. So, why would I volunteer to interview my worst enemy? Tell me that!

Trevon: Damn, I didn't know, Ash. I'm sorry for pressing the issue.

Ashlyn: (gets up to go to multimedia room) Well, now you know. (walks out of the room)

[Ashlyn bumps into Jessica and Mandy as she's walking to the media room. Jessica and Mandy are going to the production room.]

Jessica: Hey, Ash, what's up?

Ashlyn: Same ol' same ol'. (she walks into the multimedia room to hand Steve her tape) Hey, Steve, I finished the format of the commercial for next week.

Steve: (walks up to Ashlyn) O-ok. Thanks. Let me process (he grabs the tape) it and file it for next week. And we'll be all set for next week.

Ashlyn: Thanx, Steve. Steve: No problem, Ashlyn.

[Ashlyn walks out and goes back into the production room. Heath, Kent, Jessica, Mandy, and Trevon are all there.]

Heath: (turns around in his seat) Hey, Ashlyn. You finished the project already?
Ashlyn: Yep. I surely did. (she sits down at her seat)
Kent: Girl, you are a fast-paced worker. Shoot, you outta apply for the executive producer position.
Trevon: That position has been filled as of today. Ashlyn: Who's the new executive producer?

Trevon: Lindsay Cameron. She's an Anglo American in her late 30s with tons of experience working at networks including WB, PBS, CBS, and ABC.
Kent: I hope she's not a queen bee like Donna. Mandy: How is her persona?
Trevon: I don't know. We'll soon find out tomorrow. Ashlyn: Another mystery to solve. (spoke sarcastic) Jessica: You got that right.
Ashlyn: Well, well, we will see.

[Everybody is working on their project and wondering about the new executive producer.]

*The scene fades away.*
**Scene 67**

When: The next day
Where: The day care center called Kiddie Kollege

*Ashlyn has a hard time leaving Artensia at the day care. Artensia does not want to go. It is now 8 A.M., and Ashlyn is trying to prepare for her midterm exam at 9 A.M., but things are not working with the little one at the day care.*

Ashlyn: (holds Artensia) Artensia, Mommy has to go. I got to go, baby.
Day care worker: (reaches for Artensia) Artensia, come on, li'l

mama. Mommy is coming back. (she touches Artensia's hand)
Artensia: (shakes her head) No . . . no . . . no. (starts crying)
Ashlyn: (jumps her up and down as she holds her) Oh, baby girl,
Mommy loves you. I'm coming back to get you, OK? (she kisses her
and hands her to the day care worker)
Artensia: (really starts crying) Mommy! Mommy! (reaches for
Ashlyn) Ashlyn: (tears drop from her eyes) Oh, baby, Mommy's
coming back. (she walks backward and talks to the day care worker)
Take care of my baby. (she walks out, gets in her car, and leaves)

[Ashlyn arrives at the campus within 5 minutes. She parks her
car in the Hannah Hall parking lot. She gets out of the car and runs
into her cousin Trina as she's going to her journalism class.]

Trina: Hey, cuz. I barely see ya. (stops at the steps of the MLK
building) Ashlyn: (walks up the steps at the MLK building) I know.
I've been busy. (she stops at the entrance door) Shoot, I hardly go
to church now. I go once a month, 'cause sometimes I go to work
on Sundays in the mornings.
Trina: Well, I guess whenever you get a chance come by the house.
Ashlyn: A'ight. I'll probably come over Saturday.
Trina: OK. I'll see you around. (she walks away) Ashlyn: A'ight.
(goes into the building)

[Ashlyn walks into the classroom and sits down in front of the room
at the right side table. There are a few students there studying for the
midterm exam.

Ashlyn takes out her book to scan through it and review her answers
to the questions. Professor Kyle walks in 15 minutes later at 8:42 with
the exams in her hands; she greets the class.]

Prof. Kyle: (sits at her desk and places the exams on her desk) Class,
the exam is 50 percent essay and 50 percent multiple choice, OK?
Ashlyn: OK. That's fair for those whose strength is in an essay or
vice versa. Prof. Kyle: Yep. That's why I formatted the exam like
that.
[Other students are coming in the class ready to take the exam.
Ten minutes later, Prof. Kyle passes out the exam; Ashlyn is the first
recipient.]
Ashlyn: (looks at the exam) This test seems to be easy but long. (she
talks to Prof Kyle) How long is the test 'cause I have to go to work?

Prof. Kyle: It will take at least an hour, which is not bad. Ashlyn: OK. No problem. (begins the exam questions)

[Everyone in the class is taking exam. Forty-five minutes later, Ashlyn gets up from the desk to turn in her exam. Then she leaves the room. She walks to the Student Life Center where she sees R. T. signing autographs at his little signing table. Ashlyn gets in line so she can have the opportunity to talk to him.

She has enough time to do so. As she waits in line, the girls are falling apart, screaming and hollering. Ashlyn just shakes her head and keeps moving up. When she gets to the table, R. T, looks up at her like he sees a ghost.]
Ashlyn: Hi, stranger.
R.T.: Hello, Ashlyn. How are you? (he signs a picture of him for her) I see you're not expecting anymore.
Ashlyn: Nope. She's at the day care wanting Momma to stay.
R. T.: Oh, so you did have a baby?
Ashlyn: Yes, I did. And I did it without you, (grabs the autographed poster and a little basketball) you ol' sorry-ass bastard.
R. T.: You still think that the child is mine? (he laughs) You crazy. As far as I'm concerned, you need to contact that track coach.
Ashlyn: You still are a jackass. (she walks away with an attitude)
R. T.: (calls out to the next person in line) Next!
[Ashlyn goes into the store in the SCLC. She buys a Kiwi
Strawberry Ocean Spray and Cheetos; then she walks out of the store and bumps into Trevon.] Ashlyn: Trevon, what are you doing here?
Trevon: Oh, I'm here to interview R. T. since nobody else will
volunteer until Saturday at the game.
Ashlyn: O-okay. You're here for that jackass out there. I just got these items (she throws the items in the trash) from him to give to his daughter, who he doesn't claim.
Trevon: Relax, Ash. (he grabs Ashlyn and brings her to him) I know it's hard, and if you need someone to be there for you and Artensia, let me know. (he looks back at R. T.) God, I just don't believe he doesn't claim the li'l princess. I tell ya, I wouldn't mind being a father, even if the child isn't mine. Too (he hugs her) bad some brothas like R. T. are irresponsible and immature. But I'm still interviewing him for today (he lets her go) and might ask him about him having children.
[R. T. sees Ashlyn talking and hugging Trevon; he

getsa littleuncomfortable.]
Ashlyn: You do that and tell me about it later on this afternoon at work. Trevon: I will. Trust me. Now let me go interview this jackass. (he laughs and walks over to R. T.)

[Ashlyn walks out of the building.]

*The scene fades away.*

**Scene 68**

When: That evening at 8 P.M. Where: Ashlyn's home

*Ashlyn is at home with Artensia. Artensia is walking around the living room holding on to the chairs, coffee table, and love seat, smiling and laughing at Ashlyn. Ashlyn is sitting in the love seat admiring her daughter taking the initiative to walk on her own while they are looking at the Billboard Awards.*

Ashlyn: (laughing) Go, Annie! (clapping her hands) Go, Annie!
Artensia: (laughs and claps her hands) Go, go, go! (dances) [The phone rings.]
Ashlyn: (picks up the phone and answers it) Hello. [On the other line is Vanessa.]
Vanessa: Hey, Ash. What's up? I haven't talk to ya for a while.
Ashlyn: I've been busy with work, school, and Annie. (Artensia walks to Ashlyn; Ashlyn picks her up)
Vanessa: Well, I was checking on ya. Are you going to Mom and Dad's for Thanksgiving?
Ashlyn: I might, if I don't have to work. And since we have this gay racist bitch over us, it is possible she'll make it mandatory for us to work.
Vanessa: Ashlyn, are you sure she's like that? Or you just exaggerating? Ashlyn: *Excuse me,* Vanessa. This woman told the staff she's gay. Then she marked all over my final video format. None of the white people received red ink all over their final drafts like I did. Tell me if that's not racist. Jessica also told us before she came in the production room that she stated she's glad there are more of them (whites) there. What kind of the statement is that? Huh? Tell me that.
Vanessa: Oh, Ashlyn, grow up. You' acting like you did at Kemptner.

You're going to have to learn how to adapt and accept negativism when it falls in front of you so you can let them know you do not fall into the statistics of an uneducated black female on welfare who is –ghetto fabulous‖ and ignorant. C'mon, sis. You've been through the worst scenarios. This is just a test to see how you have grown. I know it's hard but beat them in their own game by adapting and manipulating those around you with your intelligence and ideas to excel higher than the standard expectations of a single-parent black female. That's life as a –black woman.‖

Ashlyn: You know what? You're right, Nessa. I'll laugh at her on how stupid she is toward me and continue to do my best without kissing her ass—because I *am* a black woman that is educated, assertive, aggressive, and ambitious. I am who God has created, a woman with integrity, dignity, and creativity.

Vanessa: I'm glad you understand. Now, do it, don't just say it.

Ashlyn: I got ya.

[There's a knock at the door.] Vanessa: Is that someone knocking?

Ashlyn: (walks to the door holding the phone and talking to Vanessa while she peeps through the peephole.) Yep. It's my supervisor.

Vanessa: Oh, OK. I'll talk to you later then. Take care of your business. Ashlyn: Okay. Bye-bye. (she hangs up the phone, then opens the door) Come in, Trevon, and have a seat.

[Trevon walks in; Artensia looks at him while she's sitting down playing with her blocks.]

Trevon: (sits down on the couch and looks around) You got a nice place, especially for a college student.

Ashlyn: (standing up) It's a li'l something-something. (pauses) You hungry or thirsty or both? 'Cause I made some baked chicken with greens, mashed potatoes, and some iced tea.

Trevon: You cook? Ashlyn: Yeah, I cook.

Trevon: Well, I can have some. (smiling at Artensia)

Ashlyn: (walks into the kitchen and fixes his plate) So, Tre, what brings you here?

Trevon: (gets down on the floor with Artensia and plays with her) Oh, I was in the neighborhood so I just decided to stop by.

Ashlyn: Uh-huh. (she brings Trevon his plate) You were just in the neighborhood. (she bends over to give him his plate)

Trevon: Thank you. (Artensia starts grabbing food out of Trevon's plate) OK, li'l mama, (he gives her some potatoes) here you go.

Ashlyn: (sits down and smiles) Trevon, what is the real reason?

Trevon: I told (feeding Artensia and himself) you already.

Ashlyn: OK. (she just stares at him)

Trevon: (feeding Artensia) Boy, this girl can eat! Can't you, li'l mama? (laughing and grinning with Artensia)

Ashlyn: Yeah, she can eat. As a matter of fact, she already ate 30 minutes ago. (she laughs)

Trevon: So, what're you watching? (continues to feed himself and Artensia) Ashlyn: (lies down on the couch) The Billboard Awards.

Trevon: Oh, I love watching award assemblies. Ashlyn: Really? Hmm.

[Destiny's Child performs on the show.] (Artensia gets up and walks to Ashlyn.)

Ashlyn: You sleepy, mama? (she kisses Artensia and picks her up; Artensia nods her head yes) OK, let's (gets up from the couch with Artensia in her arm) put you in the bed. (she walks out of the living room and takes Artensia to her room.)

[Trevon finishes his plate, then gets up and takes his plate into the kitchen; he washes his plate; Ashlyn walks in 3 minutes later.]

Trevon: Oh, I was just . . . (wipes his hands with a paper towel)

Ashlyn: Oh, I don't care. Especially, when you clean up behind yourself. (she looks in the refrigerator) You want some (takes out the tea and sets it on the counter) more tea? (grabs her glass out of the drainer)

Trevon: Yeah. (grabs his glass; Ashlyn pours tea in both of their glasses; then they walk into the living room and sit down on the couch) So, you got any movies that we can watch after the awards?

Ashlyn: Yeah. I have *Low Down Dirty Shame, Waiting to Exhale, Thin Line Between Love and Hate,* and *Nutty Professor.*

Trevon: O-okay. You have movies. (pauses and sighs) I guess you have *Love Jones*? (he smiles)

Ashlyn: Yep. You want me to (she gets up and gets *Love Jones* out of her bookcase) play that? (she holds it in her hand)

Trevon: Whenever you want to.

Ashlyn: OK. (she walks to the TV and put the movie on) There you go. (she walks to the couch and sits by Trevon)


Trevon: (scoots over to Ashlyn) What's up, Ashlyn?

Ashlyn: (laughs) Trevon, you don't—

Trevon: (kisses Ashlyn on the lips) You don't know how long I wanted to do that.

Ashlyn: (in a state of shock) I can't believe you did that. (she gets up and turns her back to Trevon) Trevon, this is too soon.

Trevon: (gets up) No, it's not. (he walks behind her and grabs her around her waist) Ash, turn around.

Ashlyn: (crying and turns around) I just don't want to lose you, so it's best for us not to—

Trevon: You're not. Just let me love you. That's all I want to do.

Ashlyn: Tre, I want you too, but every time I love a man, I always lose him. My first love was killed. My second one was taken from me by his ex. Then you. You had a history with Donna who couldn't stand me. How do I know you might do me the same way R. T. did me? Huh? I can't hear you!

Trevon: It's over between Donna and me. I want you, Ash. (he holds her and kisses her) I want you to know that. So let me show you. (he picks her up) [Within minutes, Ashlyn and Trevon are in the bedroom as passion takes over.]

*The scene fades away.*

# ACT 13

**Scene 69**

When: The next morning at 9 A.M.
Where: Ashlyn's home

*Ashlyn wakes up and smells sausage, eggs, and biscuits cooking. She gets up and looks at the floor. She notices Trevon's clothes are folded in a pile. She puts on her pajama pants and a T-shirt, then hurries to the kitchen. She sees Trevon cooking breakfast and Artensia in her high chair eating biscuit and eggs.*

Trevon: (smiles) Hey, baby, you're up finally. (making an omelet for him and her) I'm making an omelet for us, but I fed Artensia a biscuit and eggs. So, you don't need to worry, okay?
Ashlyn: (walks to Artensia) You're eating some biscuits. (Artensia laughs and kicks her legs, showing her four teeth; Ashlyn turns to Trevon) So, Tre, I see you, uh, stayed over last night and fit in. I admit I loved the lovemaking. (she starts thinking about it) Ummm, ummm, ooh boy, it was. (she gets back on track) Anyways, I appreciate the breakfast and how you treat my precious jewel, but I don't think we should be a couple, 'cause business and pleasure don't mix. I mean, I want you, (she grabs his hand as he's fixing their plate), and I cut for you, but I don't want to get hurt or lose you. I'm just tired of conflict and drama.
Trevon: Baby, (he holds her in his arms against the kitchen countertop) I understand. I just wanted to show you how much I really care for you. And treat you the way you should be treated. I admire you. You are such a strong, independent, intelligent, sexy, (he wiggles her arms in front of her body and kisses her, then smiles) mature, and ambitious black woman that drives me crazy!
Ashlyn: Trevon, uh, when I look at you, it's so hard to say I ca—
Trevon: (seals her lips with his hands) Don't say a word, 'cause, Ashlyn, you are always going to be mine, even if you continue to play the cat-and-mouse game. I will always fall into your trap. Baby, I'll wait on you until you're ready. Just let me do for you. (he sings) Baby, I'm yours, if you want me. I'm yours, baby. (he dances against her)
Ashlyn: (laughs) OK, Trevon. I'll consider us to be dating, then later on down the road—
Trevon: (interrupts) Marriage. (jumps up and down)

Ashlyn: No. (pauses) We'll be in a committed relationship. But first, we have to start on square one. Even though we made . . . um (clears her throat and grabs Trevon's butt with a crooked smile) made love, we still have to take it slow. Nice and slow.

Trevon: Well, well, can we eat our omelet later and sit Artensia in her bed for a moment? (he hugs and kisses her)

Ashlyn: Nope. We have school, and you have work.

Trevon: (puts his head down while Ashlyn takes Artensia out of the high chair) I tried. (he snaps his fingers)

Ashlyn: (talks to Artensia) OK, Arnie. Let's go take a bath.

[Trevon eats his omelet and watches Ashlyn and Artensia leave the kitchen. An hour later, Ashlyn and Artensia are ready to go. Trevon walks out of the house with them. He kisses Ashlyn right after she puts Artensia in the car seat. Then he gets in his car and leaves. Ashlyn leaves right after him.]

*The scene fades away.*

### Scene 70

When: 11:30 A.M. that day Where: KPRCT station

*Ashlyn pulls up to the KPRCT station. Trevon gets out of his car right behind her. She sees him in her rearview mirror.*
*He has a bouquet of flowers and a heart-shaped candy box with a teddy bear saying, "I Will Always Love You." He walks to her car and smiles.*

Ashlyn: I don't believe this. (she smiles and gets out of her car)

Trevon: (he hands her gifts) This is for you for being who you are.

Ashlyn: (takes it) Tre, you didn't have to do this.

Trevon: But I did. (he smiles) Ashlyn: So, where can I put this?

Trevon: On my desk or on your side in the production room.

Ashlyn: I'll put them in your office because there's not enough room at my workstation.

Trevon: OK, Ms. Thang. (he kisses her) Let's do that.

[They walk together into the building. Then they enter his office; everybody is looking, whispering, and staring at them.]

Ashlyn: Thank you, Trevon. (she puts the flowers on his desk and smiles at him)

Trevon: (walks behind her and grabs her waist) I feel naughty.

Ashlyn: (smiles) You do? (she points at the door) Lock the door. (she hops on the desk while Trevon hurries up to lock the door)

Trevon: (runs back and jumps on top of Ashlyn on his desk) I'm ready for ya, baby. Are you ready for me?

Ashlyn: (she kisses him on his lips) I'm ready for ya.

[Trevon starts caressing her body, then the next thing you know, they are at it again. On the other side of the door, Ms. Cameron is listening to Ashlyn and Trevon having sexual relations in his office.]

Ashlyn: Oh, Trevon, oh, baby.

Trevon: Oh, Ash, I'm coming, baby, oh, baby, I love you. Oh!

[Ms. Cameron's face is beet red as she stands beside the door. She knocks real loud.]

Ms. Cameron: (shouts) Trevon! Trevon!

[In Trevon's office, Ashlyn and Trevon hurry up and put on their clothes.] Ashlyn: Aw, shit. That bitch is at the door. (zips her pants and puts on her shoes, then buttons her blouse and slips on her blazer)

Trevon: (he has his clothes on) Damn, baby, I didn't know she was out there. When we passed by her office the lights were off. (he goes to the door) OK, Ms. Cameron.

(Ashlyn straightens her hair and makes sure her clothes are on correctly; Trevon grabs the Lysol and sprays it; then he opens the door.) Hi, Ms.
Cameron.

Ms. Cameron: (looks at Trevon, then turns to Ashlyn) I hope you were not having sex at the workplace. (she squints her eyes)

Trevon: That is none of your business. As long as we do our job in a professional manner, our personal relationship should not be your business or concern.

Ashlyn: I guess he told you. (she walks out)

Ms. Cameron: Humph . . . if it happens again, you two will be terminated. (she storms out of the office)

Trevon: (laughs) You just mad 'cause you don't have a Mandingo!

[Ashlyn is in the production room; Jessica, Mandy, Heath, and Kent are carrying on with their work too quietly.]

Ashlyn: OK, you guys, you don't have to be silent when I'm in the room. I know ya talkin' about me.

Jessica: Yeah, Ms. Thang. Did you and Trevon hook up?

Mandy: 'Cause we saw you two walking together and smiling.

Kent: You even had a bouquet, teddy bear, and some candy in ya hand. What you do, girl?

Ashlyn: I know you didn't.

Heath: She put dat whip appeal on him. That young stuff. He never taste it before.

Ashlyn: OK. That's enough. (she starts working on her format)

Trevon: (walks in) Hey, everybody, I'm back. (he looks at Ashlyn and smiles, then sits beside her) Hey, shorty, you a'ight?

Ashlyn: Oh, I'm fine. How about you? (she is writing down her format) Trevon: (whispers in her ear) Damn good. So, good I'm 'bout to (he stands up and shouts) *blow up!*

Jessica: Um, damn, Ashlyn, what you do?

Ashlyn: (laughs) Nothing, just being me, baby girl. Just keepin' it real. Kent: Hmm, so are you two a couple?

Trevon: We are not officially a couple.

Ashlyn: That's right, baby boy. We're dating, and we want to make sure this is what we want, you know what I'm saying?

Heath: Oh, I understand what you are saying.

Trevon: The woman has spoken. (he smiles) All right, people, back to work. Ashlyn: Yes, sir. (she laughs and continues to do her work)

*The scene fades away.*

## Scene 71

When: Thanksgiving Day
Where: The Richardson household

*The Jeff and Debbie are hosting Thanksgiving dinner at their home. Everybody is there including and Carlton and Iman, Ashlyn, Artensia, and Trevon, Darnell, Vanessa, and Darlesia. Jeff and Debbie greet the couples as they come in one after another.*

*Jeff shakes the men's hands and pats them on their backs while he hugs and kisses the women.*

*Meanwhile, Debbie hugs and kisses everybody that comes through. Speedy and his wife, Teresa, come first, then Vanessa, Darlesia, and Darnell. After Vanessa and her family, Carlton and Iman enter, then Ashlyn, Artensia, and Trevon follow. The family goes straight to the dining room. The couples sit by each other. The two grandchildren sit beside their parents. Jeff is at the head of one end of the table while Debbie sits on the other end. The youngest ones and their significant other sit on the right side of Jeff, while the two oldest sit on the left side of Jeff.*

*The family sits down and holds hands at the table as they prepare to pray over the food cooked by no other than Jeff.*

Jeff: (grabs Vanessa's and Ashlyn's hands) May we bow our heads to give thanks for this special occasion? (everybody bows their heads, then Jeff prays with closed eyes) God, we want to take this time to give all thanks to you. You have blessed us to be here one more day. You have blessed us to unite as a family one more time with additional members. (Ashlyn squeezes Trevon's hand) We take this time for you to bless this nourishment that has been prepared for us to eat. Oh, forgive us for our wrongdoings and straighten us in the narrow path of salvation and glory. Thank you, God in heaven and on earth. Continue to guide, protect, and strengthen our faith day by day, and we will continue to give you the praises, honor, and glory. Amen. (he opens his eyes, and so does everybody else and let go of each other's hands, then look at him) OK, everybody, let's eat. (he carves the turkey, then he jumps to the other side to carve the ham)
[Everybody is fixing their plates.]
Vanessa: So, Trevon, how did you and li'l sis meet? (she's putting her potato salad on her plate and Darlesia's, too, then she passes it to Darnell)
Trevon: (has finished fixing his plate with the broccoli cheese casserole, turkey with dressing, and potato salad) Your sister and (looks at Ashlyn) I met at work. At KPRCT. (he smiles at Ashlyn as she's eating her food)
Vanessa: Oh, you work together?
Ashlyn: (chews her food then talks) Yes, Vanessa. Vanessa: Um, so what department do you work in?
Ashlyn: Vanessa, that's enough. (she puts food in her mouth, then she turns to Trevon and talks to him) You don't have to answer any of her questions if you don't want to.
Trevon: Well, baby, it's OK. She's just being a big sista, trying to make sure you are treated good.
Vanessa: Trevon, if you don't want to answer, it's fine. I'm just trying to protect my li'l sis, that's all.
Trevon: I understand. (sighs) Now, back to your question. I'm Ashlyn's supervisor at KPRCT in the production dept. (he smiles)
Debbie: (almost chokes on her water) You are who? Trevon: Mrs. Richardson, I'm Ashlyn's supervisor. [Ashlyn looks at Trevon with a mean frown on her face.]
Debbie: Ashlyn, you left this out when we wanted to know who the

special person was in your and Artensia's life. Why did you leave this out?

Vanessa: (answers) 'Cause she knows business and pleasure don't mix. (stuffing her mouth with food and feeding Darlesia)

Ashlyn: (yells out) Was she talking to you? Was she talking to you, Vanessa? I think you better mind your own goddamn business!

Trevon: (grabs Ashlyn by the hand) Baby, calm down. Just let it be. (he kisses her on the hand then looks at Debbie) Mrs. Richardson, your daughter and I have already discussed our relationship on both a business and personal level. We've decided to date for a while, then go into a committed relationship. We want to take it one step at a time. So, don't be mad at her. Be glad she's being cautious of who comes in her and li'l mama's life. (he kisses Ashlyn's hand again then rubs it)

Debbie: (sighs) Well, Trevon, I'm glad you are man enough to be real about your and Ashlyn's relationship, but we cannot afford her to lose focus again on what her plans are. That's all. She's been through a lot. She doesn't need any more drama in her life.

Jeff: (turns to talk to Debbie and Vanessa) You two are being very judgmental about this young man just because he's Ashlyn's supervisor. If anyone should be upset it should be (chewing his food) me, you know? I am looking at (points at Trevon) Trevon's body language. His persona is very . . . what is the word? (he puts his finger on his chin to think) Very considerate, respectful, and ambitious. He even admires the decision they had contemplated to take the relationship slowly; not fast. It's a good idea, especially considering what Ashlyn has been through. So, let the man be the man and Ashlyn be a woman. Iman: (chewing her food) Amen, Mr. Jeff. (she looks over at Carlton) Ashlyn and Trevon, I wish you the best. (she stuffs her mouth)

Carlton: (he shakes Trevon's hand) Yeah, man. I agree; just don't hurt her. That's all I got to say. Or else it's me and you. Just keeping it real, my brotha. (he stuffs his mouth with food)

Speedy: So, Trevon, I guess you are almost in the family, (he puts food in his mouth) huh? (pauses)

All I know is my li'l sis is not a toy 'cause she's not for sale and you cannot toss her around, you hear me? Just treat her like she deserves to be treated. That's all I got to say. (he drinks his soda)

Vanessa: Trevon, thanks for being open about what's going on and who you are. Keep it up.

Trevon: Thank you.

Darnell: Just keep it real, brother. Ashlyn might consider the –M‖ word, but you gotta continue what you started.

Trevon: Oh, you don't have to worry. I'll continue to show her respect, loyalty, support, and (looks at Ashlyn and smiles) love.

Ashlyn: OK, everybody, enough discussing my personal life. Let's enjoy our dinner. (she asks Jeff) Dad, could you pass me the broccoli, rice, and cheese casserole?

Jeff: (he passes the casserole to her) Here you go, baby girl. (he talks to Trevon) Well, Tre, welcome to the family. You have (laughs) passed the test. Trevon: (laughs) I sure hope so. (he looks at Ashlyn)

[They all laugh as they continue to stuff their mouths with food.]

Speedy: Welcome to the crazy family! (laughing)

*The scene fades away.*

## Scene 72

When: Thanksgiving Evening Where: Trevon's house

*Ashlyn and Trevon are at Trevon's house to parlay. Artensia stays with Jeff and Debbie for the night. Trevon and Ashlyn are lying in Trevon's bed in the master bedroom watching the NCAA football game all hugged up in their pj's.*

Ashlyn: (asks) So, Mr. T, are we going to work tomorrow or not?

Trevon: No. Unless you want to.

Ashlyn: No. I want to stay right here. (she hugs him) You know, Tre, I've been wanting to ask you for a long time. Before you graduated from college, did you want to work at the TV station or do something else with your degree?

Trevon: I wanted to do my internship at any TV station in the production so I could get hands-on fundamentals of production. Then, within a year after graduation,

I wanted to work at a production company like Paramount, Universal Pictures, and 40 Acres and a Mule. That has always been my career goal; then in 8–10 years, I'll get my own production company.

Ashlyn: Really? So, if you forward your résumé to these companies and one of them decides to hire you, would you leave KPRCT and go to them?

Trevon: Yep, but you and li'l mama will still be in the picture. (he touches her nose)

Ashlyn: Well, at least you're straightforward. (pauses) Have you submitted your résumé to those companies?

Trevon: I sent my résumé for the past 3 years but no response. Hopefully, one day, they'll call me. If so, I'm going to be optimistic and carry on my dream. And I expect you to do the same, if opportunities should come your way.

Ashlyn: Oh, it will happen after I graduate from TSU. It surely will happen. Trevon: You betta not manipulate the situation. (he starts tickling her) Or else I'm gonna whoop your ass!

[Ashlyn and Trevon are rolling around in his bed as he's tickling her. Then the phone rings.]

Ashlyn: Who could that be? One of your hot flames that won't let you go? (the phone continues to ring)

Trevon: (picks up the phone from the nightstand) Hello. (on the other side of the line is Donna Vicks; she's at home in New York; her husband is having a fit; she's crying, all bruised up)

Donna: (crying) Trevon, I need refuge. He's going crazy. He beat me. I need to stay with you. (her husband is breaking household items) I need you, Tre. I'm so sorry for what I've done. (she gets up and runs out of the house with the phone in her hand)

Trevon: Donna, you can't come back here.

Donna: I need you, baby. I'm sorry for what I've done to you. This man is trying to kill me. (she gets in her car and drives off holding her cell phone) [Ashlyn looks at Trevon with a blank face because he called Donna's name.] Trevon: You cannot come here. I'm in a relationship.

[Ashlyn gets up out of the bed mad; mad enough to take the phone away from Trevon.]

Ashlyn: Hi, Donna. How are you?

Donna: (driving) Ashlyn? (she stops at the light) You li'l sneaky bitch! Ashlyn: Excuse me? I know you didn't call me a bitch when you call here at my man's house begging him back.

Donna: Ms. Thang, you don't know what I'm going through right now. I'm running from my husband who just tried to kill me, (she cries) and I need refuge somewhere, where he doesn't know how to find me.

Ashlyn: I'm sorry, Donna, but you can't come here. (Trevon looks worried; Ashlyn hangs up the phone)

[The phone rings again and again; Trevon and Ashlyn just look at each other and the phone.]

Ashlyn: Trevon, that's all you had to do. Just hang up the damn phone. That's it.

Trevon: Well, baby, I tried to let her know she can't come here. (he stands over Ashlyn as she lies down)

Ashlyn: Trevon, do you still love her? Be honest with me.

Trevon: I don't, but I don't want anyone to harm her either, baby. Would you want something to happen to R. T.?

Ashlyn: No, of course not. (she cries out) I wouldn't want to witness another death of someone I've loved. (she thinks about Omar)

Trevon: Oh, baby, I (he gets in the bed and hugs her) am sorry for asking that. Forgive me.

Ashlyn: (crying) I forgive you. Baby, (sighs) I don't want to lose you and please don't betray me. Please don't.

Trevon: (looks up holding her) I won't baby. Baby, I won't. (he kisses her, then he lays her down; she kisses him back)

*The scene fades away.*

# ACT 14

## Scene 73

When: Several months have passed; it's 7:30 P.M. Where: Ashlyn is at home from work

*The New Year has arrived. Ashlyn is in her junior year. Trevon and Ashlyn are still dating. Of course, they continue to mix business and pleasure at the workplace but on the DL (down low). Artensia is 1 year old and is as smart as ever like her mother. R. T. is doing well with the Rockets. Iman and Carlton are graduating from U of H in the summer of '99 and planning a wedding for the year of 2000. Jeff and Debbie are still pursuing, their careers. Vanessa, Darnell, and li'l Darlesia are continuing their lives as a family. Vanessa and Darnell are still working at U of H. Speedy and Teresa are not together anymore, so he's experiencing what Ashlyn has been through.*

[Trevon is still at work. He and Ashlyn are talking on the phone to each other.]
Trevon: (at KPRCT in the production room) Baby, do you want me to pick up some dinner on the way home?
Ashlyn: (she is cooking over the stove and watching Artensia eating her phone) That's all right, baby. I got food cooking on the stove already.
Trevon: Um, ummm, my baby can cook. I'll be home in 30 minutes.
Ashlyn: OK, (she laughs while stirring the rice) bye-bye. (she hangs up the phone and continues to cook)
[Trevon is sitting down at the workstation, organizing the video formats for next week to be preprogrammed. Donna Vicks walks in and sneaks behind Trevon.]
Donna: (kisses Trevon on the cheeks) Hey, sweet thang, I'm here.
Trevon: (jumps out of his seat) Donna, what the hell are you doing here?
Donna: I'm here (she grabs Trevon and pulls him to her) to see you, baby boy. Trevon: (pushes her off) Donna, it's over between me and you. I'm in a relationship, now. I can't be seen with you. Ashlyn will kill you and me! (he walks out of the room to his office; Donna follows) Did you hear me, Donna? I don't want you! I need you to get the fuck out! Me and you are like vinegar and water! We don't mix! (he gathers his briefcase, walks out, and shuts his office door, then locks it; Donna just stands there crying outside of his office while Trevon leaves her behind)

[Fifteen minutes later, Trevon pulls up at Ashlyn's apartment; he gets out and opens the door.]

Trevon: (walks in and doesn't see Ashlyn) Hey, baby, I'm home! (he walks into the kitchen; he sees his plate fixed with baked chicken, rice and gravy, a bean casserole, tossed salad and a roll; he smiles)

Ashlyn: (walks into the kitchen with the phone in her hand talking to Donna) Donna, you are a trip! How the hell did you get my number?

Trevon: (looks at Ashlyn in shock) Ash, hang up the phone.

Ashlyn: (rolls her eyes at Trevon while she talks to Donna) Donna, don't call here no more! I don't need any drama! (she pauses) Say what? (pauses) When did this (looks at Trevon in an anguished manner) happen? (pauses) Umm, really? You know what Donna? (she pauses again; Trevon paces back and forth looking worried) Donna, you need to (she sighs) . . . Oh, I don't need this! Bitch, don't you dare threaten me 'cause I will kick your ass enough for you to run back to your woman-beating husband to continue his daily ritual on your ass! So, don't you dare call here anymore or else you will catch a case! (she slams the phone down on its base.)

Trevon: (gets in front of Ashlyn) Baby, baby, look at me. (Ashlyn pushes him out of the way and walks into the bedroom packing all of his clothes) Baby, I didn't do nothing. I came straight home to you. I pushed her out of the way!

Ashlyn: (continues packing, then walks up to Trevon) Trevon, I told you I didn't need any more drama in my life! Now, this bitch has got back in the picture again! I can't tolerate this. (she cries) I love you, Trevon, but I will not allow any more drama in my life. 'Cause when something affects me, it effects my baby girl. And she's my heart. (Trevon shakes his head –no‖ with tears flowing down his face) Trevon, I hate to say this, but we need to go our separate ways 'cause I cannot handle your additional baggage, right now. So I want you (Trevon grabs her and cries like a baby) to leave right now. [Ashlyn tries to push away from Trevon, but Trevon will not let her go.] Trevon: (holds Ashlyn tightly) I don't want to go, baby. Baby, I love you! (he looks at Ashlyn directly in her eyes) Donna is history! You are my future!! Don't do this to me! Baby, please!

Ashlyn: (breaks away from Trevon and goes back to his clothes) I'm sorry, but I will not allow anymore drama in my life or my daughter's life. (she throws his bag of clothes at him) Trevon, you need to leave. You are not welcome (cries) here anymore. You're just my supervisor again. So, please leave before I do something I will regret, and that's calling the cops.

Trevon: (walks backward, crying) Baby, baby, I love you, I love you, Ash. (he wipes the tears as he leaves out but came back to get his plate off the counter in the kitchen then walks out the house and locks the door)

Ashlyn: (falls onto her bed in a fetal position, crying) I love you, too, Trevon. (she hugs the bear he gave her that said –I will always love you‖) Oh, God, why does love hurt? (she cries herself to sleep)

*The scene fades away.*

### Scene 74

When: Monday morning
Where: Ashlyn is leaving a classroom at TSU

*The weekend has passed, and Trevon and Ashlyn have broken up. Trevon keeps calling and leaving messages saying he loves her and Artensia and he misses them; Ashlyn swallows her tears. She leaves from her last class with Professor Kyle, the 300 Journalism course. Ms. Kyle stops her.*

Prof. Kyle: Ashlyn, can I talk to you for a minute? Ashlyn: (walks back to Prof. Kyle's desk) Sure.

Prof Kyle: I am somewhat disappointed in you on your work ethics at KPRCT. I've received a letter from the former executive producer and the current executive producer. And it is not a letter describing your achievements. They are complaints on how you carried yourself at KPRCT. So, tell me your side of the story so I can decide whether or not I regret sending you there.

Ashlyn: (frowns at her) *Excuse me,* my work ethics are fine. Ms. Vicks is upset because the guy I was dating until a couple of days ago had left her. Now, Ms. Cameron doesn't like me because I'm black and knowledgeable about the production process. She even dissected my video format with red marks all over it for no reason, just to piss me off. And the rest of the staff, who happen to be white, had as little as two red marks or none, which is impossible 'cause the writer and the editor complained about their work. Previously, they gave me an award for having a well organized, well written format.

Prof. Kyle: They told me how well you do in the department, but your work ethics are not the best. They state that you dated your supervisor right after your former boss departed, then you had sex at the workplace. I did not send you to that site to get a man. I sent you there to get a head start on your career.

Ashlyn, please don't do that again. That is very unprofessional. I don't care who does what. I want you to be better than them and be the best at what you do. So, please, Ash, try to keep business and pleasure separate from each other, OK?

Ashlyn: Ms. Kyle. I will, but those two women are the biggest hypocrites there are, and I will not allow them to manipulate me or disrespect me at all. Or else I will rebel and make sure they get the message. (she walks out, then comes back and peeps her head in the doorway) By the way, thank you for the lecture. (she leaves)

Prof. Kyle: (looks at her watch) That Ashlyn is something else. Boy, she's tough. (she gets up and grabs her bag, then exits the room)

*The scene fades away.*

## Scene 75

When: It's 12 noon
Where: The production room at the station

*Ashlyn walks into the production room at noon. Everybody is there except Trevon. They are eating their lunch talking to one another.*

Kent: Hey, what's up, Ashlyn?
Ashlyn: (sits down) Hey! (she looks at Trevon's desk) Where's Trevon? Jessica: In his office, cleaning up.
Ashlyn: Cleaning up?
Heath: Yeah. Trevon got a job offer at Universal Studios in California. Ashlyn: Say what? When did this (she jumps out of her seat) happen? Mandy: Last week. He didn't tell you?
Ashlyn: No. He didn't. (she sits down in a deep thought) Do you know when last week?
Kent: Thursday or Friday. That's all I can tell ya.
Ashlyn: Hmm, I guess I'll have a (she gets out of her seat and walks to the door) little chitchat with him. (she leaves the room and walks to Trevon's office)
[Trevon is packing his stuff in boxes. Ashlyn stands in the doorway.]

Ashlyn: (knocks on the door) Can I come in?

Trevon: (he stops and looks at Ashlyn) Yeah. Uh, sure. (points at the chair) Have a seat. (he sits down at his desk that is now bare)

Ashlyn: (sits down) So, you got your dream job. Congratulations, I'm proud of you.

Trevon: (clears his throat) Thank you. I appreciate it. Ashlyn: Well, uh, um . . . I wish you the best.

Trevon: OK. Is there anything else? (he shrugs his shoulders and leans back in his chair)

Ashlyn: Yep. (pauses) Trevon, why didn't you tell me you had got this job offer?

Trevon: Because I was indecisive about it. I wanted to be with you and Artensia as a family, but now things have changed. I have to do me just like you have to do you.

Ashlyn: That's bullshit, Trevon, and you know it! What's the real reason? Trevon: That's the truth, Ash! Plus, I don't think it's best for us to work with each other. You know how hard it is for me to be around you when I can't have you. So, I'm leaving to fulfill my dream. So, deal with it.

Ashlyn: OK. (she gets up) I guess this is it for me and you on the business relationship, too.

Trevon: Yep. You chose to do this. So be woman enough to stick to what you wanted—us to be separated!

Ashlyn: That's cool with me. (she walks to the door and turns back) Trevon, fuck you. (she walks away)

[Ashlyn runs to the restroom bawling like a newborn baby. Donna walks in.] Donna: Well, well, look who got the boot print on her face. (smiling devilishly) You need a tissue?

Ashlyn: Donna, (she wipes her face) you stay away from me! Donna: Or you're going to do what? (she gets in Ashlyn's face) Ashlyn: I am this close to kicking your ass!

Donna: Why? Because Trevon and I are back together and he's leaving with me to go to California?

Ashlyn: You, bitch! (she hits Donna in her face, causing her to fall on the floor, crying) You stay away from him. He doesn't need a two-timing ho like you messing with his heart. He needs a woman that doesn't belong to the trash bin full of STDS. (she steps over her and walks out of the restroom and goes to the production room; Trevon is picking up the video formats; Ashlyn sits at her workstation)

Trevon: (walks over to Ashlyn) Ashlyn, you have your video format done? Ashlyn: Yeah. (she hands him the format)

[Ms. Cameron walks in the room upset and in a rage. Her lips are puffed up and her face is red.]

Ms. Cameron: Ms. Richardson, I need to talk to you right now!

Trevon: (frowns at Lindsay) Don't talk to her like that, (Ashlyn jumps up all frowned up) especially in front of her colleagues. You need to correct yourself!

Ms. Cameron: Trevon, you stay out of this! Today is your last day, so shut the hell up! And get out of my department, nigger!

Ashlyn: Oh, hell, no! (she charges at Ms. Cameron, but Kent, Trevon, and Heath grab her) I *know* she didn't! Oh, boy, I can't deal with this! Let me go! Trevon: Ash, calm down; let me handle this. I never hit a woman before, but I will 'cause if you do, that will cause you to be terminated right now.

Ms. Cameron: Who's going to believe a black man over a white woman? Tell me who.

Trevon: You know what? You may be right, but this room is always recorded! So, if I was you, my head would be up in my ass!

Ms. Cameron: You know what, Trevon? Kiss my ass! (she storms out) Trevon: (turns to Ashlyn) Ashlyn, you have to calm down. Don't bite the bullet or else it will backfire on you.

Kent: Hey, Trevon, (lets Ashlyn go) you want me to go in the monitor room to get the taping of the whole scenario?

Trevon: Yeah. Go get it.

Kent: All right. (he leaves the room and Donna walks in with a black eye holding a bag of ice) Damn! (he laughs out loud)

Heath: Somebody got knocked the fu— Donna: (turns to Heath) Shut up! [Heath laughs]

Trevon: (acts shocked) What happened to you, Queen Bee? (he laughs) Donna: Your li'l girlfriend hit me.

Trevon: (laughs) Good! You deserve it! (laughs and walks out) Donna: What? (she follows Trevon) Oh, he's just going to leave me?

Ashlyn: (sits down) Ms. Cameron has it coming. She just don't know it yet. May God be with her.

Kent: (walks in with the tape) I got the tape and heard everything. Somebody is going to be terminated.

Ashlyn: Good. She needs to be. (she gets up and takes it to the head of KPRCT; she puts it inside his office while he is on the phone) Watch this. (she whispers to him, and he nods his head and waves his hand as she leaves the office) Victory is mine.

[Four hours has passed. Trevon has finished packing his belongings in his car. Ashlyn is walking to her car. Trevon sees her and walks to

her, then walks with her to her car.]
Trevon: Well, Ash, this is it. I'm gone.
Ashlyn: You be careful. (she looks at him) Come here, Tre. (she leans over and kisses him) I will always love you. (she pulls away and drives off) [Trevon is speechless. He just watches her leave with a tear falling from his eye.]

*The scene fades away. (Sad music plays)*

### Scene 76

When: Months have passed since Trevon's departure. Where: Iman and Carlton's house

*Ashlyn is a senior; she has a total of 105 hours because she took 18 hours in summer school. At this moment, track and field are not her concern. She prefers to work and take care Artensia. Carlton and Iman have graduated from U of H. Carlton is now a business manager at a car dealership while Iman is a CPA.*
*One evening, Ashlyn and Artensia are over at Iman and Carlton's house. They are all sitting in the living room watching the basketball game in mid- November. R. T. is playing in the basketball game.*

Carlton: Dang! R. T. shook him hard! Oh, all the way to basketball! Boy, that boy is cold!
Iman: He's cold enough to not claim li'l mama. (holding Artensia in her lap) Ashlyn: (eating ice cream) You got that right, sista. He is a deadbeat dad.
Iman: You know I heard he got his ex pregnant, huh? Ashlyn: Really? Um, I hope he takes care of it.
Carlton: He probably will.
[The game is going on; the crowd is cheering as the announcer is commenting.]
Carlton: Damn, the Rockets won by 15. (Carlton turns the channel)
Iman: Hey, Ash, you heard from Trevon?
Ashlyn: Nope. I surely haven't. All I know is he and Donna are together.
Iman: Ash, that boy is over Donna. He wants you. Girl, you crazy to let that man go. He was good for you.

Carlton: I admit the brotha was cool, down-to-earth, and very respectful. He somewhat reminds me of Omar, just a li'l bit more conservative.

Ashlyn: (looks at Carlton) You just saying that. (pauses) Right?

Carlton: Nope. It's the truth.

Iman: Ash, you need to contact him because I believe he's the one for you and li'l mama. (she squeezes Artensia and kisses her) That's auntie's baby.

Ashlyn: So, you think I should call him for my graduation in August?

Iman: Yep. Go get him, girl.

Ashlyn: (smiles) Naw, I couldn't. Trevon probably found somebody else. I'm not going to impose on him. If it's meant to be, it will happen.

Carlton: OK, Ms. Thang. (he gets up and goes into the kitchen)

Iman: You need to think this over. (she gets up and goes into the kitchen with Artensia while Ashlyn just sits there contemplating)

*The scene fades away.*

### Scene 77

When: March
Where: KPRCT station, CEO's office

*Fall semester has passed. Ashlyn begins her senior year. She's starting spring semester and applies at KPRCT for the position of Jr. executive producer, which is the beginning of her lifelong dream job as the executive producer at the television station after she receives her degree in journalism and mass media.*

*She goes to work in mid-March for an interview for the position. All eyes are on her as she walks through the door of the CEO of KPRCT, who happens to be white. He fired Ms. Cameron for her racist mentality. Ashlyn knows Donna dragged her name through the mud about her relationship with Trevon, who was her supervisor. So, Ashlyn is hoping as she sits in her seat in Mr. Hamilton's office, that he will focus on her organizational skills and her outstanding work performance. She smiles confidently in her nice black pant suit.*

Mr. Hamilton: Good afternoon, Ashlyn. How are you doing? (he pulls her file out of the employees' file cabinet)

Ashlyn: Fine. And yourself?

Mr. Hamilton: Pretty good. (he sighs and looks at Ashlyn's profile) Ashlyn, as I look over your progress at KPRCT, I see that you have been extraordinary and superb with your writing, editing, and video production. I tell ya, I am very impressed with your work. However, I am little concerned about your temper. You have a history here at KPRCT for not controlling your  temper against the executive producer.

Ashlyn: Mr. Hamilton, I apologize for my quick temper, but there has been cause for me to react

that way. Especially how Donna confronted me in the restroom twice over one of her staff members. Then Ms. Cameron didn't like me because I am black. I mean, she marked all over my formats for no reason.

Mr. Hamilton: I understand, Ms. Richardson, how you felt about those two, but you've got to control your anger and just walk away, then file a  complaint against whoever steps over their boundaries. So, if you become the  Jr. executive producer, how would you handle confrontation with anyone at this job?

Ashlyn: I will converse in a proper manner, then I will submit a complaint to you for further assistance.

Mr. Hamilton: (wrote down Ashlyn's response) OK, Ms. Richardson, that will do for now since I already know about your performance. I'll let you know ASAP. (he puts her file on top of the others)

Ashlyn: OK. (she leans over and shakes hands, then she walks out) I *knew* he was going to bring that up. (she walks to the production room and sits down at her workstation)

[No one is in the production room, just Ashlyn. She pulls out Artensia's picture, then she looks at Trevon's picture that is behind Artensia's picture; a tear falls from her eyes.]

*The scene fades away.*

### Scene 78

When: Two months later on a Sunday Where: St. Mark United Methodist Church

*Ashlyn is graduating this month. She's attending her father's appreciation service at St. Mark United Methodist on a Sunday*

*afternoon a week before her graduation; she's sitting in the choir stand while her cousins sing their hit single.*

*The congregation is applauding, shouting, and moving to the music for at least 5 minutes. Then the senior pastor stands up to acknowledge Jeff for his fine work at the church.*

Rev. Lockett: Well, it's time for me to talk about my friend, Mr. Jeff Owens Richardson. He's a man of God. Ever since I've known him, (he laughs) he's never been afraid to tell it like it is. He will let you know what God says. He doesn't discriminate. He's a loving father and husband. I remember when Debbie and Jeff first started dating in junior high school at Yates. I mean, that brother smiled every day the Lord sent. He pushed (laughs) his chest all out every time Debbie was on his arm, even at church. He loved that woman, and he still loves her the same way. Amen. (he smiles and looks at Jeff on the front row sitting beside Debbie)

Congregation: Amen. (laughs)

Rev. Lockett: Jeff is a scholar. He has always been smart and very well organized. He always helps around the community and even establishes a community center here as well as in Inglewood, California. He's a man with a vision. Jeff, keep up the good work, brother; keep caring and doing for others, 'cause God will continue to bless you and your family.

[Rev. Lockett sits down, and Ashlyn stands up with a poem she wrote about her father. As she walks to the microphone stand, Trevon walks into the church and sits down on the back row; Ashlyn looks at him with a shocked expression on her face.]

Ashlyn: (reads the poem –Man with a Vision‖) Standing tall, a strong black man. No wind could cause him to fall. No earthquake could shake up his foundation. That allures to hope, faith, and dreams for those dependent upon him, protecting them from self-destruction, and guiding them away from the negativism. Yet he enlightens those with wisdom, with definite accountability, by taking more responsibility; fathering others as his own, with self-assurance and compliance; to overcome obstacles before thee; and go beyond the impossible that could be seen; that could be lived in his vision. (pauses and a tear drops from her eye) Dad, you are a man with such great vision that no one can destroy it because you take it upon yourself. (she sniffles) I love you, Daddy. (she walks to the bench to hug him with tears rolling down her face) [Jeff stands up and hugs his daughter tightly with tears rolling down his eyes. The congregation applauds with a standing ovation. The sermon had already been preached earlier. Now, Jeff presents his remarks.]

Jeff: (stands in front of the altar) I tell ya, (he wipes the tears from his eyes) this has been one of the best moments of my life. I am so blessed by God to see those that have played a part in my life to be here today. I want to thank (wipe tears from his eyes) you for that. My entire family is here today. My wife, Debbie, my eldest daughter, Vanessa, and son-in-law, Darnell, and my granddaughter, Darlesia, who's talking up a storm.

[Congregation laughs]. My son, Carlton, and his wife, Iman, and my eldest son, Speedy, and my . . . my youngest, Ashlyn, and my granddaughter, Artensia. I also see my nephew, Trent, and my nieces, Tameka and Trina, with their children. All of my brothers and sisters are here, and my play daughter and son, Darnesia and Corey. Boy, I'm just overwhelmed with all of this joy that I have; all of this love coming to me. And in return, I love y'all. I love this congregation. I thank you for the support and the affection you've given to me. And to my Pastor Uncle Lockett, (he looks at him) I thank you for allowing me to do the work of God at this sanctuary. I love you, Unc. (Rev. Lockett comes down from the pulpit and hugs him, then goes back to his seat) And to everyone I have not mentioned, I thank you and may God bless you. (he sits down beside Debbie and kisses her on the cheek)

Rev. Lockett: (stands up and goes to the pulpit) Well, if there is anyone else here today who wants to make remarks and who has not done so, please come forward.

[Everybody turns their heads, shaking their heads, wondering who else would make a remark; then Trevon stands up and walks down the aisle while Rev. Lockett hands him the microphone.]

Vanessa: (whispers and touches Darnell's leg) Oh my God, baby, what is he going to say?

Debbie: (elbows Jeff) Baby, I hope . . .

Trevon: Mr. Richardson, I want to say the first time we met was on Thanksgiving. You've shown me that you are one of the elite brand. (he smiles) You don't pass judgment on anyone; you accept each person for who they are. And I admire that. (he looks at Ashlyn) The real reason I am here is to see someone who has shown the same qualities, (Jeff smiles at him) your daughter, Ashlyn. (he looks at Ashlyn) Ashlyn, I know it seems that I'm not being truthful to you, but I am. I love you and Artensia. My love for you is so deep that it is not easily identified. I came back within a year's time to see you accomplish your goals. I want to support you and love you like a husband is supposed to. (he walks to her and kneels down on one bended knee with a diamond ring in his hand) Ashlyn, I have not been complete since I departed from you and Artensia. (he smiles cause she reaches for him) You are my better half; you are strong when I'm weak; you are bold when I'm scared; you lift me up when I'm sad.

You bring such joy in my life, baby. I need you to be my wife.

Ashlyn: (cries) Oh, Tre, (she looks at him) I love you so much. Oh, baby, I've missed you. I don't want to lose you anymore. I want to be your wife.

Trevon: (hugs her and tears roll down his face) The answer is YES! (Ashlyn nods her head yes) She said YES!

[The congregation stands up again with tears rolling down their faces, including all the men.]

Jeff: (stands up and hugs Trevon) Welcome to the family, son. (smiles from ear to ear) What a blessing.

Speedy: (hugs Trevon and Ashlyn) Congratulations!

Carlton: (talks to Trevon) I'm glad you came, man. (he hugs him; Iman shakes his hand and smiles)

[Darnell and Vanessa hug Ashlyn and Trevon and li'l mama; Debbie kisses both Ashlyn and Trevon. The choir sings ‑This Is the Dayǁ; Ashlyn and Trevon lock lips in front of congregation.]

*The scene fades away.*

Part B

When: The following Saturday Where: Auditorium at TSU

[Ashlyn walks across the stage to receive her degree from Texas Southern University. Her family cheers, including Trevon.]

*The scene fades away.*

### Scene 79

When: Three weeks later Where: U of H

*Since Trevon and Ashlyn are getting married, Trevon wants to be Artensia's father. So, Ashlyn sends R. T. a letter to sign his paternity rights over to Trevon. R. T. receives the letter and signs without any hesitation because he doesn't believe Artensia is his child. Afterward, Trevon signs the form declaring he's the legal father of Artensia. Meanwhile, 3 weeks later, Trevon and Ashlyn are officially married, and R. T. visits Darnell, Ashlyn's brother- in-law, at U of H. When R. T. walks into Darnell's office, Darnell is grading papers.*

R. T.: (knocks on the door and walks in) Hey, D. What's happening?
Darnell: (looks up and stands) Hey, R. T.! (walks to R. T.) What brings you by?
R. T.: Oh, I was just visiting the campus so I decided to stop by to see the man who helped me to get where I am. (he smiles)
Darnell: (smiles) Aw, man, it's all in the heart, bro. (he sits at his desk) So how is the li'l one?
R. T.: (he sees Ashlyn and Artensia's picture with a frown) She's fine. (he picks up the picture from the bookshelf) Uh, Darnell, who's this with Ashlyn? Darnell: Umm, your daughter.
R. T.: My daughter? (he pauses and sighs) She looks just . . . Darnell: Yep. She looks like you. She's beautiful, isn't she?
R. T.: (shock) Yeah. Just like her mother. (he sits down and stares at the picture) Do you have Ashlyn's address?
Darnell: (writes the address down on a notepad) This is Ashlyn and Trevon's new address. (he hands it to him)
R. T.: (takes it and stands up) Oh, I'm going over there right now. (he walks out) Thanx!
[Darnell smiles and shakes head. Fifteen minutes later.]
R. T.: (drives up to Ashlyn's house in somewhat of a panic) OK, I can do this. (he gets out of his car and walks to the door and rings the doorbell) OK, Ashlyn, I'm sorry. (whisper to himself)
Trevon: Hey, R. T. What brings you by?
R. T.: I want to see my daughter and tell Ashlyn I'm sorry for—
Trevon: It's too late for that. You've already signed over your rights. (Trevon continues to stand in the doorway talking to R. T.)
R. T.: Look, I need to know if Artensia is my daughter, OK? Now can I talk to Ashlyn?
Trevon: No. You may—
Ashlyn: (interrupts) What's going on? (she looks at R. T.) R. T., what do you want?
R. T.: Ashlyn, I'm sorry for being an asshole. Forgive me. I want to do a DNA test. Is it possible?
Ashlyn: Yes. It's possible, but how dare you wait this long when Trevon has already signed the papers and you signed them too. You are still the same. You think you are the only thing that matters. Well, guess what? You don't. (pauses and sighs) I'll schedule a paternity test so I can say this—*I told your trifling ass she's your daughter.*

R. T.: Thanx, Ashlyn.

Artensia: Whose that man? (she hugs Trevon's legs) Daddy, who is he?

Trevon: (picks up Artensia) That's Momma's old friend. (he kisses her and walks off with her)

Ashlyn: R. T., just wait for the phone call regarding the testing. (shuts the door in his face)

[R. T. walks off and gets in his car, then drives away.]

*The scene fades away.*


## Scene 80

When: Tuesday, 2 weeks later Where: Trevon and Ashlyn's home

*The results came in on Tuesday afternoon; Ashlyn, Trevon, and Artensia are all home. Ashlyn opens the results.*

Ashlyn: Trevon, (she looks at the results that read a 100 percent certainty that
R. T. is the father) somebody is going to shit bricks!

Trevon: (runs into the living room where Ashlyn stands) Say what?

Ashlyn: R. T. is the father. Too bad, too sad.

Trevon: Yep. (pauses) Uh, baby, Mr. Hamilton called when you went to the store. He said call him when you get in.

[The doorbell rings. It is R. T. crying. Trevon goes to the door while Ashlyn walks to the phone.]

Ashlyn: (calls Mr. Hamilton) Mr. Hamilton, this is Ashlyn . . .

Trevon: (answers the door) R. T., you got the results?

R. T.: (wipes the tears from his face) Yeah. Can I see her?

Trevon: Sure. Come on in. (R. T. comes in crying but tries to hold it back) Ashlyn: (hangs the phone up smiling) Yes!

Trevon: (looks at Ashlyn) What is it, baby?

Ashlyn: I got the job! (she jumps into Trevon's arms and kisses him)

R. T.: (stands there looking pitiful) Congrats, Ashlyn. Ashlyn: (turns around) R. T., what the hell?

Trevon: Ash, be cool. (he holds Ashlyn tightly)

R.T.: Ash, I want to see her. Please. I'm sorry for doing you like that. Forgive me.

Ashlyn: Hell, naw! I ain't—

Trevon: Baby, that's Artensia's father. C'mon, baby, he didn't know. Baby, I love you. (he kisses her)
Ashlyn: I guess you can. Even though I hate—

Trevon: Baby. (he looks under eyed at her)
[Ashlyn goes and gets Artensia. She brings Artensia to R. T.; R. T. holds the child.]

R. T.: Hi, Artensia. I'm your father. Artensia: I have another one.
R. T.: Yes. (he kisses her)
Trevon: (hugs Ashlyn) It's all right, baby. She needs to know the truth. Ashlyn: I know.

*The scene fades away.*

## Scene 81

When: The next day
Where: Ashlyn walks into her new office at KPRCT

*Ashlyn reports to KPRCT as the Jr. executive producer. She walks to her new office with her name on the door. She brings her family portrait, degree, diploma, and other honors to hang up on her wall. After she organizes and decorates her office, she sits at her desk and looks around to see what she has achieved in spite of it all. She picks up her family portrait and a tear falls from her eyes. As the tear falls, she thinks about losing Omar, her fight with Christopher, her fight with R. T., her pregnancy with Artensia, the loss of her other child, and the fight with Donna and Ms. Cameron. Another tear drops as she thinks of winning the 100m dash, having Artensia, graduating from high school and college, and marrying Trevon. She smiles sitting in her new office as a Jr. executive producer. She recalls what her dad told her regarding society. He stated: "You never know what you're going to face; you never know what you're going to take; you never know what you're going to get. All you can do is live and learn, with faith day by day."*

THE END.

www.ingramcontent.com/pod-product-compliance
Lightning Source LLC
Chambersburg PA
CBHW051824090426
42736CB00011B/1637